OUR WILDEST
DREAMS

Women Entrepreneurs
Making Money,
Having Fun, Doing Good

Joline Godfrey

 HarperBusiness
A Division of HarperCollins*Publishers*

The world stands out on either side
No wider than the heart is wide;
Above the world is stretched the sky—
No higher than the soul is high.
The heart can push the sea and land
Farther away on either hand;
The soul can split the sky in two,
And let the face of God shine through.
But East and West will pinch the heart
That can not keep them pushed apart;
And he whose soul is flat—the sky
Will cave in on him by and by.

from "Renascence" by Edna St. Vincent Millay

A hardcover edition of this book was published in 1992 by HarperBusiness, a division of HarperCollins Publishers.

HarperCollins books may be purchased for educational, business, or sales promotional use. For information please write: Special Markets Department, HarperCollins Publishers, Inc., 10 East 53rd Street, New York, NY 10022.

First paperback edition published 1993.

The Library of Congress has catalogued the hardcover edition as follows:

Godfrey, Joline.

   Our wildest dreams : women entrepreneurs making money, having fun, doing good / Joline Godfrey.
      p.   cm.
   Includes bibliographical references and index.
   ISBN 0-88730-545-8
   1. Women in business—United States. 2. Women executives—United States
I. Title
   HD6054.4.U6G63   1992
   331.4'816584'00973—dc20   92-54854

ISBN 0-88730-633-0 (pbk.)
93 94 95 96 97 CW 10 9 8 7 6 5 4 3 2

Contents

Foreword

I am honored to have been invited to write a foreword to *Our Wildest Dreams* because it addresses one of the most critical issues we confront today—business values. A change in values is important because business is destroying our world. And the ways modern corporations harm themselves, and others, are peculiarly male. These values come with a host of assumptions and beliefs that permeate our lives and the marketplace. To a great extent these corporate values are synonymous with industrialism, which separated production from the land, land from people, and finally our personal values from the values of commerce.

These beliefs and ways of conducting our businesses will soon destroy the source of wealth, our resource base, and human society. In order for business to contribute to positive social change, we must revise how it acts. It would be fatuous for me to say that women can or will play an important role in this change. This is certainly true, but a role is still adjunct to an older paradigm. I believe that women's businesses are *pivotal* to meaningful change in how we shape the corporations of tomorrow. I don't believe business can lead society unless women's values suffuse and permeate all of commerce. Until that happens, corporations are incomplete, and no amount of tinkering will make them whole.

Business has become a type of addiction, a socially sanctioned addiction to money, fame, and power. Like all addictions, it is a way of not feeling; and when business doesn't feel, it is at least amoral, almost always harmful. If business economics is the study of how we add values to raw materials and processes, I suggest that you cannot add values unless you have them. Women bring important new values to commerce; they bring this courageous, heartfelt sense of connectedness to their lives and businesses—in other words, feeling. These are not merely good values, they are what will drive business forward in the century to come if it is to fulfill its role as restorer of our planet, our community, and our faith in each other.

Paul Hawken
Chairman and Chief Executive Officer
Smith & Hawken

Preface
It Began Like This

This book came into being because I got mad. In April 1989 *Inc.* magazine published its annual Dream Team article. The article featured an all-star lineup of entrepreneurs who, if you gathered them together, could no doubt invent an endless stream of new products, manage a billion-dollar company, and change the world. As the editors of *Inc.* put it in their introduction:

> What we have here is, without doubt and beyond question, the management team of our decade long dreams—the ideal people, position by position to lead the perfect fantasy start-up. So bet the ranch. Bet the kids. Heck, bet the record collection. We're ready. These are the guys.

Guys? You bet. The list was exclusively male. It included some of the fellows I admire the most: Paul Hawken, Harry Quadracci, Donald Burr, and, of course, Steve Jobs. (The Dream Team also had a group of advisors and board members, including Randy Field, husband of Mrs.) To a one, *guys*. Something happened to me when I read the article. It wasn't that I disagreed with their team; it was just that it was hard to believe that none of the many vibrant, exciting, and talented women who run thriving businesses had earned a place on the Dream Team with the good old boys.

At the time, my business partner, Jane Lytle, and I were busy running our company, Odysseum. I didn't have time to get on a soapbox. But I was mad, and I couldn't quietly let the issue pass. So I wrote to the editor of *Inc.*:

> *Inc.* you let me down. Only ten years old and already smug, self-satisfied, ossified. Four years ago I flexed my entrepreneurial muscle and joined the adventure—started a company and became one of your regular readers. You've kept me abreast of who's doing what, offered up good ideas, cautionary tales, and managerial visions I can be comfortable with. You've been a pal.
>
> But lately I've felt more irked than inspired, more bored than buoyed. Unable to put my finger on just what's wrong, I've remained loyal

reading each issue, trying to understand my discomfort. Then you sent me your anniversary issue. And in one of those awful, illuminating flashes, I got it. *Inc.,* my modern pal, my new age partner, my old friend, you're sexist.

Gulp. How could I accuse you of such a thing? Haven't you dutifully covered women entrepreneurs? Aren't you the most hip, sensitive, feminist group to come along in generations? That's the image at least, but come on guys, look at the evidence.

On page 74 of your magazine you advertise for sale a Woman in Business video. (Hip, very hip.) In the ad you tell us that women-owned businesses grew from 700,000 to 3,000,000 in the last ten years—whew! You mention that we account for $56 billion in annual revenue generated by companies owned or led by women. And we are further informed, "By the year 2000 fully half of all business owners are projected to be women." Impressive figures.

How then can you support your all-white-male "Dream Team?" How can you fliply acknowledge that it is an all-white-male team with: "We're ready. These are the guys. (Did we say guys? Regrettably. We expect a different outcome next time.)" When is next time? The twentieth anniversary issue?

Okay, so that's not enough to pick on you about? Then how about turning to your "Coming of Age" section. You know, that part of the issue where you feature wise entrepreneurs casting forth pearls. By my count you have featured forty-one "wise guys," three of whom happen to be wise women. Favorite companies? You found twelve, two of which happened to be owned by women.

Let's get this straight. Do I think you should edit your magazine by the numbers? Allot stories by gender and color percentages? No, the point is I don't think that's necessary—I think if you weren't so all fired at ease and thrilled with the "Boys Club of New Age Entrepreneurs" you'd be able to see a more diverse group of entrepreneurs.

I went on to list women who own businesses and challenged them to look around at the diverse mix of men and women—Anglo, Asian, African-American, and Hispanic—working to create a healthy economy. Anger spent, but feeling discouraged (Were things never going to change? Would women never get a fair shake?), I got back to the business of running my company.

Two weeks later I got a call from *Inc.* and an invitation to have lunch with editor in chief, George Gendron. I was surprised, but I accepted. Lunch with George was great. He is a truly thoughtful man, with one of those minds that really does enjoy the acts of engagement and consideration. He listened, questioned, joined me in frustration. "Yes," he said, "of course I want better coverage. The percentage of our readership that is female is very high. We don't want to ignore them." Feeling somewhat mollified, but skeptical, I left the luncheon hoping future issues of the magazine would begin to look different.

Shortly after that, another call came from *Inc.* This time the request was to interview me for a feature article. Feeling unsettled but not knowing why, I agreed. We were finishing the interview when I finally understood my discomfort. My intent in writing the original letter was to encourage a shift in editorial awareness, not to gain personal recognition. Although George and his colleague, Bo Burlingham, had been first-rate interviewers—not content with "sound bites" but sincerely interested in whole thoughts—I felt a little co-opted: I had no confidence that beyond this one interview the magazine (or the next Dream Team) would look very different. On impulse (an often reliable friend), I proposed to George that he let me travel the country to talk with women and create a data base that he and his reporters could use as a resource for future stories. It says a lot about George Gendron that he agreed to my proposal. He is a risk taker who has an eye to the future.

After my letter was published in *Inc.*, I had many conversations with other editors, reporters, business school professors, investors, and other women. Two realities emerged. Professors, editors, investors, and others assured me they were sympathetic to my issue, but they just didn't *see* women who were running businesses—*real* businesses, it was implied. However, I knew women who were running businesses; my friends knew women who owned businesses, their friends knew (and saw) women who owned businesses. For some reason these women business owners simply were not visible. I began to think that women who owned businesses were like Jimmy Stewart's Harvey, a wild figment of my imagination. I needed documentation. I needed proof of our existence. I know, it seems a little strange to me too, something akin to taking photos of UFO aliens. What can I tell you?

I began to organize the *Inc.* dinners. The first step was to collect names and create a data base. I called women friends who owned companies and asked them for names of other women who owned companies. I called alumni offices of business schools, women's business organizations, and chambers of commerce. I pulled names from articles in local newspapers and magazines on planes. I tapped computer networks, requesting names and referrals. Within a month, I had a long list of women who owned companies all over the country. My goals at that point were modest: to enjoy a few very good dinners with kindred spirits and to come away with stories I could pass along to *Inc.* and a data base of names and addresses of women who owned businesses. I just wanted to make it easier for *Inc.* to include women in their business coverage.

I organized dinner parties in Boston, San Francisco, Grand Rapids, Michigan, and Minneapolis, Minnesota. The parties were small, intimate, and unstructured (no agenda, no speaker, no themes). I placed a tape recorder in the middle of the table and invited women to break bread and talk.

The women at those dinners (like women business owners generally) were a diverse lot, belonging to different political parties and holding disparate philosophical views. They had varied educational backgrounds, histories, needs, and passions and represented a wide range of industries and businesses. They were united in a commitment to their customers, suppliers, employees, families, and friends and to a future built in bits every day. The dinner groups were almost evenly mixed, single and married, with and without children. Different ethnic and racial groups were represented, and women of three different generations participated: (1) women who had built businesses prior to the emergence of the current women's movement (i.e., pre-1960s), (2) women (including myself) who came of age during the struggles of the 1960s and 1970s but who have had the psychological support of consciousness-raising and feminist politics to buttress their dreams, and (3) young women entrepreneurs of the post–feminist era who still face difficulties but, armed with MBAs and a sense of limitless possibilities, charge ahead, largely oblivious to the constraints and barriers that seek to impede them.

Some of the excitement of the dinners was the electric charge of this cross-generational talk and the differing assumptions and experiences of the women. I was entranced by how actively they sought to hear one another, to exchange information and to learn. The women enjoyed being in one another's company. They quickly found a comfort level and discussed potent issues amid laughter and the heat of differing opinions. Like their corporate counterparts, women entrepreneurs frequently resist being a part of groups that set them apart more than they already are. The dinners were clearly seen as a luxury, a departure from the norm, a treat. I felt enormously lucky to experience the spirit and energy of the ideas and passions of these women. I was at home. I knew I was part of magical gatherings.

When the dinners were over and I was preparing my report for *Inc.*, I reread the transcripts of the conversations and was amazed, surprised, and excited all over again. There was something profoundly important in the repetition of themes and ideas that emerged from the transcripts. These women and their businesses had something of fundamental importance to give to the larger business community.

This book is informed by the women at those dinner tables. However, in the course of organizing the dinners, I met and spoke with hundreds of other women owners. You will hear from some of them, too. Since then, I have continued to collect names and stories of other women entrepreneurs. Everyone gives me names now, as if I were collecting coins or stamps. Friends and strangers remember my collection and add to it.

When the dinners were over I was invited to speak to a number of groups about my experience. I was struck by the level of curiosity and mystery surrounding women and their businesses and by the consistency of the kinds of questions asked about them:

What are they like?

What are their businesses like?

How did they get started?

What difficulties do they face?

How do they maintain balance in their lives?

This is not a book about all women who own businesses. We are much too varied, in culture, race, age, experience, and point of view for that to be possible. It is about some of the women I have encountered before and after the adventure of the *Inc.* letter. It is, of course, biased by my point of view, the women I have known, and my experiences; however, it will provide some answers to the questions posed to me repeatedly over the last two years. You will see real women, with real businesses, making a real difference

Keep an eye on *Inc.* magazine. I renewed my subscription, but I take no credit for the fact that more stories about women who own companies are appearing in the pages of that magazine. Like any good company, they listened.

MY STORY

I grew up in a family-owned business. My grandmother ran the company, a small commercial dairy in Maine, with great resolve and strength of character. She handled the books, the business, the hiring, and the firing. My grandfather ran the milk room, and oversaw the delivery of products to homes and stores. He provided a wise and gentle presence to balance my grandmother's forceful personality. Until my father took over the company, he worked for his mother and father.

I understood very early the demands of a business. Hours were long, everyone worked hard, and quality and service were relentlessly pursued goals. I also understood, if not consciously at the time, that there was something very good about being part of the business. By virtue of being the "granddaughter of" I felt a certain pride in the importance of the product. I was vaguely aware of the young men (and even a few young women back then) who came and went, working part-time or full-time while going to school or college. A few of them lived on the farm intermittently and were treated as family members. It was assumed that getting a college degree was important, and schedules and tasks were often juggled to make sure classes could be attended and work completed. Although I remember difficult days when milk soured, a customer unexpectedly required more milk than had been bottled that morning, or when machinery broke down, I also remember feeling as though something good happened in my grandparents' business. Nevertheless, and despite my grandmother's presence, it never occurred to me that I might become a part of the business. It probably didn't occur to anyone else, either.

After college, I surveyed my options as I had come to understand them (in the 1960s, it seemed that social work, education, or library science were the only real "professional" possibilities open to women). So, with a notion of wanting to "do good," I went off to study social work. Graduate degree in hand, and with a slightly greater appreciation for the complexities of "doing good," I joined the Polaroid Corporation as a clinical social worker.

For ten years I was a corporate woman. In the beginning it was heady, exciting stuff to be part of a large, powerful company whose name elicited respect. It was, after all, the company that had challenged the laws of physics and invented instant photography. This was also the company started by the visionary "Dr. Land"—a man who spoke eloquently of finding in business the intersections of art and science, the inventor who welcomed liberal arts graduates and assembly line workers into his labs, believing that a sense of wonder and curiosity were more important to the process of creation and invention than degrees, rules, and credentials. This was also the man who closed his company for a day in the 1970s, bused thousands of employees to a huge empty warehouse, and addressed the issue of racism with such emotion and insight that for some years many African-Americans employed by the company dared to hope they had found a welcoming institution. The people I worked for when I went to Polaroid had been Land students and protégés. I was the willing receiver of stories and legends intended to keep his values, culture, and traditions alive.

I was absolutely hooked on this company that seemed to care deeply about the value of learning and that held strong beliefs about the imperatives of ethical behavior and integrity in business. Trained as a social worker, I wanted to believe that this curious company, housed in nondescript buildings and warehouses in the shadow of MIT, cared about and respected its employees, rewarded learning and discovery, and was audacious enough to challenge science and society on all fronts.

I was at Polaroid during the Carter presidency. Affirmative action laws were on the books and, for the most part, enforced. Women and minorities felt some hope that they would indeed be able to participate in the real life of company decision making and power structures. Although blacks in senior management were fewer than the fingers on my hand (and there were no women at all) I dared to believe that change was within our grasp. I was young. I was naive. I was an idiot.

But this is not a tale of sour grapes. My tenure at Polaroid was marked by unusual opportunity, wonderful mentors, great adventure, and tremendous learning. In 1984 the CEO of Polaroid agreed to provide seed funding for a company I had been nurturing in the cellar of one of the old labs. His willingness to take a chance on me was a critical factor in my leap out of the corporation and into the entrepreneurial world. I am deeply grateful to have had his support.

But I was in the cellar for a reason. It was the only way to the top. My first years with Polaroid were reasonably conventional—for a woman. I worked in the affirmative action department and was involved in the business of encouraging managers and vice-presidents—indeed the CEO himself—to change old recruiting and hiring habits. I worked with women who wanted to break into the higher-paying, less-traditional jobs (i.e., management, engineering, chemical processing, and manufacturing), and I met with groups and individuals trying to make sense of how to "make it."

The man instrumental in hiring me worked for the president of the company. Bill Rebelsky, or Rebel, as he was affectionately known, was a University of Chicago liberal arts graduate in a company dominated by engineers and scientists. He wrote grievance responses for the president—responses that attempted to resolve employee complaints within the context of the values, aims, and policies created in the early days of the company by Land and his inner circle of idealists. When necessary, it was Rebel who helped rewrite those policies to keep them current and responsive to the needs of the employee. The affirmative action office reported to him. He reported to the president.

Progressive and intellectual, devoted to rocking the boat, he was a maverick. Nevertheless, Bill Rebelsky wielded power because he had earned his stripes: he had run several manufacturing plants for the company and opened a new plant in Holland. In a world of technocrats he had played the game by their rules and won the right to play thereafter on his terms. He wanted me to do the same. For the next couple of years he pushed, bullied, and nagged me to take jobs in the mainstream of the company—manufacturing and quality control, for example. Although he rejected the notion of career ladders with disdain ("Who on earth can imagine life neat enough to tolerate career ladders?" he would sneer), he wanted me to have sufficient credentials so I would not be blocked from opportunities at the higher levels of management.

For a while, I took assignments in mainstream divisions and departments. I began to build a "portfolio of stripes." Ruth Owades, owner of Calyx and Corolla, says that most corporate jobs are boring. Unfortunately, she is right on the money. I suppose men have been willing to "do time" because they believed there would be an ultimate payoff and an opportunity to join the ranks they reached for. For me, however, it became painfully clear that no matter how mainstream I became, no matter how many "stripes" I collected, I was never going to join the guys—my friends and peers at the top. More importantly, through a series of large-scale special projects I managed, I began to realize that by living on the fringe and avoiding restrictive titles, I could have more fun, enjoy more autonomy, and have access to opportunity, learning, and influence. For many years I had no title, no budget, no department to lose. I had, instead, a series of projects that began (unawares to me) to hone my entrepreneurial character. Without being aware of it, I stopped trying to win at a game that I didn't really enjoy and that seemed fixed against women anyway.

Many women chose a different course. They got more education, dressed for success, did time in a series of jobs meant to groom them for the top, and, in general, have tried to live by the rules of the game as presented to them. Suzanne Gordon writes of these women in a book called *Prisoners of Men's Dreams*. She calls them "equal opportunity feminists" and says they "entered the male kingdom... and were forced to play by the king's rules" (p. 4). In so doing, she contends, they abandoned the original feminist vision of transforming the game for everyone. Some of those women have done very well. Unfortunately, the glass ceiling continues to hover over too many others.

Constitutionally unable to play by the rules, I moved outside the formal structure of the organization. My ability to operate as a relatively independent agent was tolerated to some extent by the nature of the Polaroid culture (it's hard to believe I could have gotten away with such freedom at IBM) and by my knowledge base: being licensed to practice clinical psychology in a world of technocrats is akin to reigning over a pot muttering, "bubble, bubble, toil and trouble!" That is to say, there were a lot of people who believed I knew something, maybe even something important. They just didn't know what. Whatever "it" was, some people found it helpful and I was accorded respect for expertise that I was able to put to use in an interesting variety of ways: I ran a conference for women in nontraditional jobs; I brought in philosophers, ethicists, and writers and carted 250 senior officers off to a learning conference on ethics and management; I participated in the dissolution of an entire division of the company (and wrote a study on grief based on the experience); I was involved in marketing projects, human relations research projects, consulting, creating, and learning, learning, learning. In a lot of ways I had a great time. I had access to nationally known experts, money from other people's budgets to spend, and the name Polaroid behind me, which opened doors on the outside. What a time! I was not so young. I was a little less naive—not quite the idiot I had been.

My last such assignment at Polaroid was still another terrific opportunity. (Corporate women, please note how much cheaper it is for companies to offer opportunities rather than titles, promotions, or real power. There is no shortage of opportunities for a resourceful woman!) Another of my mentors, Jerry Sudbey, a true idealist, a student of Land, and the head of worldwide manufacturing (a singularly important position), was dubbed to oversee the creation and introduction of a new and, to the company, important product. The glory days were gone; Land had retired, somewhat ignominiously; sales were sagging. Professional managers with nei-

ther the vision nor the charisma of the founding man were having a
hard time putting luster back into the old gem. A hit, a killer new
product, a silver bullet was in everyone's dreams.

At Jerry's invitation I joined his new product development team.
He wasn't sure he knew exactly what he wanted me to do, but he
was pretty confident that between the two of us we'd figure it out—
and we did. I observed. Oh, I did a lot of other things too and
made a fair contribution. But primarily I observed: the dynamics of
marketing and engineering divisions at war, the staking out of turf
and loyalties among vice-presidents, and the fears and childlike be-
haviors of otherwise reasonable men desperately trying to hold on
to titles, departments, body count, and budgets in an organization
where sands were shifting and markets were changing and unpredictable. It was an illuminating time. I knew then that the game so
many women are shut out of was hardly worth playing.

Eighteen months later, the new product was moving out of development and into the production phase. The development team
I had been part of was disbanded. Jerry took me for drinks after
work one day, and we discussed my options. I could take another
assignment working for him in manufacturing, I could opt for a
mainstream job in personnel, or I could live with ambiguity for a
month or two and see what came up next. I chose the third option.

I was still a good corporate woman. Loyal to Land's original
vision, I harbored (along with many others) a secret garden in my
head that was a renaissance of the early company. I continued to
believe that his original vision of learning for its own sake, attention
to the intersection of art and science, and an organization where
people counted as much as product was still viable; indeed, it was
imperative, if the company was to regain any of its old glory. The
notion to give his ideas a fair shot by starting my own company
hadn't yet bubbled up out of the murk in my mind. I was more intent
on influencing the new inheritors—the men in suits who maintained
they had the answers. (Okay, I *was* a little crazy, but those are the
tricks you play on yourself to ignore reality.)

I went on a brief vacation to Mexico and came back with an
idea for a business. It was just that simple. Away from the distrac-
tions of corporate politics, freed of routines that kept me neatly
organized, safe from distracting phones and to-do lists, an idea sur-
faced. In a small fishing village on the Pacific Ocean, I stood looking
out over a bay and, in an epiphany, an idea was born. Who knows
what causes the substance of a thought to finally take shape, the

entrepreneurial juices to flow? Who knows why all the thoughts and experiences of a month or a decade suddenly weave themselves into a recognizable pattern? Does the scent of jasmine in an unfamiliar setting elicit a chemical reaction that causes the idea to emerge? Is it the rare tranquility of a songbird that triggers a memory? Who knows. In many brainstorming methods, there is some version of a technique called "taking a vacation." This is simply a technique that frees the brain from the path it had been following, a way to let new information come in and "do its thing." In any event, a company was born.

When I returned from vacation, I met again with Jerry and asked for six months to explore my idea. I saw this new business not as my own but as one that I would start for Polaroid. It would be the vehicle for a new model, a way to initiate a small renaissance. Jerry agreed, and for the next six months I researched, talked with people, traveled, and learned as much as I could about the viability of my idea. Convinced I was onto something, and with Jerry's full support, I began the process of "pulling others into the conspiracy," as we termed the business of gaining support and funding for the idea.

It should be clear by now that Jerry Sudbey was a prince to have in my corner. Jerry is one of those rare souls who really believes in the richness of diversity, who values the seemingly crazy idea, and who is willing to underwrite experimentation, learning, and risk taking with time, money, and emotional support. Life on the fringe would have been a great deal harder without him.

Although the path was tortuous and the challenges many, the raw idea began to assume the substance of a vision and slowly I gained support. A full year after that crystalline moment in Zihuatenejo, Mexico, the CEO of Polaroid struck a deal with me: he would fund the development of a prototype and support me for a year if I would agree to spin off the company as a separate entity in which Polaroid would hold a minority position. I agreed before he could change his mind. In an instant, I had become an entrepreneur.

Ultimately, the ugly duckling of an idea born in Mexico became a swan of a company called Odysseum Inc. Odysseum designs and delivers entertaining learning games to *Fortune* and *Inc.* 500 companies: creativity, team building, customer service, and leadership are some of the goals met through its games. Combining the best of classic, playful games of discovery and suspense with substantive content, teams of Odysseum site pros lead groups of 20 to 500 managers and executives through programs that add a shared experience to what might otherwise be staid, impersonal meetings.

Photo Odyssey, the company's centerpiece program, is an example. Teams are provided with cameras, film, and a card containing ten phrases (e.g., "leadership," "bottom line," "in the black," "membership is a privilege," etc.). The teams are instructed to create photos of those ideas. The magic of the game appears in visible results. The game leaders process the film and organize the photographs into a reasonably glitzy, large screen, sound-on-slide show that illustrates the myriad ways a single idea can be envisioned. A visceral understanding of perspective sets in. Some of the solutions are funny; some are downright sexy; others are reflective; some are quirky. They are all different. Those who protest they have no imagination or can't take a picture are startled at their creative ability. The final lesson is the challenge of making a vision shared.

Odysseum was officially incorporated on July 1, 1986. I remember the day because my partner, Jane Lytle, and I, getting into the spirit of independence, wore red, white, and blue to the closing in our lawyer's office. It was the end of one adventure—the year spent developing the company from a cellar of a Polaroid building—and the beginning of another. We were now independent entrepreneurs poised to capture a share of the $32 billion national meeting market.

You will hear stories of Odysseum throughout the chapters of this book—small vignettes that attempt to give a sense of the place. I call it a "place" because in a way it was a garden of delights. I am not a highly creative person, in the common understanding of that word. I do have some facility for bringing people together and creating an environment in which perfectly ordinary and very special people can conjure up and create original, magical ideas. Our vision for Odysseum was to create unusual yet meaningful experiences for businesspeople that would allow them to learn, feel competent, and have fun—a kind of "Sesame Street" for grown-ups.

To do that, we knew we had to create a giant "sandbox" for Odysseum employees so they could feel and experience the very things we wanted to create for others. In this way, Odysseum was also a laboratory—a place I could apply and reinterpret some of the ideas and vision gleaned from all those legends and stories about Dr. Land and his dreams that I carried around. Could I create a business that produced superior products *and* was an exciting place to work? I thought so, and this was my chance to find out.

The words "we" and "our" will crop up when I talk about Odysseum. My business partner, Jane Lytle, is a graduate of the Yale School of Management. She had been doing financial consulting for another company in Boston when we met. Jane was and is the yin to my yang and sometimes the yang to my yin. Creating a business with Jane is a wonderful adventure. Smart, savvy, and supportive, she made the creation of a company that could make money, do good, and have fun a wholly possible reality.

For the next four years our time was claimed by the endless imperatives of starting and growing a business. We met many of our goals. I am now confident that it *is* possible to create a business in which profits and people can exist in harmony. I am now sure that business as traditionally defined and operated is *not* the only or even the best way to make money—let alone, make money, do good, and have fun. Odysseum was a source of pride and pleasure. We created imaginative, high-quality products, offered a truly unusual level of service to customers, and enjoyed a commitment from employees that has set an almost impossible standard for me. Sales increased each year. We had many repeat customers, and our client list was a who's who of the *Fortune* and *Inc.* 500.

Jane and I sold the business in 1991. We did not go public. We did not make a killing. A not very satisfying relationship with our venture capital partners forced a premature sale of the company. Throughout this book I refer to the strengths women enjoy in their ability to build and maintain relationships. I speak often of this as an asset that makes our success at business less mysterious. It is also true that for a relationship to flourish there must be two parties engaged. I believe that our relationship with our venture partners was marred by the constant disquiet they displayed having their money invested in women. It was their first (although I expect not their last) such "experiment." Many factors contributed to the demise of our venture capital relationship, however, I am satisfied that by the time we sold Odysseum we had created something important. We set a standard for employees who will now always demand a little more from business; we set a standard for customers who will demand qualitative programs from suppliers; and we set a standard for ourselves, for our next company.

This is not a book about Odysseum, although you will learn something about that company through the stories told in the coming chapters. It is a book about women and their businesses, my own and others that I know. Our business is just one of many I draw on to give the reader a view of a significant sector of the

American economy, a sector that is not often written about and too often invisible. The sweeping use of the word "women" throughout should not be construed to mean all women. Although I will not be surprised if some of my experience rings true for many readers, I humbly remind the reader that this is the story of my experience and my sense of what is true for many of the women I know. I have told my story to make my prejudices clear and to give the reader a sense of the history and experience that informs my point of view.

If you think the picture I paint of the power and possibilities of women and their businesses is overly optimistic, consider this: by the end of this decade it is projected that 40 to 50 percent of all businesses will be owned by women. Like a great wave, a tsunami wave, we are coming. Like the effluence of the great rivers we are altering the landscape and enriching the economy. Flowing through your lives we are changing the very nature of business.

Acknowledgments

Thank you seems such a small phrase. Bells should ring, lights should flare, and a brass band should march to properly acknowledge how important the following people have been to this most recent part of my journey. But I was taught that thank you is a powerful phrase when it comes from the heart, and my appreciation for the contributions of my friends and colleagues surely does.

I am especially indebted to two men who were, in a way, catalytic agents for this book. George Gendron, the editor in chief of *Inc.* magazine, responded to my letter to the editor three years ago and sparked a series of events that enabled me to travel the country listening to the stories of women entrepreneurs in a wide range of businesses and industries. George's own curiosity and his support for my concerns helped transform my frustration over the invisibility of women's businesses into an active quest to bring this community to light. Later, Mark Greenberg, my publisher, became the first man to say, explicitly, "I really want your voice." His words challenged me to take responsibility for my feelings and knowledge and helped to loosen my "voice." To both men I offer my thanks.

I am rich in friends, and the loving support and encouragement I received from them got me through some rough passages. The Kellogg Fellows who visited with me in Ojai and said, "do it," were instrumental in my decision to proceed with the project. Jane Lytle, Linda Hill, and Ann Donnellon—smart, extraordinary women—read, questioned, suggested, and challenged ideas, helping me to consider, reconsider, and articulate notions not quite fully formed. Their ability to engage with me is a treasure. Peggy Barry, Kit Durgin, Elise McConnell, Ann Florini, and Heidi DiCapua introduced me to many new trails and perspectives. They commiserated, coached, and encouraged me. In this way they aided and abetted the completion of this book.

Janet Surrey and Steve Bergman are breaking new ground in their professional (and personal) explorations of the nature of relationships and the new psychology of women and men. Their work inspires, confirms, and influences my own. I am also grateful for their generous emotional and intellectual nurturing. Warren Bennis was an encouraging and thoughtful early reader. His willingness to save me from myself in a couple of instances was much appreciated! His work on leadership has heartened and inspired me; I hope its influence is evident in this book.

Sara Hughes, a recent business school graduate, and Georgeann Manville, an active entrepreneur, provided critical research support and were generous with both wisecracks and wisdom when I appeared to need one or the other. They each made contributions that opened new areas of inquiry. I feel incredibly fortunate to have them on my team.

Richard Teller gave me, as he always does, valued and wise counsel.

Scott Mathews, my agent, and Virginia Smith, my editor, get a standing ovation. As a hiker, I know the value of a great guide. The two of them were patient, knowledgeable, and always supportive, even when trying to get me to consider another view or another possibility. I'd go into the High Sierras with either of them anytime.

Without the aid of the Kellogg Foundation, which provided my fellowship and support for my learning plan, completion of this book would have been far more difficult. Bobby Austin provided advice that still echoes in my ears. To him, to the foundation, and the Kellogg Fellows (especially my first "reader," Gary Bloom), I give thanks.

Finally, critically and lovingly, thank you to the Odysseum team, for everything.

dedicated to the professor and to my teachers:
grandmother dudley, grandfather dudley, mother and father,
susie, rebel, jerry, barb and chuck, jane,
and the women (and men) rewriting the rules

Introduction

When I look into the future, it's so bright it burns my eyes.
Oprah Winfrey

Over the last decade business wisdom has been accumulating from a wide assortment of sources: from the Japanese to the One-Minute Manager, from Machiavelli to Attila the Hun, and from Tom Peters to the Tao. What all this wisdom has in common is that it all springs from the male experience and perpetuates many traditional assumptions about the nature of business. The purpose of this book is to provide balance by sharing the entrepreneurial experience of women.

Many women are leaving the giants of the *Fortune 500* to start their own businesses. Others choose never to enter the ranks of the giants. In 1992, the Labor Department released a report stating that for the the first time since 1948 the participation of women in the workforce had declined. They explained that more women were staying home to take care of their kids. That is partly true. But with the dramatic increase in the number of women-owned businesses, "the rest of the story" emerges. No longer content to spend their most productive years in organizations sealed off by a glass ceiling, no longer willing to work in companies that greedily consume all the hours of their life (leaving nothing for self, family, or friends), no longer able to blindly accept old assumptions about what business is and must be, women are voting with their feet. We are closing the door on corporate rigidity and inventing companies in which we can make money, do good, and have fun. We are creating the stuff of our wildest dreams.

Not all women run their businesses in the ways I describe in the following chapters. But there are thousands of women (and increasing numbers of men) who are a chorus, the vanguard of transformative leaders who are rewriting the rules of business.

This book is at the confluence of three streams that have been flowing in my business life. The first stream is the sale of my business, which gave me time to reflect on the feelings and experiences I had drawn on in the course of growing and managing the business. The second is the series of dinners for women business owners I hosted for *Inc.* magazine in 1990. The third stream flowing through this book is the wealth of long conversations held over the last five years with women (friends, colleagues, and strangers on planes) who own businesses all over the country. Ancient rivers like the Nile and the Mississippi regularly overflow, feeding the land, leaving behind good rich soil for planting. In like manner, I feel the overflowing of my banks, the spilling over of knowledge gained from my own experience as well as the lessons learned from other women who own businesses. Throughout this book, I draw on the voices, experiences, and conversations—the overflow—from all three streams. I hope the overflow will prove rich for others.

There is a creative force that emerges in the process of starting and building a company. No less artists than Mary Cassatt, Frida Kahlo, Georgia O'Keeffe, or Toni Morrison, women paint, sculpt, write, and compose their businesses. Like Olympic weightlifters, they stretch, flex, grunt, and rely on inner sources of strength and power to shape the fragile spirit of an idea. And wiliness, too. Like Miss Marple, they use their powers of observation, intuition, analysis, and synthesis to solve mysteries of invention, to outwit competitors, to wear down reluctant investors.

Our stories are about service. We work to demonstrate the ways in which our companies can serve clients, communities, employees, shareholders, and selves. We challenge the old values of accumulation for its own sake, numbers tell the story, buyer beware, and use it or lose it. Our tales tell of hope and creation and the sheer exhilaration of the adventure. Bungee jumping is child's play compared to the rare adventure of the businesses we are creating.

American corporations and business schools have spent time, energy, and money trying to understand the work cultures and practices of overseas competitors. However, a more fundamental understanding of and respect for one another's differences—and riches—*right here at home* can reap rewards as well. Women have learned a great deal from good men running good companies (as well as from the guys running less-than-admirable ones). But in the course of our own trials and triumphs, we have discovered some things that arise out of our own experiences as women. This book is an opportunity to share those discoveries and offer some possibilities for new ways of doing business—not just women's business, but *everybody's* business.

There are three themes that run through the book and the stories I tell. The first is the power of women's learned capacity to relate. Janet Surrey, Carol Gilligan, Jean Baker-Miller, and other researchers associated with Wellesley College's Stone Center have spent the last decade developing a "New Psychology of Women." Their work is causing a revolution in psychological theory and is intended to help us "explain ourselves to ourselves," as Gilligan puts it. The ability to grow, feel competent, and empowered *within the context of meaningful relationships* is a fundamental dimension, of women's experience, which the Stone Center scholars illuminate. It is this very aspect of our individual personas that makes a profound and positive impact on the way women start and grow businesses. This strength constitutes a new understanding of business to be shared with men and women alike.

The second theme, subtext to many of the stories, is a challenge to the definition of wealth. Most of the women I talked with in the course of writing this book make it clear that a tombstone that reads "Her net worth was $10 million [or $100 million, or $100 billion] and her ROI was 35%, R.I.P." isn't their idea of a fitting epitaph. Which is not to say that most women entrepreneurs don't think making a lot of money is a splendid idea. Many of them have revenues competitive with some of the largest companies in America. But an increasing number of women and men define wealth as a complex that includes self-esteem, integrity, quality products, family, friendships, and contribution as well as financial achievement. For many of the people described in this book, the bottom line is measured at the end of one's life, not just at the end of a quarter.

The third theme is about truth. Many of the words spoken by women here are words that have long been held secret. At last, many of the five million women who own businesses in this country have begun to say aloud what previously they silently believed was right, possible, and true. Claiming their truths, they are claiming their own identities. That "the truth shall set you free," is being felt by women throughout the land.

I hope this book will encourage those women who think about starting a business but haven't. I hope it will serve as an invitation to young women who never thought about owning a business but perhaps should. I hope that men will be tempted to apply some of what we have learned to their own business lives. For men who are husbands, lovers, and friends of women who own companies, the book may function as a guidebook of sorts. For the mothers and fathers of women who own businesses, I offer another perspective on the entrepreneur in your family. For the children of women who own businesses, it's a glimpse of mom after she's gone out the door. And, finally, for the rule changers themselves—the women who are altering the nature of business in America and realizing their wildest dreams—I offer this as a tribute.

I

NEW VISIONS

The (New) Right Stuff

> *In the different voice of women lies the truth of an ethic
> of care, the tie between relationship and responsibility and
> the origins of aggression in the failure of connection.*
>
> Carol Gilligan

I am not six feet tall. I don't wear Brooks Brothers suits. I don't own
an HP calculator (although my business partner does). I cry. I laugh,
a lot. I touch people. I talk about how I feel. I remember birthdays
(most of the time). I take time off (at least a week or two a season; I
get some of my best ideas while outside the workspace). I start work
early—sometimes. Sometimes, I start late. I don't look like I have
"the right stuff," but I do. And so do my counterparts—women who
founded and run their own companies.

THE RIGHT STUFF: WHAT IT IS, WHERE IT COMES
FROM, HOW TO GET IT

Tom Wolfe used the phrase "the right stuff" to describe the willingness of a pilot to "go up in a hurtling piece of machinery and put
his hide on the line and have the moxie, the reflexes, the experience,
the coolness, to pull it back at the last yawning moment."[1] The
men who proved themselves able to fly the fastest jet aircraft or ride
a rocket to the moon were acknowledged to have "that righteous
stuff," which defined them as giants among men. Although many
men lost their lives in these deadly darings, those who survived
were at the top of the pyramid, worthy of adulation by all those
left behind—those further down the pyramid. It was, in a way, a defi-

nition of manhood, a definition that Wolfe managed to question throughout his book, while still honoring the men—the astronauts and test pilots—who carried the mantle. The phrase, "the right stuff," came to imply a male persona—part Eagle Scout, part fighter pilot, part Superman. With all due respect to astronauts, fighter pilot jocks, and anyone else willing to hang his hide over the edge, I am taking the liberty of wresting the phrase from the grip of cliche and the exclusive domain of men. Let us consider that phrase with fresh possibility. Imagine that women are also carriers of the right stuff and that the proof of attainment is not found in looking down on those who have been left behind (with a certain degree of smug self-righteousness) but in looking around and seeing who you have been able to *bring along with you*. Further, imagine that the new right stuff is a set of values and qualities that actually bring the cliched definition into question and that, in this new vision of the right stuff, we find a way of being and a style of leadership that is growth-enhancing for all parties in an enterprise, not just for the star, that is, the fighter pilot or the executive at the top.

The right stuff required to launch a space shuttle, win a war, or head a traditional company may indeed be different from the "stuff" required to create the kinds of companies so many women seem to envision. But if the goal is different, it is not necessarily lesser or easier. Those people intent on building companies that combine good work with good lives, demonstrate qualities rare enough and demanding enough to warrant a right stuff medal. Some of those qualities include:

1. Ease in relationships and a drive for connection

2. A head, heart, and hands policy

3. Appreciation of complexity and process

4. Desire for balance and self-awareness

5. A sense of artistry, imagination, and playfulness

6. An integrated vision of business and ethics

7. Courage

In a way, the "sum" of these qualities constitute a form of leadership. Max DePree, author of *The Art of Leadership* and chairman of Herman Miller, Inc., has said that being a leader has much to do with nurturing, sincerely caring about others, coaching, guiding, and serving. Warren Bennis, author of *On Becoming a Leader*, offers the observation that leadership is, in part, the process of fully "becoming oneself." Women who start businesses often find they can create environments that give them, often for the first time, space and opportunity to fully "become self," *however unconventional* that happens to be. They also find they can lead, without apology or self-consciousness, in ways that incorporate the kind of nurturing and innovation Max DePree has written about—and practiced in his own company.

Lots of women (and men, too) have these qualities; however, not all women recognize or value them yet. (Many men who possess these qualities keep trying to ignore them. The other right stuff fantasies keep getting in the way for both sexes.) The new right stuff is rarely taught in our business schools, but these qualities have their source deep in our psyches. They are born from life crises endured and transcended or from risking, failing, and learning. For women, these qualities are, in part, the legacy of learning to survive in a frequently "woman unfriendly" world. Our resourceful adaptations to a deficit of power, rights, support, and respect have helped us hone skills and qualities that might otherwise have languished. Although many of us—men and women—may not force X-2, -4, or -15 fighter jets to high speeds, we have learned ways of creating businesses that, while they may not get us killed in an unlucky flight, may nevertheless help change the world.

Anita Roddick, owner of The Body Shop, an international retail company, is one woman who embodies new right stuff qualities. When I first heard Roddick speak, before a crowd of 500 business owners (mostly men), I cried. With passion and the credibility that comes from being the head of a multi-million-dollar international company, she challenged the audience's most deeply ingrained assumptions about doing business. She spoke fervently of business's responsibility to protect and improve the environment and of the moral necessity to help develop, not exploit, trade partners in developing countries. She described the ways she made partnerships with her employees and dared the people in front of her to explore new assumptions about the nature and responsibilities of business. I was not moved because she said something new to me, but because at last I heard another woman stand up and say out loud, without apology, what I had felt for so long. Roddick's courage—her insistence on speaking her "truth"—reinforced my own beliefs.

Like Roddick, many women are finding their voice and exercising qualities that redefine business leadership.

A PARTIAL INVENTORY OF THE (NEW) RIGHT STUFF

The list of qualities I label the new right stuff is not meant to be all in-clusive. Not all the women in this book possess all the qualities listed (and not all men lack them); however, these qualities do provide a set of characteristics that appear to cluster in women entrepreneurs who start companies and manage them in ways that meet their own needs and goals. These qualities have the effect—sometimes subtly, sometimes dramatically—of changing the chemistry, the feel, and the fabric of their businesses.

Sometimes there are paradoxes in the ways women exercise these qualities: for instance, managing a long list of complex problems while simultaneously focusing, almost obsessively, on a single goal. Similarly, women often seem to incorporate balance and commit-ment to life with commitment to their business. Perhaps women are paradoxical; at the least, they are complex and interesting human beings. And they run some terrific companies. These new right stuff qualities I see lead me to feel enormously hopeful about our future as well as the future of women who own companies, their well-being and their economic freedom.

Ease in Relationships and a Drive for Connection

This quality is different from the networking we've heard about for the last 20 years. Networking implies a set of fundamentally instrumental relationships in which the goal is mutual use of one another's resources or connections. The drive for connection sug-gests a fuller experience of mutuality—not just taking and using, but giving and being present in ways that enable all parties involved to come to know, trust, and support one another. Women have friend-ships that last for years. Women are often family caretakers. They are comfortable with relationships. This comfort with connected-ness is drawn on to manage relationships with suppliers, customers, investors, and employees with ease. This is not to suggest that women have a saintly, gene-backed advantage in business relationships. In fact, I have a few women friends I wouldn't trust to negotiate a pound of pork from the butcher. But, generally, the women I know relate better than the men I know. Argue with me if you like. That's my experience.

I can make this statement about connectedness at almost any table filled with women and knowing nods will be the response. The desire to connect and the ability to relate makes itself evident in numerous ways. Women, think of the number of times recently a man asked you, "How do you feel? What do you think?" Try to recall the last time a male colleague uttered an encouraging "mmm" or "yes" to keep you talking. Think of the last time a man listened, just listened to you without demanding center stage or, even more rare, reflected back on something you said to let you know you were heard, to check in, to *relate!!!* Now review those same questions and put women friends in the same seat. See the difference? I thought so.

When in touch, literally and figuratively, women feel right— centered, to use a dangerously New Age phrase. Women enjoy being in relationships, hearing and being heard. It's how we get our bearings, check out our instincts. If I can relate to you, I get a handle on reality. If we connect, I know there is a good chance communication will be clear. Decisions we make based on that connection are likely to be trustworthy. When we relate, I can get information from you. I can tell if we are off track or in tune. Connecting and relating are the things women do to keep track of truth, and truth is the underlying glue that keeps a woman's business steady. Women talk about, use, and trust their feelings. Among themselves, they connect and relate. When they put that ability to work in their businesses they give themselves a serious business advantage. I don't mean to be harsh toward men. Of course, I know a number of good men who relate well. But I believe they are the exception, a select group.

For too long women have felt pressured to deny and hide their emotional depth, mutual empathy, and capacity for relationships. Those qualities have been devalued and derided as soft, unprofessional, not tough enough, and naive; yet, it turns out, these qualities are particularly valuable to business. Jean Baker-Miller of Wellesley College's Stone Center maintains that women's discomfort with claiming their best qualities (the capacity to feel, relate, be emotional) comes from a deep awareness that our culture has declared, "men will do the important things in life; women will take care of the lesser realm of fostering the growth of other human beings." "Women," she says, "have learned empathy and tend to value relationships. In the overall, men have been encouraged to turn away from learning about relationships, to develop in other directions, lest they be seen as 'womanly.' "[2]

The body of work done by researchers at the Stone Center over the last decade is valuable because it confirms what we know intuitively to be true. When I listen to researchers Janet Surrey and Jean Baker-Miller discuss "relational empowerment," I get it. I know immediately they mean that our feelings of self-worth and self-esteem come from our ability to relate to others. This makes us feel powerful. It is not terribly mysterious; it is simply confirmation of our experience. And it is wildly exciting. At last, scholars who study women's psychological development are framing our experience in theories that explain relationships as a means of personal growth and intellectual development. Prior to their research, our desire, indeed our yearning, for connectedness had been diagnosed as proof of our weakness—a neurotic neediness based on our inability to separate, to be strong and disconnected like our ideal male models. We have needed "fixing" for so long, according to the gospel of Freud, that many women buried these parts of self that were most useful and hid them in shame.

We know that the more numerous and diverse the relationships we enjoy—that is, the more we connect with real feelings and shared experiences with others—the greater is our sense of being both connected to and empowered to respond to others. That knowledge has been denied for generations. Trying to adapt to the rules of corporate America is just one way some women deny their ability, their assets. Yet the happy fact is that our friendships, family relationships, and love relationships provide a training ground for that sense of familiarity and comfort we take in being connected on various levels to employees, customers, investors, colleagues, and the full constellation of people involved with our businesses.

Baker-Miller has used the word "zest" to describe the effect of connecting and relating on our well-being. *Zest*, what a word: "relish," "gusto," and "piquancy" are synonyms for "zest." That fits. Often in a meeting or in the middle of a project when ideas are flying and people are cooperating and working together, I feel gusto, *without* the beer. Janet Surrey explains my delight this way, "The joining of visions and voices creates something new. Connection and participation in something larger than self does not diminish but rather heightens a sense of personal power and understanding."[3] I knew that.

At the heart of the Stone Center's investigations is the idea that women's development involves the "self-in-relation." This term simply refers to an understanding of oneself that comes from seeing oneself relating to others. How do I talk with my best friend? What do I share of myself with others? Do I feel rapport and enjoy conversation, exchange, and dialogue? Or must I command center stage, grab all the attention, take more than I give? "Growth of self-in-relation" is the development women report as they experience relationships with significant others, children, friends, colleagues, family members, and others. Using this ability to relate in business relationships is a clear benefit to the woman business owner.

Judy Rosener, a faculty member at the University of California at Irvine, surveyed members of the International Women's Forum (which includes many corporate executives and business owners) and matched them with men who held comparable executive and entrepreneurial positions. She found, not surprisingly, that women's business relationships are more likely to be based on trust, empathy, and engagement, while men tend to base their business relationships on pure power or hierarchical arrangements of organization. She described the leadership style of the women she surveyed as "interactive"—that is, characterized by four active qualities: (1) encouraging participation, (2) sharing power and information, (3) enhancing the self-worth of others, and (4) energizing others. These are all elements of relating and connecting.

Rosener was also aware of the difficulties that have been associated with women's style: "because information is power, leaders who share it can be seen as naive or needing to be liked."[4] How do we all know that women who lead and run businesses predicated on the assumption that participation and respect and engagement are smart ideas are considered naive? We just know. We have been told. It is a message repeated to us in a million subtle (and not so subtle) ways, in movies, books, on television, and in the interactions we have with traditionalists who dismiss women's ways of thinking and behaving, not as different, but as wrong.

Power derived from one's position in the organizational hierarchy is, in part, the legacy of systems invented to achieve large scale projects—from the pyramids to the railroads, from castles to factories. With the rise of industrial society, the urge to organize, bureaucratize, get faster and more efficient, was a relentlessly pursued goal. For a long time, the simplistic equation seemed to be that more was better—more bureaucracy, larger organizations, and more control. Organizational position, numbers of employees reporting to (and *under*) that position, and the size of one's budget were qualities that automatically embued some people with more power than others and implied rights of authority and control, largely unchecked, in many cases.

But where "more is better" once prevailed, now "less is more" may be more functional to the tasks of modern management—less control, less bureaucracy, less concentrated power. The skills Rosener identified in her leadership study (communication and an ability to relate, feel empathy, understand, and make oneself understood and respected) are now the skills that more often produce the kind of motivation, loyalty, and reciprocity that so many companies seek from their employees.

Not all women are whiz kids at relating, any more than all men are relational nerds. But what we know about the socialization of women in Western societies is that more often than not we have learned how to relate by the time we are five, and after that the process is one of simply honing our skills (for the sake of survival as well as for the pleasures and practical benefits that strong relationships bring). Now that socialization is paying off. We are seeing that hierarchy and bureaucracy are less effective at moving mountains than mutuality, respect, and the ability to relate, listen, and be heard. When Tom Peters started pushing "skunk works" and smaller, flatter, more agile organizations in the 1980s, he gave notice to corporate leaders that the "bigger is better" philosophy would turn them into dinosaurs. Many companies heeded Peters's advice, but smaller alone is not enough. Paring down and "flattening" organizations doesn't do any good if people don't know how to relate inside those new organizations.

Historically, the ability to relate (in fact, to acknowledge feelings at all) was sand in the wheels of hierarchical, bureaucratic organizations. Both men and women were trained early on (first by Frederick Taylor and his cohorts, later by business school professors) to leave the ability, indeed, the *desire,* to relate in any real way outside the office door. Well-behaved men did—often to their own personal loss. Women, deemed highly unreliable, emotional, and unpredictable (we pay attention to our feelings and you know how unpredictable that makes us), were hardly given a chance to behave. Finally, in the 1970s and 1980s we somehow made it clear that we would dress right, talk right, and try to fit in, and we traded off our feelings and the right to use our ability to relate fully for the dubious privilege of entering corporate America.

Happily, many women now running successful companies boldly claim as right stuff the so-called womanly abilities, reveling in the freedom to use relational skills nurtured over many years and challenging old notions of what constitutes the important work. One business owner from Grand Rapids, Michigan, put it this way:

> Women are naturally attuned to helping other people do their very best—being supportive, coaching, and guiding. Each person requires a different kind of attention. I think women are very sensitive to those things and are ready to be leaders.

Such generalizations are tricky; however, making meaningful connections that work for yourself, for others, and for your company does require a willingness and a facility for nurturing. Enabling people to feel connected to one another, as well as to the goals of the business, is one way to gain from employees the motivation, loyalty, and commitment to purpose that too many owners and managers think they can buy or demand.

Studies show that owners, employees, and some investors (note the success of socially responsible investment funds) believe that money alone is not a sufficient motivator. They want meaning, balance, and connection to higher aims than producing more widgets than were made last year. The age of self-assessment via the net worth statement is retreating. People seek connection to purpose as well as to others. By giving themselves free rein to nurture and encourage relating and relationships *within the context of their businesses,* women are creating those connections and tapping a well of power that helps build strong, stable companies. In those companies, morale, motivation, and commitment to mission flourish like seeds in good soil. "That sense of human community is a wonder; [it's] very satisfying somehow," said an entrepreneur from Boston.

Women who own businesses often express as much pleasure in the relationships required to make the business work as with excellence, increased profits, and growth in self-esteem. But the ability to create and maintain relationships does not mean that women (a) do not fire employees or (b) are soft marks. "In relationship" implies an ability to relate, exchange, dialogue, and make decisions while maintaining a sense of self. Men and women who enable employees with drug and alcohol problems to get away with shabby work or long absences are not "in relationship." Women and men who ignore poor performance and symptoms of employee dissatisfaction are not "in relationship." They are out of relationship, unwilling to engage; they are denying not dealing.

Connectedness is that sense of self and caring for others that demands involvement and presence in the toughest of circumstances. It requires the ability and willingness to explore the causes of bad performance, set limits, assert rights, take difficult stands, defend values, and set standards. These actions are respected and have credibility when a relationship exists. Where there is no relationship, there is no connection—no basis upon which to gain respect or achieve understanding. But where a relationship exists and connectedness is present—for men as well as for women—growth, understanding, and healthy companies can be the result. Until men more commonly claim their own capacity to grow in their relationships, women will enjoy an edge in their ability to motivate employees, inspire colleagues, and develop alliances with suppliers and investors.

Whole People: A Head, Heart, and Hands Policy

Since the mid-1970s, companies have talked about "fully utilizing their human resources." This jargon suggests that they employ androids and not people. By tightening a few screws, redesigning an arm, or programming a new way of thinking, the android can be made more productive. I hate the term "human resources." It makes me think of jobs that just require left arms or perhaps a right ear. Instead of material resources stowed in bins, we can go to the closet and pull out the part of a human required at the time for a particular job or function.

A head, heart, and hands policy recognizes that a whole individual comes to work. That is, ideas are welcome; individuality is viewed as an asset; and the full set of qualities embodied in employees, colleagues, and associates are valued as present and future treasures. Particularly where capital resources are scarce, a head, heart, and hands policy is more than just a humanistic approach to business—it is a *no-nonsense* approach to business. A right arm, a left ear, or a facility analyzing flow charts is just not enough to fill a place on a payroll. A whole person—one who brings the abilities of mind and creative spirit, devotes caring and heart to the welfare of colleagues, customers, and company, and willingly rolls up sleeves and gets his or her hands dirty making something happen—is the sort needed and appreciated by all businesses. Such a policy may require companies to adapt to people, but the current norm of insisting that people adapt to companies is both dehumanizing and limiting. Ultimately, selecting "parts" of whole people shortchanges the companies they work for as well.

Inviting a whole person to work does mean that, in addition to a specific "resource," you also accept the messier parts of their humanity. With their laughter may come times of moodiness. With their energy and imagination may come days when attention wanders or is totally absent. With their concerns about work come concerns about family and other outside pressures and interests, which will sometimes impinge on work. Most companies are uncomfortable with whole people. They are hard to manage, to understand, and to cope with. But women seem to expect whole people to show up for work.

A graphic artist who once worked for our company on layouts and brochure design was also a cartoonist and a pretty good writer of creative fiction. On learning of these talents, which we had neither advertised for nor knew about when he was first hired, we were able to expand his role in the company in a number of ways. This provided him with opportunities to be more of who he was and provided us with skills we would not otherwise have had. Another employee (hired to be in charge of operations) was also a first-rate actress. We put her talent to work as a spokesperson for the company, again emphasizing her strengths. This same person was a master of organization and detail (which is why she was hired as head of operations), she was experienced in theater production and had a powerful appreciation for what it took to present to the public, nail down the most specific directions, and keep everyone on track and following a plan. Those qualities, as critical as they were, did not live easily under the same roof with my personality. Quite unintentionally, we often drove each other crazy; yet she was vital to the success of the company. It was essential for me to learn to live with those parts of her being that were so different from mine. I didn't always succeed (such are my flaws), but I understand that people are not like Lego pieces. You cannot use one part and isolate the rest in a place where it won't inconvenience you.

In companies where the business owner herself (or himself) is struggling to juggle business, family, and other obligations, there is often natural empathy for the trials of employees. Women, comfortable with a wider range of emotions, tolerate a wider spectrum of behavior. Although expectations for excellence may be very high, the expectations for laughter and celebration also signal an acceptance of spirit and individuality. It is this individuality that many of us are determined to incorporate into the running of our businesses. As a business owner from Grand Rapids, Michigan, said:

> I tell people when it stops being fun you need to leave the company; you don't belong here if you're not having fun.

Look at pictures in annual reports or corporate board meetings. The men in their dark suits all look alike. The efforts of Armani and Calvin Klein aside, individuality is anathema. Although the day of the *Organization Man* and *The Man in the Grey Flannel Suit* is theoretically behind us, and although IBM apparently allows blue shirts in addition to white now, the tendency to repress individuality for the convenience of management seems to live on. Not so in firms owned by women I know. Are they simply more tolerant of deviance? Probably not. Entrepreneurial men in Silicon Valley are renowned for their zany exhibitions of individuality. But women, anxious to be individuals in their own right, are likely to grant the same right to others. Consciously or intuitively, they understand that a whole person has more to offer than a well-pegged human resource. Women come to their businesses too often having been pegged themselves: as girls, mothers, secretaries, helpmates, and/or minority women. According to a business owner in Minneapolis:

> When I went to school you were either a teacher or a nurse, and there weren't many other options. You only worked to help your professional husband finish school and then would have children and stay home. Well, I started that pattern but when "happily ever after" didn't work out, I had to figure out what I would do to support these two little children I had.

Having experienced limitations (in expectations, opportunities, pay, recognition, and power), women have a particular empathy for and ability to be encouraging of others' needs for individuality and self-expression. It's a little hard to demand something so basic for yourself, if you're not willing to grant the same to others. Respecting and appreciating each person's individuality is the key to an authentic head, heart, and hands policy.

Appreciation of Complexity and Process

In one way the experience of women entrepreneurs is very different from their male counterparts. Women entrepreneurs don't have wives. There may be a nurturing spouse or significant other, and sometimes there are nannies, housekeepers, and other paid staff. But none of these people takes the place of a wife—the person who worries about hiring the nanny, assigning duties to the housekeeper, and getting the kids to their required appointments. That so many women juggle factories and families as well as they do is a testament to the presence of Amazons among us. As a business owner in Minneapolis said:

> No matter how successful any of us become, many of us still do the same things we did when we made $15,000 a year.... Still responsible for every holiday, the food, the groceries, getting the kids to wherever. Here we are running multi-million-dollar corporations but I've got to make sure the laundry gets done.

Regardless of whether this phenomenon is good, bad, or indifferent, it is real. And it is this experience that women bring to their businesses that helps them to manage a complex of concerns—the conflicts of marketing requirements and operational imperatives, the competing claims of customers and investors, the varying perspectives of new and senior employees—with some facility. As a business owner in Boston put it, "A lot of things are thrust upon you, and you just learn to handle them or to juggle a lot of things."

The management of complex problems in organizations is the focus of much business school study. How do you manage inventory, respond to the market, take advantage of favorable supply prices, cut warehousing costs, determine optimal work force size, and remain flexible—all at the same time? (Now add to that dentist appointments, softball games for kids, a death in the family, and community obligations and you get a *real* sense of complexity!) Most of us can solve any one of these problems independently, but working them together like pieces in a puzzle requires a different kind of problem-solving ability as well as a certain tolerance for what are sometimes termed "wicked" problems. Business professor Ian Mitroff explains that such problems are wicked in the sense of being "like the head of a hydra, an ensnarled web of tentacles. The more you attempt to tame them, the more ensnarled they become."[5] For example, you may buy triple quantities of a critical material to take advantage of a supplier sale, but if you have cut inventory to reduce warehouse space and sales projections for next year are not yet clear, it is possible to solve one problem (supply savings) only to create another (raised warehousing costs). Both problems can be solved or further aggravated by new data on sales projections.

Most people involved in business are all too aware of wicked problems. Awareness, alas, is not the same as being comfortable with it. The rise of business organization and management science can be explained by the ever-elusive quest for control, which the forefathers of industry associated with efficiency. To some extent we can explain hierarchy, organization trees, chain of command, and other inventions of modern management as part of the constant drive to make organizations rational, efficient, orderly, and manageable—that is, controllable. And it wasn't so long ago that the social organization of America, men at work and women at home, reinforced this quest for the rational life and enabled us to foster an illusion of neatness that implied that work things happened at work and home things happened at home. "Don't bring your personal life to work" was a common admonition. Between the development of management science and the social organization of men and women, a myth of order and control in the business of business emerged. Comfort with complexity is, in part, being at ease when you are not in control or when you are sharing control. It is trusting that all the loose ends, with participation from others and your own clear vision, will come together properly.

As single men and women, dual career couples, single-parent families, and other iterations of contemporary society have become the norm rather than the exception, old illusions about the compartmentalization of work and personal life have crumbled. Simultaneously, technology, communication, global competition, and the speed at which change fractures stable practices, markets, and ways of doing business (not to mention routine and predictable lives) have unsettled many of those folks who are only truly comfortable when everything is in order. Getting kids to the dentist, caring for elderly parents, juggling his and her schedules and earning a degree at night while working during the day, and trying to find time to read the paper on the weekend are new heads added to the hydra. Learning to live with an exponential growth in complexity—that is, learning how not to get crazy when you are not in control and maintaining a sense of humor, health, and a few good relationships, is key to a healthy entrepreneurial spirit.

Comfort with complexity often extends to comfort with process. Although women are as capable as men of bungling process, they more often make an attempt to attend to it. Has everyone in the staff meeting been heard? Were ideas given sufficient air time? Did we explore why the silent one in the corner didn't offer an opinion this morning? Once again, this is explained in part by the value women place on being "in relationship." To relate, to be connected, one must pay attention, and paying attention is what process is all about.

If comfort with complexity is the ability to hold and deal with conflicting problems all at once, comfort with process is a tolerance for the gradual unfolding of surprise. Allowing process to unfold takes a certain amount of trust—in the people involved, in process itself, and in one's own ability to maintain direction and purpose in the midst of chaos. It means being willingly out of control while process does its thing.

Women have been out of control for much of their lives—out of control of their rights, their financial well-being, their physical safety, and their access to opportunity. Women are rarely in a position to mandate anything, whether in politics, business, or often even in the home. In spite of that, women get things done. And they have learned to create, to influence, and to be powerful anyway. To be out of control is nothing to fear, it is an old friend, a familiar adversary that has caused us to develop other skills—skills that appear to work very well for our businesses, thank you.

According to Stephen Bergman, a Boston novelist/psychiatrist writing about male psychological development, some men experience being out of control as a diminishing of power. While women in similar circumstances (that is, in the context of tending to relationships and being part of a process with others) may experience a sense of empowerment. This difference in response to the experience of being out of control—and the differing source of our feelings of power—is vital to understanding women's experience of business. That experience can guide us in training and socializing young managers, both women and men.

DIMENSIONS OF PROCESS.   It is important to understand three dimensions of process in business: the creative process, the group process, and the operational process. Comfort with process, that nonlinear, often messy, time-consuming dynamic of unfolding, provides a competitive advantage in all three areas.

Comfort with (indeed, enjoyment of) the *creative process* is the difference between wanting a slick new brochure and understanding that the way you get that brochure will affect everything from employee relationships, vendor success and motivation, the quality of the finished product, and customer satisfaction. This includes setting aside time for a creative brainstorming session, taking time to get input and reactions from all appropriate parties (salespeople, product designers, customer service representatives, etc.) on design samples, or saving time for a heated exchange or an impassioned plea for another approach. Such openness to input empowers others.

It also frequently results in a better product: an environmentally conscious assistant may remember to plug for the use of recycled paper; a customer service representative may remember an often-asked question that can be answered in the copy; or a naive query from someone taking a quick glance at the design may result in a fresh look at the goals of the brochure. A willingness to take time with process does not mean that everyone will be allowed to comment on everything, that a democratic vote will be taken on the final product, or that authority is being abdicated. It is simply a recognition that there is power and creativity in the collective ideas of a group or team. When the energy and involvement of that group is sought, the resulting product is usually richer and more thoughtfully realized than ideas (products, services, materials) created under controlled conditions, in a vacuum, or apart from the hothouse of competing views and differing perspectives.

Trusting that this is so and giving time and space for process to unfold can test the strength of the most sensitive entrepreneur. There were days when I preferred (and chose) the methods of a benign (mostly) dictator. But time spent in staff meetings, in informal consultations, and in organized imagining sessions goes a long way toward tapping the full power and energy of the "resources" available in the humans who are part of any entrepreneurial venture.

Facility with *group process* is seen in the difference between a staff meeting in which the leader talks, gives orders, and sticks strictly to the agenda and one in which there is time and room to explore issues that are new, troubling, or confusing—or just time to share, brainstorm, or laugh. Judy Rosener contrasts the "command and control" style of leadership associated with men with the interactive style described earlier. Women's tendency to empower, share power, invite participation, and be supportive of others is in marked contrast to the style often employed by men in which there is an ongoing series of transactions, exchanges of punishment and reward for tasks or services performed, a clear reliance on gaining power over another, and a real discomfort with empowering others. This difference in leadership style creates significantly different group experiences. Certainly it takes more time to be conscious and attentive to the needs of the group—the process unfolding (time for disagreements or further exploration of a new idea), and sometimes employees (or investors) may be thrown off by a request for input, especially if it is not subsequently used. But many women seem willing to trade off the extra time (and patience) required for the involvement of the group. A transactional style may foster the expectation that involvement should accrue as a simple right due by virtue of one's position in an organization or by the power one may hold over pay or promotion. Group loyalty and participation may be acquired in these more traditional, transactional ways, but it may not have the full heart of the person or group with whom the transaction is made.

Every group has a life of its own, a process it goes through in an hour and in a year. Sometimes those groups are healthy, energized work teams, and sometimes they are depressed and depressing groups of people who can obstruct the simplest goals. Leaders who engage their groups—whether a group of investors, a senior staff, a department, or the whole employee group—may enjoy higher levels of morale, employee motivation, and loyalty. Running groups by transaction rather than interaction may make a business owner feel more in control, or safe, but that may not be in the long-term best interest of the company.

As a woman business owner from Boston said:

> I've learned that if you are going to take money from someone, the more you keep them involved, the more they buy in to who you are and what you are going to give them. Long term, that's better for you. Because if decisions get made and they don't like what they see, they have been part of the process and at least understand. It's foolish not to involve them.

The wisdom of her insight extends to all the stakeholders associated with a business. Involvement, attention, and a willingness to listen, to reflect, and to be moved are all indications of respect. The ability to be "in relation" is not just growth enhancing for owners and entrepreneurs, it is a signal to everyone participating in the adventure that you recognize, appreciate, and respect their contributions. In the end we each seek respect and recognition. (Bob Schrank, philosopher, sage, and observer of work in America, once told me that he thought that much of the angst people feel could be resolved by giving them cassette tapes that had nothing but the sound of clapping on them. They could listen to these tapes on the way to work and arrive with a sense of recognition and affirmation. Bob was joking, but he calls attention to the human need for recognition and appreciation.) It is as important to spend quality time with employees, investors, and customers as it with children. Women (and men) who take pleasure in the relational process experience satisfactions and results that more than compensate for time "lost" and uninvited input.

Finally, *operational process* is attending to the systems and procedures for making things happen in reliable, efficient, and qualitative ways while seeking a balance between the needs of a system and the needs of the people who have to make that system work. The owner of a car dealership in Michigan mused:

> For me, one of the challenges that I find fun is the cycles—the ups and downs and problems. Making things work, from differentiating yourself from your competition to changing the buying public's perception of your salespeople. It's the actual process of making a business operate smoothly that I think is fun.

My business partner, Jane Lytle often says, "I like to work at making a business 'hum,' to get all the parts working in concert." Operational process is solving the puzzle of how to get hamburgers in the mouths of customers in a way that is hygienic, fast, inexpensive, and manageable for employees. Ideally, it includes the design of systems that are not dehumanizing to either employees or customers. Operational process is solving the puzzle of dispatching freight trucks for optimal scheduling while maintaining safety standards and respecting the health and welfare of drivers. Operational process is solving the puzzle of designing quality control in a service business with multiple variables that affect the delivery of the service. You have to be a little (ok, maybe a lot) compulsive to create and maintain good operational systems, but you also have to tolerate deviance to new ideas to ensure that the system constantly responds to and works for the humans in it. An obsession with process and a tolerance for deviance, as well as the ability to balance the two without resorting to a blind reliance on rules, are qualities that many women entrepreneurs (yes, and some men, too) nurture in themselves and others.

PROCESS AND PASSION.   In her acceptance speech for the San Francisco Chamber of Commerce Entrepreneur of the Year, Pam Laird, founder of PSL Marketing, spoke of Pam's Four P's: passion, plunge, perfecting, and partners. "You must have passion to plunge and enjoy the PROCESS of perfecting with partners," she told the audience.

Recently a young woman came to visit me. She was thinking about different business ideas. "I go back and forth," she said, "between ideas I think will make money and those I have some real passion for. How do I choose?" Pam Laird would probably advise the young woman to follow her passions. It is our deepest desires that provide us with the strength and the willingness to attend to the tedium of process when we otherwise would turn off the light, close down the meeting, or just lose interest. When people follow their hearts, they equip themselves to grapple with process. Late at night or on the road, my partner Jane and I often marvel over the fun we suddenly realize we are having. "It's a good thing," Jane will remark, "if I didn't enjoy the process of putting a business together, it would be a lot harder to keep going some days." Operating a business for the sheer pleasure of it, the enjoyment of the process of creation rather than as a means to something else (wealth or fame, for example), is part of what Jane is talking about. Her feelings are echoed by this owner of a fleet of charter boats:

> From financing to actual building took five years. Building the California Spirit was an act of love. I love my business.

Contrast this with the attitude of a male developer who spends as little time as possible with employees. When I asked, "You don't really enjoy interacting with employees do you?" he replied, "I do what I have to do."

Doing what "you have to do" will result in a very different business from the one that is lavished with love. I get a real charge out of each new form designed, an improvement in a customer survey, the creation of product enhancements, or just a suggestion to make staff meetings more fun. It is the building, "piece by piece, bit by bit," that gives me the creative surge of bringing something new to life, which is inherent in the process. Rare is the gardener who toils among the weeds for the mere pleasure of placing roses in vases. The feel of the soil, the satisfaction of engaging with nature, the process of learning about plants, soil, weather, and the frailties of some seeds are part of the process of gardening. Rare (I hope) are the parents who bring children into the world to watch them graduate from college. Raising the child, like raising the company, is the adventure. Businesspeople who start businesses to get rich or to simply exploit an opportunity, who seek the goal and resent the process, miss all the fun.

Desire for Balance and Self-awareness

Women owners are conscious of seeking balance. They don't all get it and when they get it may not sustain it indefinitely, but it is a value they consciously seek to integrate into their lives. Women are aware that although work is integral to life, it is not *all* of life. This knowledge is illusive in a world where all the messages imply otherwise. Nevertheless, for many, there is a stubborn refusal to abandon the quest for balance, as the following quotes from women entrepreneurs suggest.

> My greatest triumph has been to do exactly what I wanted to do with my life and make a business out of it. There are very few men who have their careers, let alone their businesses, founded on something like that. I continue to think that it is extraordinarily valuable that women hold on to the sense that their lives are a whole lot more than their work, their careers, and businesses.

> I don't think that women want the same things that men do. I love to feel powerful and I love to make money and I love the drive. But I

love my four beautiful children and my friends as well. I like the fact that I can cry and feel. I get support from my friends. I don't want to emulate men. I don't want to lose the good qualities that I have.

I cross country ski, I run, I do yoga, I like restoring old houses.... My frustration is that there are a lot of community things I would like to get involved with and there never seems to be time. This culture is so focused on the idea that what you do for money is all that is important; that really irks me. I'm now raising money for AIDS. The people who are involved in activities like that are really good to be around.

This last comment came from a venture capitalist from Boston. She has a solid record of impressive company dealings. Her choices of which companies to invest in and to nurture do not come simply from a strategic plan that targets a certain niche and requires a specific rate of return before being considered. Her choices are informed in part by her interests and values—interests she uses to stay in touch with the world and to develop more of herself, interests developed apart from business and outside the traditional work structure. This is a person who hikes in rainforests, stays abreast of issues in education, and cares deeply about developing opportunities for women. Not all of her investments are socially conscious, but all of her decisions are affected by her involvement in subjects and issues outside the narrow world of finance. Her success is attributable in part to her balance.

The 1980s were characterized by a profound lack of balance for both men and women. The make money, get ahead voices that seemed to ring in the head of a generation of careerists created scenes that look like a film in fast forward. Men have lived unbalanced lives for generations and considered it normal. Of course, total concentration on work, business, career, and growth at the expense of intimacy, relationships, and more varied interests wasn't considered unbalanced, it was simply what you did to prove your worth as a man, to get ahead, to succeed. Some women followed suit. In the quest for equality, economic independence, and entry into heretofore inaccessible realms, many women ran faster to catch up, worked harder, juggled the three fronts of work, home, and self, gained a toehold in the new frontier, and lost time and space to think and reflect on just what had actually been gained.

Fundamentally, finding balance is a matter of breaking rules— rules about hours of work, job design, and the nature of work.

Traditionally, our work models have not encouraged balance. Being present in the office, working long hours, and a boundaryless work life all contribute to the image of being a serious, good, dedicated businessperson. But these are social or cultural agreements, not laws we are biologically bound to live or die by. And there is mounting evidence (medical, psychological, and sociological) that lack of balance is not good for either people or businesses.

At a seminar offered during the 1990 *Inc.* 500 conference in Milwaukee, Wisconsin, about 20 entrepreneurs met to discuss ways to create more balance in their lives. Business owners are as prone to the seduction of the 28-hour workday as are corporate careerists. American entrepreneurial legends communicate the notion that you aren't a real entrepreneur if you aren't devoting every waking minute to the fulfillment of the business. But being an entrepreneur is in part about the quest for autonomy—the desire to create new rules for running one's life—as well as the desire for creating new products and finding economic independence (autonomy by another name). Entrepreneurs are celebrated for their vision, and the quest for balance is to some extent a matter of personal vision and needs. For some, balance is the freedom to spend guilt-free time with children and significant others; for others, balance implies attending to one's physical well-being, spiritual needs, cultural interests, and community concerns; for still others, balance is simply a matter of setting limits and maintaining a sense of oneself apart from one's business. Increasingly, leaders with the right stuff are expanding the visions of their businesses and organizations to include an eye on the development of self. Whatever the goals, the key to achieving balance seems to be flexibility. As a business owner in Minneapolis said:

> We have tremendous flexibility among the staff, working sometimes at home, sometimes in the office—it requires a lot of trust and a lot of flexibility. There are still traditionalists in my own organization [who are] not comfortable with this new way, but I think everyone is going to see the benefits of more job sharing and flextime.

In my own business I maintained balance with a strict commitment to seasonal sojourns. Occasionally, I also found balance (and encouraged the rest of the organization to seek it, too) by building it into the workday. At the end of a particularly hectic period of meeting schedules and fulfilling contracts, I might arrange a staff field trip to a movie during the workday; eating popcorn, we shared an experience that was illicit by most standards, yet it provided a break and a recognition of the idea that work is not all of life. Sometimes we would later use the experience to develop ideas and make connections back to our work, but the goal of the experience was to acknowledge the need for balance in the working schedule.

Physical endurance, broad perspectives, openness to the new and the unfamiliar, a degree of equanimity, a sense of humor, and the capacity to be both giving and receiving in relationships are all right stuff qualities that many women entrepreneurs understand are critical to the long-term well-being of a company. However, these qualities are hard to maintain when you are preoccupied with the daily grind of business operations; burned out; out of touch with yourself or your friends, family or world events; and weary from spreading yourself too thin.

I am struck by the ingenuity of the women entrepreneurs I meet and by the plethora of ways they divine to claim the balance they demand. Some have learned to recreate extended family networks, either with their own families (parents, aunts, uncles, sisters, and brothers) or with friendship networks in which shared care of children is arranged and managed. Those able to afford it get on a cruise ship or go to the mountains where they cannot be reached except in case of emergency. One woman business owner arranges regular theater trips to New York with her children; a woman entrepreneur from Manhattan rents a house in the Berkshires and allows herself to watch videos and nap on weekends, finding replenishment for the week ahead. Many entrepreneurs recognize that the practice of staying in daily contact with their company is more a reluctance to be out of control than a response to a true need their staffs may have to be in constant touch.

What about those entrepreneurs not yet flush with success? They walk, hike, garden, and make time for potluck dinners with friends. They fiddle with schedules that allow breathing space, rejecting traditional work hours/work week rules. They alternate working at home and at the office, and some days they may dress in jeans — in short, they take the liberty to make themselves comfortable.

The woman from Grand Rapids who said, "My greatest triumph has been to do exactly what I wanted to do with my life and make a business out of it," may have put her finger on the real key to finding balance in one's life. She has, in the words of Joseph

Campbell, the late anthropologist, "followed her bliss." Ruth Owades took time off after selling her first business, Gardeners Eden, and spent a large part of her time in her garden. A year later, recognizing what she cared about and how she wanted to spend her time, she started a second business that enabled her to be intimately involved with fresh flowers. Marti McMahon, enamored of boats, found a way to design and sail charter boats on San Francisco Bay. Karen Fenske, an impassioned environmentalist, chose to start a recycling business that meets the needs of the Michigan furniture industry.

The choices of these women stand in stark contrast to denizens of Wall Street who still think it is perfectly normal to give ten plus years to building a portfolio and net worth statement, spending precious years earning the right to do what they want. They live as though life were out there waiting to be purchased with ten years and a collection of IRAs. Following one's bliss, pursuing a passion, feeling the license to integrate work and life in a way that meets multiple human goals of growth, learning, contribution, creativity, relationships, and financial savings may be the best way to achieve a sense of balance in one's life. However, many people still feel it is slightly illicit to enjoy themselves during the day. The psychological baggage that equates work with suffering and a perverted sense of virtue is tough to unload. But right stuff business owners travel light.

A Sense of Artistry, Imagination, and Playfulness

After I finished giving a talk one night to a group of women, a few people stayed around to continue the discussion. One woman who did not own a business asked one of the female owners present a question. This owner, a building contractor, started to answer the question and then interrupted herself—"I just love having a business!" she said, half to herself. There was glee in her voice, a delight in herself and her business that she almost couldn't believe. I've seen that same sort of pleasure in children at play, in artists whose work is bearing fruit, and in other people engrossed in and pleased with what they are doing. Play, imagination, and a feeling of pure artistry are intangible products of business, but they aren't often discussed.

We talk about the need to be creative in business and the various

satisfactions that come from creating products and running successful businesses, but we too seldom say aloud that having a business
is fun and that part of the fun comes from an inner awareness of
self as artist or creator. It is pure, plain delight to create something
in your imagination and breathe life into it. We can talk all we want
about the difficulties, pain, and the hardship of choosing a life as an
entrepreneur, but the fact is that part of the charm, the seduction,
and the joy associated with owning a business is that it's fun.

I am not a painter (although in my next life I would like to be).
I have never appeared on stage (although I generally hold season
tickets to two or more theater companies). I am not a photographer,
sculptor, or poet (well, I have written a rhyme or two). But I have
spent a good portion of my life in the presence of artists and have
long been intrigued by the creative process, the muse, the chaos, the
muddling, the angst, the search, and the struggle to give substance to
a vision (whether it be a painting, photograph, symphony, sculpture,
or novel). Building a business is similarly an act of creation. It is a
cursed and glorious life—the struggle to shape something new out
of clay, get a painting to the gallery or a script to the stage is much
like bringing a business plan to a profitable reality.

In Stephen Sondheim's musical *Sunday in the Park with George*,
the main character, French postimpressionist George Seurat, is found
at an art opening lamenting what it takes to realize a vision:

> *A vision is just a vision if it's only in your head ...*
> *If no one gets to see it's as good as dead.*
> *Bit by bit, putting it together, piece by piece,*
> *Every moment makes a contribution, every little detail plays a part ...*
>
> *Gotta learn to trust your intuition ...*
> *Remember your objective, keep it in perspective.*
> *Everything depends on execution, time and perseverance,*
> *With a little luck along the way ...* [6]

Sondheim might as well have been talking of business. Perhaps
the existence of business plans and the language of business give
a misleading impression of business building as a rational process.
But, as any entrepreneur can confirm, starting a business is very
much a series of fits and starts, brainstorms and barriers. Creating a business is a round of chance encounters that leads to new
opportunities and ideas, mistakes that turn into miracles. Just as
a lyricist teases a line to life, a painter brings magic to color, and

a sculptor imbues clay with movement, the creative entrepreneur realizes new ways to reach customers, involve employees, and trim overhead without compromising quality. Attention to detail, trusting one's intuition, and seeing something that others cannot see are all aspects of the creative process that are brought to bear in the act of creating a business. Those who approach their business like a painter greets a blank canvas are proud of what they create and understand the importance of giving time and room to the creative process. One woman, a general contractor, put it this way:

> When I finish a house and hand the keys over to the buyer, they are on cloud nine and I know I have created something of beauty. . . . I feel a pride beyond description.

The owner of a trucking firm waxes eloquent about her trucks:

> Our trucks are a dark red, with a little rust to it. Our trucks are very beautiful, lots of polish, voluminous, big, big trucks. And not only do we look good, we perform well. And that's very important to me.

Vision and imagination are aspects of art that are integral to the creation of a successful business. But a "vision's just a vision if it's only in your head," and there are many people with ideas, for both paintings and business. It's the true artist who brings the idea, the vision—the business—to life. The work of the artist is hard, often physically exhausting, frequently tedious, and repeatedly discouraging. It is the vision held in the head, the almost physical presence of the way the finished piece will look, feel, sound, or work that lays claim to all the artist's resources, compelling—demanding—that the work be finished. So it is with the creation of a business. The business owner as artist is a metaphor rarely entertained, yet, when I look at Georgia O'Keeffe's *One Hundred Flowers,* I see the same attention to detail that Ruth Owades, creator of Calyx and Corolla, invests in her business. I see the sensuality that comes forth in the displays used by Judy George to show off her furniture in a lush store on Newbury Street in Boston. The painstaking contribution of time that resulted in the *One Hundred Flowers* is evidenced as well in Marti McMahon's boats and Edith Gorter's growing fleet of freight trucks.

Georgia O'Keeffe's flowers grew to be a collection of more than 200 paintings of flowers over the course of her life. Her flowers caused surprise and outrage in some quarters for the feelings they aroused in her viewers—feelings connected to the newness of her experiment, the lack of familiarity with her subject, discomfort with the power of the work coming forth from a woman. Artists and entrepreneurs endure similar discouragements in the creation of their works. Sounding suspiciously like a skeptical venture capitalist rather than her husband, Alfred Steiglitz, on seeing her first flowers, asked, "Well Georgia, I don't know how you are going to get away with anything like that—you aren't planning to show it are you?"[7]

Creating a business is in part about finding your way. It is about detail and life, about a work that when viewed at different stages appears like phases of an artist's body of work. There is plenty of backbreaking tedium and discouragement in the life of the artist; there is also more art in the shaping of a business than business school professors or venture capitalists are willing to acknowledge. But it is in the intersections of art and science, intuition and intellect, chaos and order, creativity and routinized activity that painters and entrepreneurs find common ground. A lot of right stuff entrepreneurs are closet artists.

Edwin Land hired graduates from liberal arts schools, untrained as scientists, to join his labs at the Polaroid Corporation. He believed that if you do not know what you do not know you won't put up barriers to learning. If you do not know that the laws of physics prescribe against a certain reality, you may imagine a new reality. Unhindered by the boundaries of given assumptions, you may test, play with ideas, imagine possibilities, and question realities that have become too ingrained to be seen as mere collective agreements about reality. Imagination is food for the soul. It is also the lifeblood of innovation and company health.

I love to visit companies where the flicker of childlike joy exerts itself in the playfulness of the businesses. Such companies feel good. Often they look good. Usually, as you walk through their doors you sense that this is a good place to be. The wind of serious, deathly toil doesn't blow in your face. Ray Bradbury has written:

> If you have starved him [the boy existing in every man, the girl in every woman], if you have forgotten how to have fun, how to play, how to love, then no matter what you set out to do, you will not do it well.[8]

Women know that. Some women know it outright, and others know it intuitively; the knowledge shines through their businesses.

Bradbury raised the question of what a writer like himself (a creative science fiction writer, no less) had in common with people running businesses. "We are not different in any way," he answered and went on to prescribe how to feed and nurture the child within: "Stick your head in an office meeting just after lunch and say, everyone the hell out, go swim, go make love, come back at four for that meeting! If you do that and people go swim, jog, run, jump, love . . . you might get more done in one hour of chat than three hours of pressure."[9]

Now I can't cite any entrepreneur other than myself who actually does such a thing, but I suspect that's because it's the kind of thing we don't usually broadcast. In any event, some entrepreneurs do give permission to the presence of play; they actively employ the good collective imaginations of their people, and they go at their businesses like an artist with a brush. You can feel it when you walk in their doors.

An Integrated Vision of Business and Ethics

When I was growing up, my younger brother and I often played board games—Parcheesi™, Sorry™, Monopoly™—classic games of accumulation and chance. With apologies to my brother (who grew up to be a good man), I can report that he often cheated. Winning was VERY important to him. I was always struck (and not a little aggravated) by that. I liked playing. I didn't understand what was so bloody important about getting to the finish line first (or having the most chits) that made cheating worthwhile. It spoiled the games as far as I was concerned. I can hear traditionalists suck in their collective breath. I can see the raised eyebrows. "With an attitude like that we'd never be competitive again!" (And women will never be *Fortune* 500 CEOs.) But running a business is not like playing Parcheesi. And though some of the folks on Wall Street forget this occasionally, running a business is also not a simple matter of playing Monopoly. In Parcheesi you roll the dice and move; in Monopoly you collect little plastic (or metal, if you still own them) houses. In businesses, sometimes you figuratively toss the dice, but, hopefully, you do so armed with some information and experience. The houses you collect are real, with real people inside. Sadly, those early lessons of accumulation and winning have too often translated into attitudes about business and "how to play the game" as though it really were just a grown-up version of a game.

"It was just a business decision." That phrase has been used countless times to explain away or rationalize business decisions. (Indeed, I remember a time, when I was still at Polaroid, I used to think women who saw a moral dimension in so-called business decisions were hopelessly naive. I had been too well indoctrinated by my stint in the "real world" of corporate America.) Too often business traditionalists explain their decisions in terms of business decisions (amoral) and ethical decisions (moral). At a conference on business ethics at Yale University in 1982, I listened to a business professor argue that such a separation was shortsighted and ultimately damaging to American business. I sat spellbound as James O'Toole described the importance of "moral symmetry" in business, and I drew strength from his remarks. He articulated my strongly felt intuition. His ideas gave me a tremendous burst of self-confidence and courage at that time. A few years later in *Vanguard Management,* he wrote:

> There are no rules for managing households. There is no one best way to constitute, coordinate or cohere the various members of the family. Instead, household management is an ongoing process, the success of which depends on a perception of justice or fairness by all family members. Sue may not get her way this time; but her time will come. And, at all times, her claims are considered; at all times she is shown respect. For the French root (ménage) of the word suggests, management is similar to the care of a household. The image is that of husbandry [his ideas on ethics were so refreshing that I let this sexist metaphor go unchallenged—then]: through the judicious use of resources, the good parent cares for *all* the members of the family, *all* of whom are seen as having legitimate claims on the group's collective resources. Sometimes junior must be favored; other times, all must come to the support of sister. But the family bond will erode if it is perceived that one member always commands an unfair share of household resources—financial or emotional.[10]

Women have known this all along, but saying it aloud was suicide. It was proof of our lack of business acumen. But lots of women business owners have long understood the wisdom of practicing husbandry (of course, wifery in the dictionary is a pitiful word meaning "to be wifely"; as it is most often the wife who practices *husbandry—you go figure!*).

Women were, and frequently still are, laughed off the stage, like actors delivering inane lines, every time they venture to make a case for applying ethical standards to business decisions. "Well that's fine for a woman's business," you might hear, "but of course that wouldn't work in a *real* business." This attitude is patronizing and insulting. Nevertheless, many women business owners hold on fiercely to their values; despite the obstacles they face, they cannot see any other way to do business except in ways that are essentially human, mindful of the complex of parties with a stake in their companies. Quietly, they persist in running their companies in a way that demonstrates an integration of business ethics and personal ethics. As a woman business owner from Minneapolis said:

> When we started out, my partner and I said we were going to treat our employees and suppliers the way we treat our clients, with respect.... We have been more successful because of those values. Our integrity, our consistent application of those values is part of our particular success.

Professor O'Toole, observing the going-for-broke attitudes of the 1980s and warning that such recklessness was against business's own self-interest, was foresightful. Finally, many business schools have begun to explicitly address ethics in their curricula. Many businesses now acknowledge moral dimensions of business decisions. The Business Enterprise Trust, based at Stanford University, annually recognizes acts of courage that appear to take the high-road in business decision making.

Obviously, lots of men practice business ethically. The point is that women less often entertain a separation of business and personal ethics. It is this assumption of integration that women bring to their businesses, not naively, but wisely; not as a result of being enticed by an award or taught in a business school class, but as a sense of what works in relationships among people—in and out of business. Health Plus is a company that conducts health planning for corporations and helps those companies prepare disaster programs (for earthquakes and other acts of God and man). A statement from founder Regina Phelps's mission statement sums up this ethical sensibility nicely:

> Health Plus practices business with honesty and integrity. Operating with the philosophy that what goes around, comes around, we are in business for the long term, not the short term.

The hardest thing I have ever done is to lay off people who worked for me, worked with me, supported my vision, and gave of their own energy, hope, and vitality to realize a dream. But when it became a necessity, I did not rationalize that it was a business decision only; I knew it had a moral dimension. People's lives were affected and, although I couldn't change the decision, I could control the way I handled it. My partner and I did not surprise employees with pink slips one afternoon and dismiss them from their desks like creatures we were ashamed to look in the eye. We met with them, talked with them, and included them in our contingency planning. Several days later my partner and I returned from one more meeting to plot another strategy to move the business forward; our recently laid off employees met us at the door with a bottle of champagne and a commitment to work part time as long as they possibly could. We had notes of encouragement left under our doors, warm hugs, and a sense of camaraderie and commitment from our employees. We did not have particularly unusual employees (although each of them is special), but we did have people who felt they were treated with respect and not dismissed with patronizing explanations of business decisions.

A final word on ethics is expressed by a woman entrepreneur in Grand Rapids:

Act ethically and do what is right, no matter what everybody else is doing. Even if you get burned a couple of times, fine. But keep your head up, and don't let them cause you to act unethically. If you do you are not going to be around in years to come and you are just promoting everybody else doing unethical or rotten things.

Courage

Too often in our society courage is equated with a willingness to (A) kick ass or (B) bungee jump. Well-publicized successes at war and daring athletic feats no doubt do much to contribute to these perceptions. Women often exhibit physical prowess, defy death, and even choose to skydive, hang glide, and bungee jump; however, the courage I speak of here refers not to warrior skills, physical prowess, or death-defying acts. *Webster's Ninth New Collegiate Dictionary* defines "courage" as "mental or moral strength to venture, persevere, and withstand danger, fear, or difficulty" and lists "spirit," "mettle," "resolution," and "tenacity" as synonyms. With apologies to Webster, I take the liberty of adding "grit" and "grace" to that list. "Grit" is "unyielding courage in the face of hardship or danger," and "grace" includes "a sense of propriety or right . . . the quality of being considerate or thoughtful."

Everyday acts of courage demonstrated by women who own businesses include a determination to meet payroll, endure financial insecurity, hold out for quality standards that may appear impossible to others, say yes, say no, sell the house, take the loan, reject an investor, apologize to a customer, and confront an errant employee. It is these wearying, commonplace decisions that crowd the working hours of the owner and call on the resources of courage, grace, and grit. There are visible, celebrated acts of courage that should not go unnoted. Anita Roddick's call to arms to change the most basic assumptions about the purpose and methods of doing business is an act of courage. It was courage that enabled Regina Phelps, the first female board chairman of the San Francisco Chamber of Commerce, to lay out a new vision for the chamber's involvement with small business. When Susie Tompkins of Esprit put tags on her garments reminding people to think about whether or not they need a new piece of clothing and urging environmental awareness, she challenged conventional wisdom about the business of marketing and challenged the textile industry to match her courage.

Risk taking was a subject I raised at the *Inc.* dinners. I asked, "What enabled you to take the risks you have over the years? What helped you risk the terrors of starting a business?" At the table in San Francisco, Sudha Pennathur, founder/owner of a large retail company called House of Pennathur, recalled that her mother was one of the first pilots to fly the Himalayas:

> Whenever I get frightened or feel overwhelmed by something happening in the business, I think about my mother. Men were refusing to fly in those days, they kept slamming into the Himalayas. It was very dangerous. I think about how frightened my mother must have been at times, and that gives me courage to take risks.

In many cases it is a role model who gives us the inner strength to dare the absurd. In my own case, it was the legend of Edwin Land, inventor of the instant camera, that fortified me with steely resolve to proceed with a decision. Land was famous for the "impossible" demands he placed on colleagues to surpass their own limitations. Frequently, those demands resulted in new inventions that for many years made his company, Polaroid, a company of "magic."

My company developed Photo Odyssey, a learning game often used by other companies to encourage creativity and imagination among their management teams. This photographic learning game requires a minimum of two days to play and produce and is usually held at an offsite location. One day a request came from a particularly important client who wanted the program for a meeting but needed the production to be completed in an afternoon, not two days. I saw the difficulties involved. It would be expensive, physically demanding of employees, and would tie up virtually all the people and resources of our company for almost a full week in preparation for the event—and it might not even be possible. I knew that the successful execution of the event would cement the reputation we strived for as a high-service, high-quality company. I also knew that if we delivered an inferior program, due to the limitations of time, our reputation would be tarnished, possibly ruined. I talked with several key employees and the director of operations (who was absolutely sure it could not be done). After hearing everyone out, I decided to gamble on the skill and talent of the team in charge of the program. The next few days were a period of terrible morale. Since the director of operations was convinced the task could not be achieved, there was great resistance to begin developing plans. Finally, it came to a showdown. I was told again it could not be done. I replied that it *would* be done.

As it happened, Peter Wensberg, who had been Polaroid's vice-president of marketing for 25 years and one of Land's most talented negotiators, was now involved with our company. He happened to be available during this week of tension and conflict. Perhaps because he felt the old thrill of suspense and high drama (Could they do it? Was it one risk too many?), Peter assumed the role of the negotiator between the operations team and myself. He was brilliant, managing to maintain a sense of humor and a line of communication. It was clear he was not taking sides. He told me the team felt very sure they could not perform under the client's conditions; they proposed several alternative solutions, none of which really measured up to the client's expectations. Throughout the shuttle negotiations, I held my ground, constantly asking myself what Land would have done. I had observed the feats of achievement he had wrested from disbelievers time and again. Although I knew he had also made terrible errors in judgment, it appeared that more often than not he caused people to exceed their own expectations of self. I did not back down.

The day finally arrived. The plans had been made, but no one really knew if we would succeed. An abbreviated method of playing the game had been rehearsed in a mock performance, but that was not the same as the real thing. We would fail or succeed in full view of the client. The staff delivered a wildly successful program that day. The client was impressed and delighted with the discoveries that came from the game. The staff was full of the triumph of success. And I finally breathed. If it had not gone well, my credibility, the reputation of the company, and the trust of the staff would have been destroyed. These are not the kinds of risks you take every day. Defying your director of operations is not a practice to repeat often. But having the courage to call for the best of your people's talents is a responsibility of leadership. It is an act of courage that is at least as breathtaking as jumping from a bridge bound by a rope around your ankles. Without a role model, I might not have had the courage to hold out.

Role models are just one source of courage for women business owners. Confidence in one's own ability to survive, no matter what happens, is another. As one of the women in Grand Rapids explained:

> I knew I could always sell shoes. I wouldn't starve. And Ginny [another entrepreneur at the table that night] knows she can wait tables, she can make a living, she won't starve. One of my friends, a founding member of the Association of Women-Owned Businesses once said to me: "When you are about to take big leaps, take a look at the worst possible thing that could happen, and if you can live with that, go for it. Knowing that I won't starve, that I can live, and that I am aware (insofar as possible) of the worst that can happen, I am able to take risks.

For entrepreneurs there appears to be a threshold of normal risk tolerance that is at some point surpassed. This is an adaptation to the entreprenerial life. At that point, there is a changed awareness of what actually constitutes risk. What is at first terrifying to the beginning entrepreneur (precarious income, fear of failure, bungling a big contract) over time acquires less threatening dimensions. Frequently, this is because your worst fears *are* realized (the payroll slips, a client is lost, a hoped-for investor backs out), and you discover that in spite of the unfolding of worst case scenarios, you don't actually die. You find a way to survive—and sometimes to prosper. The definition of risk is constantly revised. At the same time that the perception of risk diminishes, a corresponding growth in self-esteem and self-confidence emerges, enlarging one's capacity to act in courageous ways.

Finally, I have come to believe that only when you are being laughed out of the room (or have a whole pack of people mad at you) are you on to something original, something new. Human flight and instant pictures were visions so unfamiliar they made people uncomfortable; they generated disbelief and hostility. In Warren Bennis's book, *On Becoming a Leader,* he observes that those who have emerged as leaders, "have come to know themselves" and have carried on with their mission—that is, they held on to their visions even when the world discouraged their drive to become "self." It is in this instance that the courage of your convictions takes on serious meaning. As women grow and become "self" in their companies, they demonstrate courage daily.

DO YOU HAVE THE RIGHT STUFF?

The right stuff is, of course, not the sole province of women who own businesses, but many women who own businesses have it. The women I write about are survivors ("I knew I wouldn't starve"). Either through necessity or will, many of them have a fierce need for independence, autonomy, freedom of mind, and spirit. As one woman said, "Autonomy is power. Power over one's life is ultimate power. And autonomy gives you that." Often they were self-supporting from an early age, but just as frequently circumstances forced them to become the sole support of families and selves later in life. Some were not able to find jobs that would sustain them—no one would hire a woman without previous experience. Others could not leave small children or sick family members and had to find a way to make money from their homes. Owning their own business was a way to have flexible time schedules, autonomy of movement, and control. Again from Bennis, "At bottom, becoming a leader is synonymous with becoming yourself. It's precisely that simple and it's also that difficult." Women business owners know that. The right stuff comes from claiming the best parts of yourself and "becoming." As one owner put it:

Until just about 50 years ago, we couldn't even control our reproductive processes. Our role has traditionally been wife and mother. We are among the first generation of women able to be political and business leaders. We are defying our traditional roles, becoming what we can be, what our potential is as human beings.

Women with the new right stuff are, ultimately, learners. We learn about ourselves and our abilities, our customers and their needs, our employees and their strengths. We learn about the environment within which we do business, the goals of our investors, and the ways we can make contributions to the community and the future. We learn how to listen to and trust ourselves. We learn to claim those qualities we possess that constitute the right stuff.

This book is intended in part to encourage more women to join the adventure by starting businesses of their own. Many times I hear, "I wish I had," "I didn't have the confidence," "It didn't seem possible." For those of you with similar thoughts, please consider the possibility. Many women business owners are late bloomers. Increasingly, young women are graduating from business schools and getting on the entrepreneurial track right away, but some women come to value their abilities later in life than their male counterparts do. The process of claiming and becoming self takes awhile. Learning to trust yourself is harder if the messages you have grown up with do not include encouragement to be the one in charge—the owner, not the employee. I do not think this is a disadvantage. By the time some women start their businesses (either out of pure economic necessity or simple desire), they have collected a richness of experience and knowledge that is a valuable asset to their business. Late bloomers have many strengths: they are not easily rattled; they are able to reflect on past experience; and they have the confidence that comes with age and survival.

The self-assessment provided in Table 1.1 is not a scientific tool to ascertain business aptitude. Many people who reject the value of right-stuff qualities start and own businesses that make money, and they can be found on lists like the *Inc.* and *Fortune* 500. But for those of you who are unsure about whether or not you have the right stuff and are thinking about starting a business, the questionnaire in Table 1.1 will provide a tool for self-assessment. Those of you interested in developing more of your right-stuff strengths will be able to identify the areas on which you should concentrate.

Table 1.1   Self-assessment tool.

	Yes	No	Sometimes
1. Do you have good relationships?	___	___	___
2. Are you trusted?	___	___	___
3. Are you reasonably accepting of idiosyncracies and eccentricities, of your own and others' "strange" ideas? (The litmus test used by Ben Cohen and Jerry Greenfield of Ben and Jerry's Ice Cream is "Are we/is it weird enough?" That is, are we doing something original, new, unusual?)	___	___	___
4. Do you juggle multiple obligations well? (If you can run a dinner party for 8, you can juggle. If you can attend to the needs of children and friends and self, you can juggle.)	___	___	___
5. Do you have a sense of fair play?	___	___	___
6. Do you have an internal radar about what is "right behavior" with friends, associates and strangers?	___	___	___
7. Can you set limits?	___	___	___
8. Do you say "no" before you feel overwhelmed?	___	___	___
9. Are you clear in explaining expectations and needs?	___	___	___
10. Are you in good health?	___	___	___
11. Do you eat right?	___	___	___
12. Do you sleep well?	___	___	___
13. Do you pace yourself to prevent becoming rundown and worn out?	___	___	___
14. Do you ask why not more often than you explain why not?	___	___	___
15. Do you encourage others and give rein to your own sense of experimentation and exploration?	___	___	___

(*continued*)

16. Do you take the "road less traveled" sometimes?

17. When others are ready to give up and walk away, are you willing to tug and pull and reach for that extra strength required to finish the job?

18. Do you have a sense of how you would survive—that is, what you would do to keep a roof over your head and food on the table if all else fails?

19. Do you have a strong sense of humor?

20. Are you able to see what is absurd and ridiculous in the grimmest situations?

21. Can you sort out what it *really* serious from daily aggravations and lighten up on the daily aggravations?

22. Are you courageous enough to "become yourself?"

23. Are you willing to try using parts of yourself not tested before? Are you daring enough to discover possibilities that will lead to a long list of unknowns—possibilities that may in fact change the most basic realities of your life?

24. Eric Hoffer, the late bard of the Embarcadero, said, "The learners will inherit the future, the learned will be prepared for a world which no longer exists." Are you a learner?

Scoring:

Rate yourself with the following point values: Yes = 5; No = 2; Sometimes = 3.

90 or more points—You are a role model. Send me your business plan!

70 to 90 points—You've got potential. Work on your no answers and take the quiz again in six months.

Under 70 points—Send your résumé to the *Fortune* 500, they'll be happy to see you!

Item: In 1992 four women made the BE100 industrial/service companies: Isabell Cottrell, Lonear Heard, Louise Johnson, and Shirley Moulton.

A POSTSCRIPT FOR MEN AFTER READING
CHAPTER ONE

By now you may be musing, "This doesn't sound so different from what I think. It's not just women who have been dissatisfied with traditional organization and conventional business. And some of us guys have a lot of the qualities she describes. Why is she making such a big deal about women?"

I suspect some of you are friends from whom I've learned a thing or two, and maybe a few of you have argued with me over various dinners. I know we share values and world views that make your businesses and mine look alike. I don't think different visions of business are a matter of genes or gender or that women have innate ability, inaccessible to men, which replaces the old dominance with a new one controlled by women. So, with you guys in mind, I started to write the book in a way that would be clearly inclusive of you— gender neutral as it were. But I ran into trouble. I lost my voice. I felt crabby. My thoughts wouldn't flow. I couldn't understand why I wasn't having fun anymore. So I shut off my Macintosh and went for a long hike up a canyon not far from the house. Following the creek, kept company by water music and the flight of hawks over my head, I tuned in trying to understand why I resisted being more explicitly inclusive of you in this book. The fact is that I am very excited about what is happening to (and for) some men these days, and the values and vision I write about are alive and shining in companies owned by many of you. As our worlds increasingly overlap, I feel a growing camaraderie between us. Men and women are often buddies now; we share visions and dreams of a better world, a world that is just and clean and open to the diversity we all represent. Increasingly, we talk about using our companies to realize those dreams and look for ways to emphasize environmental activism, to divert funds to peace efforts, to feed the hungry, and to introduce work policies more sympathetic to the needs of working parents and their children. It is one world, and we are fundamentally in it together.

So what's my problem? Why couldn't I write in a gender-blind way? Well, business has always been the domain of men. Although there are variations in the ways men choose to run their businesses (Max DePree and Harold Geneen were hardly cut from the same cloth), the fact remains that men are ascribed the right to run those businesses in whatever way they choose. Wall Street might complain, and those who invested in ITT may not invest in Herman Miller and vice versa, but variations in style are explained by endless studies of corporate culture. We accept that the cultures of IBM and Polaroid are different and attribute that, in part at least, to the differing personalities of the founders, Tom Watson, Sr. and Edwin Land. However different their individual businesses might have been, they were both lauded as successful business*Men* who were part of that club of leaders, those guys who advised presidents on business policy and domestic and international issues. As business*Men,* they were accorded credibility whatever their eccentricities or styles. As business*Men* they were automatically given membership in the fraternity of fellows that drove the wheels of commerce. Although women have always owned and run businesses, they were kept on the fringes outside your domain

Do you remember the treehouse scenes in the film *Stand By Me?* I envied those boys. I have always wanted a treehouse. But it wasn't the treehouse by itself that exuded magic, it was the relationships among the boys that were so wonderful. Filled with mystery, adventure, squabbling, and caring, that treehouse was rich with the textures of learning, living, and loving. In part, those boys learned about themselves by establishing boundaries between "us" (the guys) and "them" (the girls). I can argue the downside of this segregation. Even so, I am sure that the bonding those kids did in their treehouse gave them strength and self-knowledge that was vital to their development.

This book is a kind of treehouse for me and my entrepreneurial women colleagues. Of course, I am going to descend from the tree and carry on the business of life and business with you. The times are exciting, and we have lots of work to do. But I have a sense that this time up here with my women friends is important. Up here we flex our muscles, try out ideas, and test ourselves and each other without having to hear from "experts" (the men who have historically controlled and ruled the realm called business). Up here we share our wisdom with one another and find strength in common and uncommon dreams. We have begun to appreciate the assets we bring to business and resist apologizing or hiding those qualities deemed unsuitable for so long. (I know, I know, some of you never thought they were unsuitable, but you aren't women—you were not banished from the kingdom for taking issue outloud.)

Most men have not had to change laws or change their dress and language to be a part of business. You can change your mind and be called flexible (not indecisive). White men have not had to fight for the right to join business clubs like Rotary and Kiwanis and posher establishments like the Somerset Club in Boston and the Metropolitan in New York. You have not had to hide your intuition (because it's called having a hunch). You could play by the rules, change the rules, or rebel against them because, after all, it was your game, your realm.

When my business partner, Jane, and I acquired venture capital it was a big deal. We were the first women to have received money from an august firm. What a novelty we were. We were reminded of just how great the novelty was the night of the annual presidents' dinner, the night the venture capitalist's portfolio companies were honored for being part of the club—and a real club it was. Tradition had it that gifts were given to the presidents before dinner. The gifts included a tie. That was the first time I became aware of the extent to which membership is real. Those ties were identifying markers, like prep school ties or fraternity pins. They were all the same color and style, of course, so presumably if worn at a dinner or meeting you could identify a fellow member by his tie. Quite a revelation that was! But we got a good chuckle out of the consternation our presence caused at that dinner. What on earth were they going to give these two women, aliens after all? They gave us ties. Tradition is important, you know. We had to fit in. God forbid anything should change just because we showed up.

We accepted those ties. We did not stand up and say how silly we thought the whole business was. We were ultimately alone. We did not want to get kicked out of the club (we needed the capital for our business—or so we thought then). But up here in the treehouse it's different. We giggle among ourselves and howl over how truly ludicrous those ties were. And, by extension, how silly so many other "traditions" are.

I know some of you laugh with us. I suspect many of you are in fact relieved that there is a critical mass of us waving a red flag at so many of the old rules. Some of you are role models for "right stuff" qualities, others of you are finding ways to develop those qualities. The "new rules" so many of us are practicing in our companies are evident in some of yours as well.

But it has not been easy to to talk openly and easily about alternative ways to do business. And the luxury of this little time together as women (like the fleeting time in the treehouse in *Stand By Me*), testing new ideas and possibilities, is giving us strength and courage. We are learning to hold on to our convictions, even in the face of tremendous resistance—from traditional capital sources, business reporters, and other critical business resources.

But even if we recognize our common ground, there are still real differences that create a chasm in the assumptions men and women employ in the creation and management of our businesses. The evidence grows that women gain validation, strength, pleasure, and a sense of empowerment when in the midst of relationships and that men still feel more comfortable when in a "power over" mode. Boston psychiatrist Steve Bergman has observed that the very notion of relating, being vulnerable and open, is antithetical to the nature of maintaining "power over." "Men," he said "can come to think that sensitivity to the welfare of others drains power and is hazardous."[11]

Many women welcome Bergman's new work. It confirms what we have known all along. We have felt the discomfort so many men exhibit when we attempt to connect and be open. We have worked in companies in which being "in-relation" was considered unprofessional. We have tried to discuss the discomfort we sometimes feel in the air, only to be told, like the child who whispered "the emperor has no clothes," that we were wrong. Our perception of reality, we have been told over and over, is not right. Our experience is challenged. Our truth is challenged.

"In-relationship," "mutuality," "reciprocity": these words and phrases are jargon for simple acts of talking together, hearing, nurturing, and attending to and sharing experiences and resources. These skills—women's "domain"—are being reconsidered and revalued in the light of new criteria for success and a changing consciousness about the requirements of leadership and management. Many men are beginning to think there might be something to this business of learning how to connect. But women still need (indeed have earned) the luxury of time and validation to fully claim their strengths without apology. I really believe that speaking directly with women for the course of this book will help solidify ideas and values that we can then share profitably with you.

Differences between men and women are rarely simple or absolute, but there are patterns that are the heritage of our cultural assumptions and habits. These differences are at the heart of what we must understand separately and together. So this book is addressed to women, but as though in a fish bowl. If you sit in a circle around us and listen, then later we can talk together with a common language.

Yes, lots of men are helping to redefine the right stuff. Every day more of you are understanding the wisdom of claiming qualities you have had to shun as "unmanly" for too long. I recently talked with Zak Terry, a teacher at a private school in California who teaches a course called "Mysteries." "Sherlock Holmes?" I asked when we met. "No," he laughed, "male development and rites of passage." Once a semester, he takes his students off to a remote valley north of Los Angeles for several days of roughing it, reflection, and learning.

> When I first offered the course, I thought that what was important was to give these teenage boys an opportunity to test themselves against nature, learn to be tough and strong and spend time on their solos, learning independence. They repeatedly showed me that was not what was important. What was important to them was to connect. They would subvert my every effort to keep them separate from one another. They'd sneak into one another's tents, devise strange adventures of catching and eating lizards, or tell stories and stay awake until they fell asleep exhausted. By their actions, they told me repeatedly that they wanted to connect. Now I have made changes in the class to support that instinct. We have begun to explore ways to make real connections that go beyond the exploits of eating lizards. And I have stopped encouraging young men to disconnect and define themselves in terms of the rugged individualist, man against nature and all that.

Zak Terry is one of a growing army of men who are in the vanguard of redefining the nature of manhood. It is not my intention to polarize the sexes or to elevate women business owners as fundamentally superior to male business owners. As men and women both reevaluate their strengths and gifts, I feel certain we will come to share more common ground in both business and society. Our human qualities, not our gender, can be put to the service of running creative, successful companies for the good of our customers, employees, investors, community, nation, and ourselves.

TWO

New Ways/New Rules

Life's what's important. Walking, houses, family. Birth and pain and joy. Acting's just waiting for a custard pie. That's all.

Katharine Hepburn

Most people want a life. They want time away from work to be with family and friends or just to be alone. Lots of people would like to make a greater contribution to community or society, pursue hobbies or, heresy itself, even spend a little time lying on the grass watching the clouds go by. Just being off schedule and guilt-free is a luxury all by itself. Unfortunately, contemporary imperatives for earning a living and supporting a family (however nontraditional that family may be), combined with cultural norms regarding what is appropriate to give to one's work, make the dream of a life apart from work ever more elusive.

"Telecommuters" is the term now used to describe those people who can work from their homes. They are connected to a corporation many miles away thanks to the wonders of modern technology. It is a development that promises tremendous flexibility to thousands of men and women for whom children, aging parents, transportation problems, or simple preference make it an attractive means of achieving job flexibility.

But technology sometimes has the same effect as the speeded-up assembly line Charlie Chaplin showed us in *Modern Times*. Now that a number of firms have trimmed down and made themselves leaner, many employees and managers have responsibility for work formerly done by two or three people. Many middle managers have been supplied with the technology (workstations and fax machines, for example) to complete work at home. Now instead of being freed from their workplace, they find that work simply follows them home, extending the work day and the work week, clinging to the rest of their lives like an albatross around the neck.

This modern affliction of the unbounded work life is pronounced among entrepreneurs. In our culture, there are old and ingrained assumptions about entrepreneurs that embody a "make money, get rich, grow fast, devote your whole life to this thing" way of thinking. Lone eagles, driven, single-focus inventors are images, mostly male images, that tickle our collective unconscious when the term "entreprenuer" is uttered. We *expect* entrepreneurs to work all the time, sacrificing personal lives for the brass ring of fame and fortune. Men (and women) who embody qualities of staunch independence, obsessive devotion to work, superiority, and power bring to mind the characters celebrated by Ayn Rand in her novels—those superhuman men and women embodied her notion of the best of the American industrial way. Not all entrepreneurs have bought the fictional and media-enhanced model of entrepreneur as rugged individualist. There are other models, other ways, and many women business owners are defining and designing them. And they are making them work for the good of their companies, their families, their communities, and themselves.

Make money, have fun, do good. This is what I want out of my businesses. Some people want to balance family and business. Others want to make money and help solve world problems. Some entrepreneurs want money and independence or money and fun. Some want flexibility and freedom. Increasing numbers want to use their business for social change. What you *want* should determine the way you design and grow your business, even if that means bucking the impulse (and cultural pressures) to prove how serious or good an entrepreneur you are by constantly expanding the number of hours spent in the office or otherwise adopting tired assumptions about "the way business is."

Women who once were part of the corporate scene often say, "I'm not going to do it their way, I'm going to build a different kind of company." Women in business for the first time may not be saddled with traditional ways of getting work done. Melanie Griffith spoke for thousands of women when she said to her secretary at the end of *Working Girl*, "Call me Tess, only fetch me coffee if you are getting some for yourself, and the rest we'll make up as we go along." This notion of "making it up as we go along" is one of the great possibilities of building a business. If there are no previous models—no rules for *how* to do it differently—entrepreneurs who reject old assumptions are free to invent their own models of how a business should be designed and administered. Long-held entrepreneurial myths often do not work for the kind of lives women either live or want to create; thus their businesses may not look like the entrepreneurial businesses we are used to seeing.

In her book, *Prisoners of Men's Dreams,* Susanne Gordon describes two groups of feminists: the equal-opportunity feminists and the transformative feminists. She maintains that during the 1970s and 1980s, equal-opportunity feminists entered large corporations and worked hard to make it, to fit in, and to be accepted. In so doing, they accepted corporate rules as they were, thus increasing their own burdens (that is, to do it all) and did not challenge corporations to change and adapt to them or to change for the benefit of men also. Although Gordon paints an extreme picture to make a point—certainly American companies are different from the way they were in the early 1960s, when women were not seen at all, except as secretaries—she is in large part correct.

In *Men and Women of the Corporation,* published in 1977, Rosabeth Moss Kanter eloquently describes the costs of being different inside a large company. Using simple X's and O's, she illustrated the ways a lone O (anyone who is different from the dominant group by virtue of race, gender, or other discriminating factor) can be singled out, ignored, stereotyped, or otherwise treated as a token.

X X x x X X O X x X

Using the O to stand in for the token woman or token minority, Kanter demonstrated that

> If one sees nine X's and one O, the O will stand out. The O may also be overlooked, but if it is seen at all, it will get more notice than any X. Further, the X's may seem more alike than different because of their contrast with the O.[1]

Kanter explains that O's (Gordon's equal-opportunity feminists) experience three kinds of pressures as a consequence of their very "O"ness. They get attention, which may translate to being more closely watched, as under a microscope. They are seen in contrast—that is, they are seen apart from the dominant group. This may result in stereotyping (one woman or one minority member becomes the representative of all), which causes them to suffer the loss of their own unique qualities. The last thing that the equal-opportunity feminists wanted was to be seen as any more different than they already felt. It is no surprise that they worked hard to become as much like X's as possible in order to fit in.

What about the transformative feminists—those women intent on changing the rules? I think it is these women who are starting businesses in record numbers. They are the women who decided they couldn't or wouldn't adapt to the expectations of corporate America as it was. And they wouldn't build companies that replicated entrepreneurial stereotypes. To paraphrase an old saying among women's groups in the 70's, "if they were going to play the game, they were going to *change* the goddamn rules!"

They would design companies, not according to the images of male myths and business conventions, but in the images of their own needs and desires. They would build companies that could accommodate the realities of their lives. They would build companies where employees and customers would be treated with respect. They would build companies that would "do good," and would meet their multiple needs to create, play fair, make money, and be responsive to family and self. And they would build companies in which they could have a little fun. Tired of trying to break through the glass ceiling, they began to leave large corporations, in part to create a new system that works better for them.

As business owner Regina Phelps said in her inaugural speech as chairman of the San Francisco Chamber of Commerce:

> The rules, the games and the players are new and different. We have to find new ways to deal with old problems.

I adopt Gordon's "equal opportunity" and "transformative" terminology cautiously. With sadness, I understand that many businesswomen still carefully reject the label of feminism, even though, in some profound ways, they behave as feminists. At the dinners I hosted for *Inc.* magazine, there were several women who were uncomfortable with the term (although they sure sounded like feminists to me!). Of course, there also are countless women business owners who have not challenged conventions and who run their companies in fairly traditional ways. But I rely on Gordon's term "transformative feminist" to identify those women—dropouts from large corporations or women who rejected or were rejected by corporations from the start—who are building something new in their businesses. They are starting companies to get what they want—and what they want is not necessarily the same thing that conventional entrepreneurs have historically wanted. It is these differences that are transforming the nature of business.

Earlier, I mentioned that *Inc.* magazine claimed they weren't adequately covering women-owned businesses because they couldn't *find* them. Some business school professors echo the same plaint: "Gee, I'd love to have more cases on businesses owned by women, I just can't *find* them." (Why is it then that women professors at some of the nation's most prestigious business schools seem to have an easier time tracking down case material on women?) The business media and business school professors across the country are looking for X's. They are looking for something familiar, something they are used to looking at—that is, fast-growth, high-profile companies headed by hard-driving young men. When an alternative model presents itself, it is hard to see it. The new *is* hard to see. We are often surprised to finally notice things that have been around for awhile but don't register at first. For example, read the following text:

What's
wrong with
with this sign?

How long did it take you to notice the repeated word? This example illustrates that we have expectations about what we are supposed to see. Frequently, the brain "helps" us see what is not really there; it maintains reality for us as a kind of efficiency mechanism. In this way, constructs that do not fit into our familiar ways of understanding business may be altogether invisible or explained as exceptions, flukes, or "women's businesses"—not *real* businesses. (Just as Kanter's O's were not real businesspeople, not real X's, of course.)

Women's businesses may appear much like the text with the repeated word. We may look at them and overlay a familiar (but inaccurate) image, never realizing we are doing so because our brain has made us see what we already "know." Because women do not always follow the *rules* of entrepreneurialism—that is, do not always fulfill stereotypes of the way we "should be" or "should look"—we sometimes grow differently, organize our businesses differently, and sell our products in different ways. Because our values may be unconventional by traditional business standards, the way we behave and the decisions we make may not be considered really businesslike, when in fact they may just be different and unfamiliar.

Every business reflects the belief system and assumptions of its leader. Knowing what you want, what your assumptions are, and what is important to you is a weighty responsibility, because what you assume and what you want will influence how you design your business. Determining what you want is a decision that dictates the nature of the business to which you will commit your time, energy, and passion.

Warren Bennis has written a great deal about the importance of leadership in the last decade. He has studied some of the most interesting leaders of our time—conductors, film directors, CEOs, and visionary politicians—and has found that leadership is a "process of becoming." Realizing a vision means being in touch with and holding to the values and goals that inform that vision, no matter how unpopular or unfamiliar they may be to others.

People who have not yet figured out who they are have a hard time taking the path less traveled because they lose the signposts that tell them who they are. If you have not struggled with the process of becoming yourself, choosing instead to merely adopt external signs as proof of who you are—corporate executive, entrepreneur, accountant, etc.—you will not have the strength of self and the strength of conviction to buck the trend, to show something new, or to challenge convention. Women who have struggled mightily with discovering who they are are prepared to answer the question of what they want. The self-confidence that accrues with self-awareness, enables women (and some lucky men) to build a business that accommodates the full self. That is very different from the old way of building a business, which is based on conventional expectations about who we should be and how work must get done.

Determining what you want takes on tremendous importance. Whoever said, "Be careful what you want, you may get it," had the right idea. It is a rigorous yet vital process to answer truthfully the question: "What do you want in your business?" It will reflect intimately who you are. ASK Computer is a reflection of Sandra Kurtzig, and Pacific Marine Yacht Charters looks a lot like Marti McMahon. Odysseum was a strong representation of my business partner, Jane Lytle, and me. Each of us, in touch with who we are, designed companies to give us what we want.

The process of becoming self is a lifelong one. Only after you have traveled down the road a piece do you have insight on who that self is becoming. For this reason, I am convinced that late bloomers— women who didn't know they wanted to be entrepreneurs when they were nine—have an advantage. Having spent time on the path, becoming themselves, they develop the self-confidence to design exactly the kind of businesses that work for and have meaning to them.

DESIGNING A BUSINESS THAT GIVES YOU WHAT YOU WANT

Here are some of the questions women entrepreneurs I know have asked themselves to determine what they want in their businesses:

Do I want meaning? What meaning?

Do I want to grow, explore, and discover?

Do I want to devote all, some, or most of my life to this effort?

Do I want to have fun?

Do I want to create an environment within which others can have fun, too?

Do I want to work with a few or a lot of people?

Do I want to make a difference?

Do I want to do this alone?

Do I want to be richer than Midas?

Do I want to have time with family and friends?

Do I want to make a contribution to the war on environmental degradation, the well-being of indigenous populations, or the education of the young?

I do not believe that anyone can have it all or do it all, at least not all at one time. I am not willing to foster or condone the myth of Superwoman or Superman. (As appealing as Ayn Rand's characters may have been when I was 14, they are less attractive to me at 41.) There are trade-offs for our choices, but it is that process of envisioning and choosing, and then consciously making the necessary trade-offs, that enables us to create businesses that adapt to our needs rather than continuing to build businesses that force us to adapt to ill-fitting conventions.

You can design a business that allows you time away every few months. You can design a business that is part of the solution, not part of the problem, in relation to the environment. You can design a business that is fun and welcoming to the human spirit. But to succeed in these designs requires a vivid imagination, a willingness to make up rules as you go along, a determination to constantly question old rules, to make conscious trade-offs, and to fend off the seductive call of traditional cultural values regarding what we "owe" to work. These are the qualities, right-stuff qualities, that are required to rewrite the rules of business.

REWRITING THE RULES

How do you rewrite the rules of business? First, you begin. You start with an assumption that it *is possible* to find ways of doing business that are essentially human and that meet the needs of customers, employees, investors, community, family, and self. You discard the notion that there are inviolate business "laws." You trust your own instincts about what is right and what is possible. And you begin. An idyll?

Compare some of the old conventions of doing business with some of the new rules that are being instituted in the companies of my kindred spirits.

New Rules	Old Rules
1. Work, live, love, learn	Work, work, work
2. Seek meaning and money	Seek money—alone
3. The web	The pyramid
4. Do no harm	Buyer beware
5. Sustain it	Use it or lose it
6. Grow naturally	Grow fast
7. Work and family	Work or family

These new rules are not female rules that are in simplistic contrast to male rules. Paul Hawken of Smith and Hawken, Ben Cohen and Jerry Greenfield of Ben and Jerry's Ice Cream, and Max DePree of Herman Miller run companies in which these rules make themselves felt in exciting and important ways. They are *human* rules, which offer a less cynical vision of business than we are used to. They are rules that are related more to one's values and expectations than to one's gender, and they are almost always found in companies in which the owners have consciously determined how to run their businesses in accordance with their own needs and vision, defying tradition and conventional wisdom.

No doubt many readers will cite additional new rules that are not covered here but that are alive in their own companies. Women have not held a convention to put forth a platform of new rules by which they will manage their companies. Instead, practicality and individual ingenuity have stimulated the emergence of new assumptions about the nature of everyday reality in their companies. The rules discussed here are just a few of the social inventions women are creating.

Rule 1: Work, Love, Live, Learn
versus Work, Work, Work

One of the standard tests for true entrepreneurial zeal is the extent to which you are willing to pledge your life to the business endeavor. An assumption promulgated in American business is that the more time, energy, commitment, and single-minded focus you shower on your company, the greater the chance for success. More is better. It is true that focus and commitment are necessary and that developing a business requires many long days, long nights, and the doggedness of a marathon runner. However, the single-minded focus entrepreneurs are generally encouraged to foster is rarely good for anyone—whether it be entrepreneur, company, customers, or significant others—and it is a single-mindedness that few women have the luxury or the desire to indulge.

If you are totally absorbed in a business for 365 days of the year, some part of yourself is lost and the business loses, too. If you don't nurture the energy and creativity in other aspects of your life, you have less to put back into the business. (Remember, the idea for my company emerged while I was sitting on the terrace of a small Mexican inn taking in the azure sea.) You don't do your business any favors by being completely immersed in it. You have to go outside to get perspective, energy, knowledge, and ideas. The challenge is to determine how to do that, because there are not a lot of models around.

Entrepreneurs who immerse themselves in their businesses, devoting all their time and energy to it, may control a business but may lose control of their lives. They are held prisoner by their companies—and that's not good for a business. Companies, like people, need to be fed and stimulated with as much food for thought and inspiration as possible.

Owners who take time to travel abroad or even across country (not the two-day business trip, but a two-week or two-month tour of a South American country or of Japan) are more truly global leaders; they are better prepared and more likely to take their companies in new directions. People who have real relationships with friends and family will have real relationships with customers and employees. Relationships are at least as demanding as push-ups at the gym, but the entrepreneur who is at ease with many different kinds of relationships will invest time and energy in getting to know customers and employees and will have a deeper appreciation for the imperatives of respect and trust. Owners who feed their souls drifting down a river on a raft or with a night at the theater or hiking a trail with grand vistas stimulate their senses and intellect in ways that bring unexpected benefits to the company. Experiences that result from living, loving, and learning are dividends that can be invested back into one's business.

Perhaps because women have traditionally had to juggle, they less often seem to devote all to their companies.* These are some of the charges brought against women to show they are not serious about their companies: they have babies and take time away from their business; they have relationships and run a business; they only want to work part time. These actions seem inappropriate only because they are not part of the entrepreneurial stereotype—they challenge convention—not because they are inherently wrong. Women who insist on finding a way to work *and* live, love, and learn are inventing new kinds of companies—companies that may be more flexible, adaptive, and innovative (and profitable) over the long run.

Staying in touch with the world outside your factory or office doors is a challenge. Companies are seductive. There is always just one more phone call you can make, another letter to write, a manager to check in with. It takes tremendous discipline (and some

---

*A wonderful article in a British Newspaper, *The Independent,* written by columnist Neal Ascherson, argues that "if you want to see the future of work in the 21st century, you should ask your mother." Ascherson describes what used to be called "women's work." He says, "Here is a woman buttering two scones, crossing the kitchen to pick up a fallen child, buttering another scone, answering another knock on the door and exchanging information while clutching the child and wiping it's nose, glancing into the oven, going into the backyard to take down the washing, returning to the kitchen to turn the oven down, changing a nappy, taking down the washing, looking for the jam and rearranging a cupboard shelf, going for the last sheet left on the line." Ascherson contrasts the complexity of managing a household with what he calls his own well-learned male ideology that "if I am doing two things at once I must be doing both inadequately." He very sharply observed that in "women's work, many operations are being conducted at once—often as many as three—with attention shifting rapidly from one task to another and back again ...Many time scales are in play, different in length and predictability...there is no such thing as an absolute priority." Although Ascherson notes that his example is a caricature from the past, replayed to make a point, many women would argue that although the specific tasks may be different, the style is the same. Women juggling work and family can only succeed because they are able to operate on serveral levels (perhaps in several "zones") simultaneously. Ascherson concluded his piece by describing how his work has changed—a function of technology and organization—and acknowledges his difficulty adapting to this more flexible style in which "random interruption is a component of the production process." See Neal Ascherson, "If You Want to See the Future, Ask Mother," *The Independent,* July 7, 1991, p. 23.

imagination) to keep from being swallowed up by the endless needs of a growing company. Early on, when my company vision was still just a glimmer of an idea, one of my mentors listened to me describe my experience of starting a company up to that point. Wisely, he said to me, "You need a buddy. Not just a partner, but a buddy." He had hit a chord. If this really was going to be fun (one of my earliest understood goals), I needed someone to share the experience with and someone who would share the demands of the business in such a way that I could keep an eye on life outside the world of the business. Finding a buddy who could be a good business partner was no easy task. But the act of finding such a person was a key decision and made possible my ability to build an organization that allowed me to live, love, and learn as well as create and build a company.

My partner, Jane Lytle, and I made a few agreements that were sacred. One was that we would each take two weeks a season and get away from the company. If either of us balked, the other was to push her out the door. This worked. Jane went on a European biking trip with a well-known company and came back filled with excitement about ways to improve customer service techniques. I went to an international business conference in Helsinki and followed that up with a trip to the Soviet Union, returning with a better perspective on the needs and challenges of going global.

We also agreed to travel together occasionally. In a partnership, ideally you can divide the business, each partner being responsible for a separate sphere. To a large extent we did that; however, because we wanted to have fun (feeling that fun was vital, not a luxury), we knew we had to have some shared adventures. A favorite was a train trip between Chicago and Santa Fe to meet with a new designer working on our sales materials. We were both feeling the need for planning time, and it occurred to us that 24 hours on a train, away from phones, customers, employees, and anyone else who had a claim on our time, would be the opportunity we needed. We booked a first-class sleeping compartment to share and spent the next day getting a new perspective on America which helped us to remember that our own urban setting was not the universe. We also had some quiet time to rest and catch our breath, and we had plenty of time to talk, create to-do lists, and consider goals and needs for the coming months. And we had fun. Watching the western landscape slip by was invigorating. By the time we arrived in Santa Fe, we had been immersed in color and light that no doubt fed our senses as we considered colors and design for a new brochure.

Jane was fondly known as our "cheap financial officer." We never entertained at expensive restaurants, and we didn't have much use for "trappings" (we both drove old cars and lived in modest apartments). At work we recycled because it was cheaper, not because we were conscious (although we were). But we also knew there were times when it was important to spend extra money to invest in the health of our company. For us, the time and dollars invested in our train adventure resulted in less stress, more creativity, and time to plan and be reflective—learning and living. We watched the western landscape roll past and drew strength and perspective for our company.

Jane and I were both involved in strong love relationships with men who supported, indeed celebrated, our mission. We honored the time one another spent away from the business nurturing our relationships. Love is important. If you are cared about, you can care. Sacrificing marriages and relationships for your business is one of the most misguided follies of entrepreneurial tradition. We all need the care and feeding of a relationship to be whole. Whole people are better equipped to lead companies. They have balance, humor, perspective, and probably good health, which are vital to the constancy required in being true to a business. Women who are involved with children and significant others keep a handle on what's important. "Life's what's important," said Kate Hepburn.

Debates about whether women are serious about their businesses, whether their businesses are as big as or as profitable as men's, and arguments over whether or not women's businesses measure up to men's businesses miss the point. The question is not, do women's businesses measure up to men's; the question is, do men and women live their lives deliberately in ways that celebrate their lives and the businesses they create?

Rule 2: Seek Meaning and Money versus Seek Money—Alone

In the course of raising capital for our business, we were frequently given a test. The potential investor would ask, "Why are you starting this business?" For some, the only right answer was, "To make money, to make *a lot* of money." To make money *and* anything else was the wrong answer. They just wanted to know if they were placing their money with people whose sole obsession was to make money. I confess that was never my sole goal. A goal, surely. But I have always felt that there is so much to be done in the world that seeking wealth by itself is a frittering away of one's allotted time, a frivolous use of life. Virginia Woolf told us that every woman needs an income and a room of her own. I agree. I think that having your own business is a way to ensure both. To me, having "a room of one's own" means having space where you have autonomy and power over the rules, the use of that space, and the activities that occur within it. A business, a literal room of your own, provides a way to create a space for achieving meaning in concert with money. Recently, a friend of mine, a man who runs a food bank in Atlanta, told me about business owners he knows who are searching for meaning:

> Executives come to me and they are in pain. They want to know what they can do to help me; they want to be involved with helping the food bank. One owns several companies, and the other is president of his own company. They are looking for meaning and can't find it in their companies. They are really sad cases.

E. F. Schumacher, author of *Small is Beautiful,* offered three purposes of human work:

1. To provide necessary and useful goods and services.
2. To enable everyone of us to use and thereby perfect our gifts like good stewards.
3. To do so in service to and in cooperation with others, so as to liberate ourselves from our inborn egocentricity.[2]

Schumacher didn't argue for wealth, but for a decent living. He didn't advocate rampant consumption, but lobbied for a nonviolent, sustainable lifestyle. He wanted creative and satisfying work and habits that left the planet healthy and capable of supporting life. Pursuing these goals, rather than wealth for its own sake, enables entrepreneurs to integrate meaning with the attainment of a decent living.

Women who choose this path may be considered unwilling to participate in the real world of business and commerce, where the stakes are big and the goals can be quantified. ("Are Women Hungry Enough?" "Do They Have the Killer Instinct?" read business headlines.) Yet as the consciousness about a sustainable lifestyle grows (and make no mistake, it is) and the realization that business *as we have known it* is antithetical to the needs of a sustainable planet, the models women are creating begin to look awfully sensible.

Moreover, work as we have known it is undergoing a revised consciousness. In *Modern Madness: The Emotional Fallout of success,* Douglas LaBier studied careerists between the ages of 25 and 47. He described their "battling goals," the conflict of their ambitions and work habits with their values and emotional needs. He found that "the new careerist seeks overall a deeper sense of meaning from work."[3] In particular, they believe that "the paycheck is not the only reward."

A new paradigm is emerging. It integrates the quest for profits with these three criteria: the search for meaning, a sense of fair play, and an attitude of respect toward people, planet, and society. Women are on the leading edge of this new paradigm. La Bier's new careerists might take a cue from women business owners. What today is considered fringe, idealistic, even womanly, will be seen in coming decades as vital to the survival of American commerce, to the life of the planet, and to the psyche of those who lead our large companies.

I am not constructing a fantasy. Women (and growing numbers of men) actually are creating companies that bring together their need to become economically self-sustaining and their need to engage in the kind of work Schumacher was describing in the mid-1970s.

In 1990 Avon issued *The Avon Report,* the results of "A National Attitude Survey of Successful Women Entrepreneurs." The 450 applicants for the Avon Women of Enterprise Awards during 1987, 1988, and 1989 were surveyed either because they had been asked by a local group to apply for the award or because they were confident enough of their own success to apply. One of the items on the questionnaire was intended to illicit information on why women were starting businesses. The results were as follows:

Happiness/Self-fulfillment	38%
Achievement/Challenge	30%
Helping others	20%
Sales growth/Profit	12%

This is neither an unbiased survey nor a good assessment of all women; however, it is a glimpse of what is important to many women. It supports the notion that money and meaning do not have to be mutually exclusive.

Women are finding many ways to integrate profits and meaning. One is to be involved with products that bring them pleasure. Pam Kelley, founder of Rue de France, a mail-order catalog that sells exquisite lace curtains, focuses attention on "the craftsmanship and traditions of the Provence artisans." At Womanswork, a company that began by manufacturing work gloves for women, the goal is to support "Strong Women Building a Gentle World." Engineer/psychologist Deborah Kearney is the founder of Work Stations, Inc., a company that designs and builds complete workstations for physically challenged employees. Kearney's products are based on the conviction that every "person has the right to meaningful and productive work." Her company tries to assure they have access to such work. Nancy Alexander, founder of Peach Blossom Diaper, sees her company as the work of one mother helping other mothers create a better world for their children. Gwen Kaplan, founder of ACE Mailing, a multi-million-dollar success started almost 15 years ago, located her company in a San Francisco neighborhood so that she could hire, promote, and develop young people from minority groups who would otherwise not have access to work. The stories are numerous.

Too often people equate doing good and finding meaning with nonprofit organizations. They too easily accept the convention that serious business is about making money and not about making money *and* finding meaning or making money *and* doing good. I have yet to understand why this simplistic either/or choice rather than an emphasis on "and" is considered an acceptable expectation of business.

When planning a business, an entrepreneur must first seek out markets and fill needs. On this planet that doesn't require the analytic skills of a rocket scientist. There an abundance of needs to be filled. And there are opportunities to integrate business and meaning everywhere. Maybe you won't start the first airline whose niche is the transport of food to famine-struck countries. But let's say your company produces nuts and bolts. Where's the meaning in a factory that produces nuts and bolts? Maybe it's in the style of governance of the plant—that is, the authority employees have over safety and decision making. Maybe it's the 2 percent of nuts and bolts provided to small businesses in developing countries, or maybe it's in the model of environmental ethics the plant exercises. In any event, there is almost no excuse for running a business just to make money. As Anita Roddick reminds everyone who will listen to her, "This is not a rehearsal. You can learn in business, you can grow." The notion that one must compartmentalize making money and finding meaning is old-fashioned, wasteful, and cynical. Integrating profit and meaning is the new imperative.

Of course, women are mindful of profits; however, profits for their own sake seem to connote a sterility of purpose and activity that many shun. Success, meaning, and money are intimate partners. In the next chapter you will hear more about the ways women view success.

Rule 3: Webs versus Pyramids

When Jane and I first started to circulate our business plan, we included an organizational chart that placed us side by side. We were clear on our separate spheres of operation, but we wanted it to be understood that we shared decision making and power. This chart became so problematic to potential investors that we finally dropped it. We agreed between ourselves to show them whatever they wanted to see, while continuing to operate as we thought most effective.

In retrospect, I think that the notion of sharing power is so incomprehensible to most men that it must seem completely absurd—an inherently contradictory concept. I think hang gliding is pretty nutty, but plenty of people do it. Just because something is incomprehensible is no reason to believe it is not possible. Yet that is what we were told: someone had to be at the top to make the final decisions. We tried, in many ways, to explain that we could achieve the clarity of decision they desired with the organization we wanted. Most of the time, we met a stone wall of disbelief.

Yet in her book, *The Female Advantage: Women's Ways of Leadership,* Sally Helgesen describes a style that sounds comfortingly familiar. The web, as she calls the alternative to traditional hierarchy, is a design in which women position themselves in the center of the organization connected to all those around them as if by invisible threads constructed around a center point. Indeed, when our company was just starting, before we had parted from Polaroid and had space we could design as we wished, I often left my office to sit at a large table in the middle of our common space. I called this "managing by sitting around." We all thought that was a good variation on Tom Peters's notion of "managing by walking around." But it was in fact my favorite place to work. I was accessible, and I was aware of the mood of the team, the pace of a project, problems, and triumphs. I could focus on my own work and still feel tuned in to everything going on around me.

Ruth Owades, the owner of Calyx and Corolla, mentioned that when her company had grown to such an extent that she was forced to move the operations center to another floor, she felt as though "some part of her body was gone." When the order center was close to her office, she had a kind of subconscious awareness of the flow of orders, the problems her customer representatives ran into, and the energy level of her team. As the company grew and the order center became physically distant, she found she had to invent ways to gain access to the same kind of knowledge without recreating old styles of formal hierarchy and chain reporting.

Helgesen explains that, "hierarchy values position, individual achievement won by competition, while the web puts a premium on affiliation, on staying close." It is a style that many of the women I spoke with employ to varying degrees. It is the style of choice of Frances Hesselbein, the national executive director of the Girl Scouts and the woman that Peter Drucker maintains "could manage any company in America." In an interview with Sally Helgesen, Hesselbein described her "circular management system." "Here's me in the center," she said as she set her glass in the middle of the table. "And this is my first management team." She had surrounded her glass with more glasses and cups. Helgesen then described how Hesselbein constructed more circles, building outward concentrically, linking them with knives and forks. The director of the national Girl Scouts told her, "The great thing about the circle is that it does not box you in. You can connect with any other point. As the circles extend outward, the fabric becomes more interwoven."[4] These remarks stress the importance of connections and interrelatedness and the irrelevance of traditional mechanisms of power and control. Women simply seem not to find the old chain-of-command style very appealing. I haven't the patience for it, and many women find that the freedom and responsibility that employees experience when hierarchy is lessened results in a more energized organization.

The web, Sally Helgesen argues, has advantages. Because position is less important than in traditional hierarchy, an organization can achieve flexibility without lowering morale; if there is no up or down there can be no demotions, no losing face. In a web, information flows more easily and quickly. Says Helgesen, "The web's more direct, free-flowing, multi-connected mode mimics the workings of the microchip or the circuit board and is more appropriate to today's environment than a model first developed to serve the needs of Caesar's army."[5]

Rule 4: Do No Harm versus Buyer Beware

If you consider business a zero-sum game—that is, that every deal has a winner and a loser—then each transaction has the potential to harm at least one of the parties involved. Each transaction is also a move in the game, an attempt to outwit or outsmart the other player. If I make an extra 10 percent from a deal by substituting goods of an inferior quality and you don't spot the difference, don't blame me. Watch out for yourself. Buyer beware.

This is a short-term, transactional approach to doing business, and it is in direct contrast to the "do-no-harm" school of business. This school assumes that business is a series of *interactive* relationships that must be nurtured and maintained. You give value for money now in order to assure the next sale and to build trust with the customer. The do-no-harm school assumes that each transaction has a consequence, and thus it is in the overall best interest of the ongoing business relationship to do no harm. Of course, the do-no-harm principle goes beyond the simple concept of buyer beware and is relevant to all parties in a business—suppliers, employees, investors, the environment, the community, even the future. It is a tall order, a lofty aim. This is also the rule that demands the best right-stuff qualities to administer well.

Treating and trading fairly (rather than exploiting trade partners) is a variation on the do-no-harm way of business, but it is different in that it recognizes the relational aspect of each business to the larger world community. Business is often described as the successful exploitation of opportunity. Exploitation also implies overpowering conquest. The alternative—treat/trade fairly—acknowledges the reality of our small global village and offers an alternative kind of power—mutual empowerment (yes, we are back to the importance of being "in relation" again!) rather than conquest. Sadly, loathe to give up these traditional notions of power and conquest, most companies continue to follow a path intended to maximize dollar investment returns, without thought as to the consequences. Thus we have policies that encourage the dumping of hazardous waste in developing companies and interference in the politics and economies of third world countries.

Women who insist that fair play is a valid business value either turn away from exploiting such "opportunities" (risking once again the label of being lesser risk takers or of not being ambitious enough) or find some way to make opportunities truly fair to all parties. Touting "trade not aid," Anita Roddick's company, The Body Shop, has built a soap factory in a poverty-stricken section of Glasgow, Scotland. The factory will provide jobs for people who have been unemployed for as long as ten years. The Body Shop obtains the ingredients for many of its products from people and areas connected with rain forests. Roddick believes that the Indians are the custodians of the rain forests and that it is our obligation to support their stewardship, not by buying the wood they clear-cut, which destroys the forests, but by helping to develop and purchase products and raw materials that sustain the land instead. In that way, trade forestalls the need for governments to intervene with aid, which sustains dependency but does not sustain the planet, the people, or the connection between the two.

Traditionalists argue that business should not be involved in social activism of this type. Unfazed, Roddick maintains that the only thing stopping us from solving many of the world's pressing problems is the way most people think business should be managed. It's hard to argue that the status quo practiced by those same traditionalists is not dramatically damaging (perhaps beyond repair) the world and the people in it. Experiments of the sort Anita and people like her are practicing are overdue for a serious trial.

Finding ways to run a business that do no harm requires an artist's soul, endurance, imagination, and an integrated view of business and ethics. It requires a conviction that there is another way to achieve our goals, however illusive or difficult it is to see.

Rule 5: Sustain It versus Use It or Lose It

Consuming is at the heart of business. Oversimplified, business consumes raw material to make products that customers can consume. The conventional wisdom was that if I do not use this raw material someone else will and they will reap financial gain, not me. Thus, I'd better use it or lose it. In Western thinking, there appears to be an almost childlike faith in the natural replenishment of raw materials, or at least a comparable substitution. Not to be part of the cycle of consumption is often viewed as not being competitive.

But those business folk climbing on the "sustainable" bandwagon have a different view of their place in the cycle of consumption. They attend more carefully to what they consume, how they consume it, and what they do with the refuse of their consumption. Paul Hawken and other entrepreneurs who sell furniture or other products associated with rain forest woods or material are now careful to buy raw material from those suppliers who are maintaining sustainable sources. Gail Mayville of Ben and Jerry's Ice Cream became aware that ice cream wastes were polluting Vermont waterways. Realizing that irresponsibility to the water system was a direct violation of the values that Jerry Greenfield and Ben Cohen stand for (not to mention her own), Mayville devised a program to fund Vermont farmers to buy pigs, which would eat the waste that was going into the water system.

This sort of thinking turns the business of business on its head. What does the future hold for those companies rethinking their responsibilities with regard to consumption? Will it lead to customer loyalty, unforeseen opportunity, or financial ruin? Will investors invest in companies that openly and aggressively challenge our assumptions about consumption? So far, the answer seems to be that many investors prefer to invest in such forward-thinking companies. They are betting that in the strange, new world to come, it is just those sorts of challenges to the old order that will help business to create the future, not destroy it.

Frequently, we are told that environmentalists are sabotaging business and undermining the bottom line. Karen Fenske, owner of Lubber's Resource Systems, challenges that. She argues that the bottom line is simply a matter of perception.

> There are a lot of companies wavering on where the bottom line is— at the end of a quarter, the year, or at the end of the decade. The real cost of waste disposal, for example, is now figured in terms of decades. Three years ago in Grand Rapids, companies paid $9 per ton for waste disposal; in 1989 they paid $23 per ton; and this year they will pay $40 per ton. And the ten-year cost of waste disposal anyone can calculate as you drive from here to the Grand Canyon and watch the landfill pile up. So where is the bottom line? It's misleading to say that the bottom line is just a quarterly measure. It's much more complex than that.

This question of determining just where the bottom line rests is at the heart of the conflict between the use-it-or-lose-it school and the sustain school. And Karen makes it clear that if you put your eye to the horizon and look at costs over the long term you have a different perception of where the mythical bottom line rests. She is untroubled by the implied complications of this long-term view. Premature judgments of people, art, the weather, and bottom lines lead to distorted views and bad decision making. Redefining the bottom line is one of the liberties many women are taking with their businesses.

Rule 6: Grow Naturally versus Grow Fast

In the spring of 1991 *Inc.* magazine ran an article reconsidering the heretofore unquestioned virtues of growth. Conceding that the growth of the 1980s was a function of a particular set of conditions, authors John Case and Liz Conlin outlined the differing conditions of the 1990s and what was augered for business. Demographics, business climate, a changed marketplace, and less support for entrepreneurial ventures will combine to make fast growth a sexy memory, but not a present companion, they implied. Once, this would have brought a chorus of dismay. But Conlin and Case went on to document companies in which slower, better-managed growth actually improved profit margins, customer service, and customer satisfaction.

The new biogenetics does make it possible to force some species of plants into faster growth; in countries where people are starving this is a life-saving advance. However, not all living things benefit from forced growth or growth for its own sake. As with children and a good stew, *not* hurrying things is sometimes the better course. It takes some companies years before their technology and their markets find one another.

Digital Equipment Corporation was blessed with a founder and investors who understood that it takes time to grow a sturdy tree—to set the roots well, prune the branches, and try a variety of fertilizers. They were investors who believed attention to the care and feeding of a company paid off over the long term. General Georges Doriot, often referred to as the father of venture capital, was known as a patient man who stayed with his entrepreneurs. It was Doriot who agreed to invest in Digital Equipment Corporation. Doriot once said:

> When you have a child, you don't ask what return you can expect. Of course you have hopes—you hope the child will become President of the U.S. But that is not very probable.... I want them to do outstandingly well in their field and if they do, the rewards will come. But if a man is good and loyal and does not achieve a so-called rate of return, I will stay with him.[6]

Doriot stayed with Ken Olsen and Digital Equipment for 30 years and became very wealthy over the course of that relationship.

Biographers Glenn Rifkin and George Harrar described founder Ken Olsen:

> He bucked the tenet of the day "start a company, grow quickly, then sell out to a larger company for a big profit." Olsen was in it for the long haul. He wanted the company to *grow naturally*.[7]

It is likely that in the environment of the 1980s DEC would not have made it past the start-up phase. The imperative to grow fast and provide an exit for investors became such a high priority and investor attention spans became so short that companies began to use cash and debt like steroids in an effort to force growth before it was organically ready.

According to a *Harvard Business Review* article, "How to Write a Winning Business Plan," "Entrepreneurs frequently do not understand why investors have such a short attention span. Many who see their ventures in terms of a life long commitment expect that anyone else who gets involved will feel the same." (How silly to think that commitment might be an appropriate business behavior!) The authors go on, "When investors evaluate a business plan they consider not only whether to get in, but also how and when to get out. Venture capital firms usually wish to liquidate their investments in small companies in three to seven years."[8] The three-to-seven-year investment schedule is unquestioned as a business law. Maybe three to seven years is reasonable for some companies; it may take eight to twelve years for others. In any event, the "laws" of investment return, however rational the "lawmakers" may wish them to be, often turn out to defy the wishful thinking of the impatient investor in wildly irrational ways. George Gendron, editor in chief of *Inc.*, once said to me "We are just beginning to understand that if you make it to ten years and survive you're doing great."

Organically grown companies may not seem natural to the investor who views fast growth as an entitlement. But for women, a historic lack of resources, growth more intimately tied to available resources, long-term vision, and adaptations to opportunities and life needs have forced a different view of growth. Women were less likely to participate in the fast-growth conditions of the 1980s. Ready money and tax abatements simply were not available to most women entrepreneurs, nor did they have the same support as their male counterparts; fancy accounting companies and hot shot lawyers were less likely to take on women as clients precisely because the stereotype of women-owned businesses is that they do not grow fast. The power of a self-fulfilling prophecy is overlooked by those who insist on invoking the stereotype as fact.

But as overleveraged firms led by cowboy entrepreneurs teeter on the brink of financial fragility, some women business owners are in better financial health for not having been able to leverage. One woman with a start-up firm (a very smart woman with all the right "credentials," banking experience, and an MBA from a prestigious school) made this observation:

> I have my eye on a company near where I live. It was started by a couple of guys who graduated from college just two or three years ago. They started a brewing company, and I see their brand new little mini trucks tooling around the city. I see the beautiful plant that they had built. The father of one of them is an investment banker. I'm sure he helped

them get their capital. For a while I asked myself, "Am I starting my business the wrong way? Am I starting with too small a vision? Am I wrong to put just $25,000 in capital and start with four customers on the first day, when what I want is a company of 3,000 customers and my own fleet of vans?" Finally, I decided that the way I will succeed is by learning on a small scale—doing it right small and then duplicating it. It is a deliberate building strategy which works for me.

Another woman described her growth strategy:

I don't mind being invisible. You build a company slowly, build the root system, branch out as much as you can, then when you have a steady base of customers and sales, when you have a real head start on the opportunity discovered, then you let the world know what you are doing.

Simplistic assumptions now held about rates of growth, investments, and return on investment are due for a fresh examination. Study of the organic growth of businesses owned by women may prove fruitful for all businesses.

Rule 7: Work *and* Family versus Work *or* Family

Women have turned up the volume on the debate about work and family. Women who have juggled businesses and family learned a long time ago that you cannot maintain a neat, uncluttered separation of work and family, work and humanity and keep a business running smoothly. Dual-career couples, single-parent families, young families caring for older parents, and people who are single and want a full and balanced life are designing companies that acknowledge the integration of human lives and the realities of competing claims on a working person's time and attention.

Many women are designing companies in which flextime is an assumed operating standard; they are working out ways to share childcare, and they work with employees to find ways to handle the emergencies and demands that go with having a life. Speaking at a Congressional hearing, Jeannette Reddish Scollard, owner of SCS Communications in New York, said:

The corporate structure was designed for men who had wives. Well women don't have wives, we are the wives.... The only way women can have it all, as men do, is to take charge of her destiny. If she is the boss, she gets to write the rules, new rules. She can design her schedule around her family's need. She can delegate to her assistants when Johnny is sick, instead of apologizing to her boss.... When she likes, she can take the office to the nursery or the nursery to the office. She can do this without losing one iota of professionalism. We are seeing this extremely capable segment of our workforce abandoning the corporate halls and creating a most exciting and vibrant part of our economy, new businesses that create new jobs for our economy.[9]

Fran Rogers, one of the founders of Work/Family Directions, has built a successful company with two underlying assumptions: (1) that business is a good thing and (2) family is a good thing. Rogers saw that these two independent statements were increasingly troublesome for employees and employers. Her company has become one of the leading resources for large corporations trying to find a way to make both realities work in concert. Rogers and her colleagues appreciate the complexity of accommodating the needs of work and family, but they are also clear that the accommodation can and must be made.[10]

At last, more traditional companies are reviewing and altering policies (in some cases clumsily, in other cases with care) to make it easier for work and family to coexist. Companies such as IBM, Xerox, Johnson & Johnson, ADP, and Levi Strauss are viewed as forward thinking for adapting to a set of demographics that compels them to acknowledge the way family and life have entered the workspace. And indeed they are, in a way. But what some of these large companies are struggling to do, women business owners have been doing for years as a simple matter of necessity—and choice. Women do not want to have to choose between work and family, not if it means causing harm.

OWNING AND APPLYING NEW RULES

My business partner, Jane, will read this section and laugh. "Joline hates rules," she will say. She's right. Tell me to do something one way and I seem genetically required to ask, "Well what if we try it another way?" Suspicious of so many rules that haven't been very good for women, I suppose I rebel as a matter of habit. Perhaps this section more appropriately should be called "Rules and Anti-Rules." Fundamentally, what the new rules or anti-rules encourage is questioning and experimentation as a way to make organizations work for people, to create a sustainable planet, and to allow people to live. My purpose in proposing alternatives to the old rules is to show it is possible.

The rules I offer here are at work in many companies owned by women. I used them in my own company. But it's been hard for me to own these rules, to talk and write about them outside the safe circle of friends and kindred spirits, men and women alike. It's hard because they sometimes sound foreign, illicit, or forbidden. Yet I know they are rules that are sound and which provide a firm foundation on which to build a business that one need not be cynical about. For a long time I have felt the intuitive rightness of these ideas and the truth they hold. Only recently have I had the confidence of anything more than my intuition and my own experience.

A New View of the Self

Thanks to the work of researchers at Wellesley College's Stone Center, I now have more than my own truth on which to base the rightness of these rules. Over the past ten years, researchers there have been working on developing a new psychology of women, a central theme of which is described by Stone scholar and author Jean Baker-Miller:

> Women's sense of self becomes very much organized around being able to make and then to maintain affiliation and relationship.[11]

Jean Baker-Miller, Janet Surrey, Carol Gilligan, and their colleagues are shining a new and illuminating light on our lives and looking at them, not through the lens of the male experience, but by looking directly at us. They challenge basic ideas that have been the filters through which women are traditionally viewed. For example:

1. *Relationship and action are separate.* Girls relate, boys act. "No, no," says Janet Surrey, "girls act within the context of relationship. They get things done by INTERacting." This is radical stuff. This implies that women can rub their tummy and pat their head at the same time!
2. *Power is a zero-sum game—the one with the most power wins.* If you aren't scrambling to get the most power you must be: (a) afraid of success and power, (b) passive or (c) a wimp. Hogwash. Again Surrey, "The 'power over' model assumes that power is a

resource associated with size, strength, and dominion. The alternative model, that of mutual power or empowerment, enables us to play a new game in which the outcome is not always win-lose, but more frequently can be win-win."

3. *Strength looks like John Wayne—strong, silent, and invulnerable.* "Oh, please," groan the women working on the new psychology of women. Strength lies in the courage to be honest, to be present with, and responsive to. John Wayne was a wimp.

Studies such as those conducted by Judy Rosener, referred to earlier, and the work of the women at Stone Center are beating the same drum: women are likelier to enjoy a greater ability for relatedness, emotional closeness, and emotional flexibility than are most men. For girls, "being present with" psychologically is self-enhancing; for boys, it may come to be experienced as invasive, engulfing, or threatening.

Women who own companies question and challenge assumptions about the business of business. This is happening in large part because what they have seen and, in some cases, experienced in traditional companies just doesn't work for them. What makes sense, what works, is to build businesses based on the tenets of mutual respect and relationship. What works is to pay attention to the realities of their lives and of their needs and build companies that are responsive to those realities.

At one of the *Inc.* dinners, one woman mused:

> Imagine what would happen for all those hundreds of thousands of budding enterprises out there if the ideas we are discussing became the new set of messages they received. What might happen if they could hear [that] there is a wide range of ways to develop and grow an enterprise that the important thing is to do it authentically, integrated with who you are, your own style, your own values.

Once we can see women-owned businesses, it will be easier to learn from them. Increasingly, the nature of the entrepreneur's reality and the desires about how to deal with that reality are defining the way businesses are designed and grow. In the process of building the companies of their wildest dreams, women show themselves to be forceful, competent, growing, and dynamic. They show themselves as able managers of the new rules.

THREE

Success: If Not Wealth and Fame, What?

> Here is a holy landscape, the village enclosed by walls with
> helter skelter angles so both sides of the tiny houses and
> walls are visible—a world that a god would see looking
> down that day on the town—the way a god sees both sides
> of all human choices.
>
> From These Are For Your Consideration by Emily Hiestand

KEEPING SCORE

In America, a company is hailed a success if it gains and maintains
membership in the *Fortune* 500. And the entrepreneur is hailed if
cited in the *Forbes* list of wealthiest people in the United States.
These measures are clear and easy to determine. A simple standard
of dollars determines whether one is or is not on the list. Membership on these lists is celebrated. The companies receive attention both
as case studies of success (or failure, if later they fall from the list)
and as a kind of bellwether of how well the country is doing. Wall
Street assigns specialists to study the successes and failures of these
companies, *People* magazine covers their leaders. The *Inc.* 500 serves
a similar function for keeping score of new and emerging companies. The leap from the *Inc.* 500 to the *Fortune* 500 is the measure
of true success. It's the badge that says one has made it into the
BIGTIME.

Business magazines and newspapers cover businesses much the
way sports are covered—keeping tallies, running stats, dissecting the
players. Who's ahead, who's winning, and who's losing is a running
theme through the pages of *The Wall Street Journal, Business Week,*

and *Fortune* magazine. The 1989 issue of the *Forbes* 400 organized its table of contents in this way:

Who's New
Statistics, et al.
Rules of the Chase
Forbes 400
Who Dropped Off the List
Who Almost Made It

Although business itself is filled with ambiguity, our ability to discern success and failure in those businesses is startlingly clear. Are they on the list or not? Do they have the POTENTIAL to make the list? It is in part the mystery, the suspense, the unpredictability of those answers that holds our attention. Will our hero or heroine make the goal? Will the company triumph? There is a mythic quality to the quest for membership and understandable interest as the adventure unfolds and fate (and the Herculean efforts of the entrepreneur) dictates the ultimate outcome. Once a year the measure is taken. Once again the rosters of success and failure are established.

This is, of course, an oversimplification of the nature of success within American business. But the point remains that inherent in our culture is a powerful drive to measure a person or a company in terms that allow us to rank order against tangible standards like the *Forbes* 400 and *Fortune* 500.

"Is That All There Is?" Peggy Lee crooned during the 1970s. Perhaps it's no accident that song resonated when big business was ascendant. "Uh uh," now seems to be the answer, "not for me." Women (and increasing numbers of men) are rebelling. Unwilling to accept that the answer to the song is "Yes," they insist on making their businesses count for something more than a place on a list; instead, they use their businesses to make a real contribution to the greater good.

ECONOMIC INDEPENDENCE AS ONE MEASURE OF SUCCESS

Women's greatest opportunity to achieve personal and economic independence is through the establishment of their own companies. Although other means are possible in this country (e.g., earned salary, investments, inherited wealth, marriage), the potential to be "Captain of my ship, Mistress of my Fate" is amplified by the ownership of a company—creating and delivering products and services that are exchanged for money. Although still subject to the absurd injustices of sexism, racism, and classism, women may achieve financial independence not otherwise available in a world of glass ceilings and bureaucratic pigeonholing by gender and race. What is exciting, astonishing, and change-making is that so many women (and more and more men) are not content to make economic independence the *only* measure of their success.

Success is a multilayered concept. For myself, for many of the women who speak in this book, and for many of my entrepreneurial male colleagues, there are many qualities that provide a measure of success: self-esteem, balance, long-term growth in lieu of short-term "wins," contribution, excellence, endurance, mutual relationships, inner peace, spirituality, love, laughter, and learning. Few of my colleagues are satisfied that wealth and celebrity are *sufficient* indicators of success. As the Avon Report indicates (see Chapter 2), the pit-of-the-stomach measure is the one most of us use to judge attainment of success.

Success is personal. And dynamic. It is lit by our age, our personal stage of development, and the context of our lives. It is not an absolute state. During the 1980s when young "masters of the universe" discussed, in absolute terms, net worth figures as measures of success ("If my net worth is $5 million before my thirtieth birthday ... ") I wondered, then what? Then what, turned out to be a series of "raising the ante" exercises ("If my net worth is $10 million ... $50 million. . . . ") This view finally collapsed with the leveraged fantasies of those years.

The uncluttered notion that success was a place (like Omaha or Oz) that could be reached by following the map and stopping the car at the right stations seemed strangely unrealistic for otherwise worldly people. But those masters and ms.'s were rushing so wildly for "Omaha" that they had no time to ask why they were going, what they would do when they got there, or, more importantly, what was between here and "Omaha?" Anyone who did ask those questions was considered hopelessly out of touch with the opportunities of life in the fast lane. Nevertheless, women (and more and more men) began to drop out of the fast lane, establishing businesses that, while difficult and absorbing, provided some opportunities for them to make life work, to define success for themselves, and to rewrite the rules of business.

REDEFINING SUCCESS

For a long time I kept my ideas about success to myself, like subversive thoughts that needed to be hidden. But I have developed a guerilla warrior's instinct for identifying kindred spirits in the business community with whom I can discuss my apparently heretical ideas. At each of the *Inc.* dinners I hosted for women entrepreneurs, sometime just before dessert was served and the women were feeling comfortable with one another, I posed this question: "What does success mean to you? How will you know when you have been successful with your business?"

I remember feeling at home during those dinners, in the company of like-minded friends; however, it wasn't until later as I read transcripts from the dinners that I understood why I had felt so warmed. The great majority of these women shared my subversive thoughts and were engaged collectively and individually in a redefinition of the meaning of success, creating a paradigm shift as naturally as they breathed. The women represented a wide range of businesses. Some had owned companies for 10 to 20 years, operating consistently in the black. They were reinvesting in and growing their companies. Some were struggling with the traumas of start-up—too much growth as well as too little growth—some were coping with still being in the red; and others, having sold at least one company, were working on the establishment of new ones.

Only 1 woman out of 50 responded to my question without hesitation, "Success to me is what I want to make of my life, and I want to be rich and famous." She was the only one to answer in that way. Indeed, in another city, at a different table, another woman observed, "My father was very rich and very famous. He was dead at 49 of alcoholism. I don't think my father was a success at all."

The other 48 women offered more complex explanations of their own standards for and definitions of success—definitions related to financial measures but not limited by them. They did not appear to be measuring themselves against one another or by any of the standards common to business reporters. There was no mention of either *Fortune* 500 or *Inc.* 500 status as a standard of success; no dollar figures were presented as net worth goals to be attained. No one seemed to believe that if they were worth $1 million or $10 million or even $100 million (as measured by either net worth or business revenues) then the question of success was settled. Success is not a place to them. Instead, the women offered a broad array of meanings

seldom explored by business reporters. Explained one entrepreneur
from Minnesota:

> Success means being able to have an ever-increasing sphere of people
> in my life that I care about and can help. When I was a little successful,
> I could help myself. As I got more successful I could pay for my chil-
> dren's education . . . then I was able to provide employees with a higher
> quality of life, vis-à-vis the paycheck that I could give them and the
> quality of the work life. Now I am helping other women, mentoring
> and becoming involved with the community. That's what I consider
> success—helping others through my efforts.

This entrepreneur made no explicit mention of return on investment, profit, or financial goals and no mention of fame or fortune.
There is an underlying assumption that financial growth not only
supports the achievement of these measures of success but that it is
critical to the attainment of ever-greater levels of success—first for
children, then employees, then community. The woman who spoke
is a successful businesswoman whose company is growing steadily.
But financial growth in her definition of success is a *means,* not an
end in itself. This is one of the most dramatic commonalities among
the women and men who share the right stuff and operate by new
rules. This view—that profit is a vehicle, a means, not an end in
itself—is central to the new rules so many entrepreneurs are now
adopting. And the shift from means to ends is at the heart of a
challenge to the notion that the business of business is business. By
a large majority, the women who attended the dinners rejected the
assumption that making money for its own sake is either enough or
even defensible. Furthermore, they reject it with a kind of amused
indulgence, as though sorry for the poor old dinosaurs still clinging to old definitions of success. One woman, speaking with some
optimism, said:

> There are men growing up with different values and ideas, rejecting the
> old-fashioned notion that you devote your entire life to your company,
> you get rich, you get famous, and those are your marks of success.

This view, that the old standards of measurement for success
are dated, is one indicator that these new entrepreneurs are rewriting
the book on business. Neither apologetic nor self-conscious, these
owners are betting the farm on their chosen strategies and definitions
of success. They know deep in their souls that children cannot be
judged by how many inches they grow or how many pounds they
weigh. They know that a flower that takes a year to bloom is not

inherently inferior to one that blooms in a month; it is just different. Although they may not talk about this or refer to these analogies specifically, there is a refreshingly commonsensical approach to making judgments about what constitutes success in business. They scoff at the notion that numbers alone can tell a tale. Never disputing the imperative of financial indicators as one source of data, they do not allow themselves to be fooled into believing this is sufficient data upon which to base judgments. What are your goals? What is important? What are your values? These are the questions that they pose. Only after these questions are answered can some true determination of success be assessed. The willingness to consider such questions may not be quantifiable for inclusion on a neat list in a business periodical but may help explain why women-owned businesses are failing less often than those of their male counterparts (by some reports, up to 24 percent less often).

Sudha Pennathur, a former general merchandise manager with Levi Strauss and Co. and now the owner of an international design, manufacturing, and retail organization, was very successful as a corporate woman. She made a high salary, had great benefits, and enjoyed many opportunities. However, she felt she was never going to be in serious contention for any of the most senior management positions of the company, and she would not have had the opportunity to exercise her credo of success. Sudha left Levi Strauss and established a company of her own. She has enjoyed recognition, profits, and the exercise of her creative and managerial talents far beyond what might have come had she stayed at Levi Strauss another 20 years. But that is not what Sudha focuses on. For her, success has another dimension:

> I have 2000 people in India working on the various designs in my collection—2000 people in 14 cities and a lot of villages—every item is handcrafted, nothing is made by machine. These people have ten generations of crafts behind them, and to help revive those crafts is thrilling. My credo of success involves improving the quality of life of those people who have something wonderful to contribute to the world. If we don't give them opportunity, their craft will go, their skill will disappear, moreover, they will not have a tomorrow. There is no challenge or glamor to just measuring success in dollar sales. I see a generation growing up that has been told, "Success is a dollar sign, bottom line, climbing that ladder, stepping on people to climb that ladder." I was told that if you step on someone to climb that ladder, you've just broken and fallen down a few rungs. I want to see young people being given other options for defining success in the way that I was given.

PARADIGM SHIFTS

Pairing business success with means instead of ends is a paradigm shift. In 1964 Alfred Sloan wrote that General Motors was in the business of making money not cars. In the 1970s and 80s, entrepreneurs such as Ben Cohen, Anita Roddick and Paul Hawken began to tell us that business should do more than make money, create jobs, or sell products. Business, they argued, should help solve major social problems—not by contributing to charity, but by using all their resources to come up with real answers. Not everyone takes as literal and wholehearted an approach to this notion as the owners of Ben and Jerry's Ice Cream, The Body Shop, and Smith and Hawken but most of the women I spoke with aligned themselves in the make-money-*and*-do-good camp. This shift, connecting one's business with a conscious intent to use it to do something more than simply create money, implies a process of reflection and choice. What am I doing this for? This is the question faced, either explicitly or implicitly. Just to make money? To get rich? To pay back shareholders? "That's not all there is," they sing. (Those people who take issue with the idea that business is a means to solve our most debilitating social problems (and create something good for self, family, employees, and community) ignore the extent to which business has been used as a means of influencing domestic social policies, overthrowing foreign governments, and otherwise throwing its weight around.)

Whether solving problems, making a contribution, or infusing cultures with new life, as Sudha Pennathur does, this new view of business assumes that success is integrated with the use of business as a vehicle for achievement and contribution, beyond the conventions of return on investment or simple accumulation. This paradigm shift carries with it implications for the future of business and business owners.

Imagine how bankers, investment advisors, management consultants, and corporate CEOs who believe "the business of business is business" react to this new view. Humans do not change their driving assumptions easily, and humans who assume that Alfred Sloan had the right attitude will make a particular set of decisions relative to investing capital, offering advice, and making introductions. Those people who assume that Anita Roddick represents a more effective point of view will make vastly different decisions about investments, advice, and resources. Those entrepreneurs seeking capital from people who hold a radically different set of assumptions from their own may find it difficult to secure resources for their company. Conversely, investors and entrepreneurs who seek a new vision of business, reparation of the environment, responsible growth, and are open to a more complex interpretation of the meaning of success will set new standards for measuring the bottom line.

Kathryn Keeley, the founder of numerous successful businesses and director of the WOMENVENTURE in St. Paul, Minnesota, adds another dimension to the experience of success.

> Success means being able to change something...I have to be able to develop new models, new ways of doing things, new ways of looking at situations. Then I take those models and grow them into bigger things so they become national and international.

Keeley has an impressive track record of starting and growing companies. However, to her, success is not the attainment of international scope—that, she assumes, is the natural outcome of her efforts. Real success for this woman comes from being innovative—that is, creating new models and finding new ways to operate, to solve problems, and to do business. In other words, success lies in the process, not simply in the results of the business.

Many women at the dinners argued further that results, as measured by traditional standards, are actually improved by a shift in emphasis on process. None of the businesswomen I spoke with advocate inattention to the numerical bottom line, a lack of attention to financial indicators, or business sloppiness. Although some of them are wild-eyed dreamers, they are also sharp-eyed business owners and entrepreneurs. Yet, because they are relatively new to business ownership, they are not bound by the conventions, assumptions, and practices of the past. Unfettered by tradition, they make choices in concert with their values and experience. The pleasure of creating new models is part of the exercise of artistry discussed earlier; it is the part of the business that requires your most imaginative strengths—strength to envision a new recruiting system or to reinvent customer responsiveness, for instance.

Creating new models is part of the transformative challenge that many women are committed to. Finding ways to help working women respond to the needs of their children and their clients is one such goal. Establishing flexible schedules, child-care sharing systems, and "mobile offices" are methods women are devising to create a new reality in the workplace. Creating new models that can be replicated and that can make this new vision of business a reality is part of the adventure for the transformative feminists. Kirby Sack, a Yale School of Management graduate and an entrepreneur in San Francisco, articulates this transformative drive:

> Our capital markets have had a narrow focus on certain sets of numbers, which were met by having certain people maintaining the home life and other people devoting themselves to their business life and focusing on a narrow set of financial performance goals.... You have to have a broader set of evaluations. I have people working for me who have been here for 12, 15 years in positions which, in our industry, turn over every couple of years. There's a reason for that, and it has to do with how we do our business. It takes commitment and diverting funds, and you sacrifice certain measures of success in order to do that for your people. If our large corporations took the time to look at the long-term impact on a broader set of people than just their shareholders, they would begin to define success differently.

REMEASURING SUCCESS

Do these new constructs of success being realized by thousands of entrepreneurs around the country mean an eventual end to scorelike listings of "most and least"? Probably not. There is something peculiarly American about the need to measure, and it is hard to resist the mythic adventures of our heroes and heroines battling the odds for a place in history (or at least a place on the *Fortune* 500). However, these new definitions of success bode well for everyone in that they reveal many new pathways for experiencing a sense of achievement and self-esteem. That now-cliched phrase of the 1980s, "The one who dies with the most toys wins," made it clear that who we were was what we owned or could tally as net worth. The entrepreneurs I meet with roll their eyes at such lunacy.

Now success can be measured in the balance achieved between home and work. It can be measured in the positive impact the business and its employees have on their community or on the planet. It can be measured in the mutuality of respect held among employees, customers, suppliers, and investors and in the creation of innovative ways of making a profit and providing jobs. As one woman owner said:

Success isn't any of the things I thought it would be....I thought it would be the diamonds and the fur coats. And it turned out not to be outside validation, not external things. No, it's me feeling good about me.

New Measures

Success is measured in many ways. It is measured annually, quarterly, and nightly:

- Did I listen to myself?
- Did I listen to others?
- Did I risk?
- Did I work from truth?
- Was I fair/just?
- Did I do as well as I could?
- Did I add something?
- Did we make a difference?
- Did we meet payroll?
- Did we meet sales projections?
- Did we manage costs wisely?
- Did we meet marketing goals?
- Did we spend rightly?
- Did we improve quality or product?
- Did we help one another to grow?
- Were we responsible and respectful of our goals: environmental, human, financial, creative?
- Did we change, learn, grow?
- Did we make money, and did we use that money well?
- Are we in harmony with all our stakeholders?
- Did we reflect as well as achieve?
- Did we balance the competing claims of clients, employees, families, investors, suppliers, and selves in ways that can bear the harsh light of public examination?

What may be most important about these questions is that the examination is both reflective—a conversation with yourself—and participatory—a conversation with others. Do customers feel you have successfully responded to their needs? Do investors, community, and suppliers have respect for your methods and meeting of goals? In the middle of the night, are you satisfied that you have been true to your values and ethics? Are you meeting your own goals, whatever they are? Wall Street, conventional business journals, and venture capitalists may not cite you on their "sports listings" of successful companies, but women and men unconcerned about the old scorekeepers will share in the dividends of multidimensional definitions of success. Never before has such a wide array of validating achievement markers been available to so many people. Ordinary women and men, building large and small companies, can now design companies to meet their own standards of success and are no longer held hostage to rigid conventions that measure achievement like baseball standings.

GAINING CONFIDENCE

Claiming your own definition of success is a part of the process of gaining confidence as a person and as a business owner. It is part of the process of "becoming self." Taking your definition of success out of the closet and letting it shine is the act that will most profoundly aid the emergence of a new vision of business. It has taken me almost 15 years to speak out and to write about the strengths that the new breed of women and men bring to business. Identifying our values, our ability to build and sustain relationships, our access to emotional insight as assets and not baggage to be jettisoned in the process of climbing to the "top" (wherever that is) takes a certain amount of audacity. It takes courage that comes only from a sense of self secure enough to stop apologizing for qualities that are not inappropriate, but are merely unfamiliar, in the realm of business.

FOUR

Time for Fun

*Each day, and the living of it, has to be a conscious creation
in which discipline and order are relieved with some play
and pure foolishness.*
          May Sarton, The Quotable Woman, p. 169

I am a tireless advocate for the integration of fun with work. Fun is not frivolous; it is essential, play is imperative. Playfulness is the door to surprise, possibility, invention and breakthroughs, team cohesion, and energy. By using play, we learn to experiment, challenge rules, dare the absurd, and focus on common goals.

What if the sea were made of lime jelly? What if time stood still? Why can't I have a kangaroo? What if I eat dinner standing on my head? Why not paint my room in polka dots and put stars on the ceiling? "What if" and "why not," the questions children can ask to distraction, represent insatiable curiosity and a driving sense of possibility. What if lightning could be tapped for electricity? What if people could fly? What if you could send your voice through wire? Why not see a picture in seconds or send a package overnight? The people who ask these questions are not simply visionaries; they are adults who never lose their childlike wonder and who treat their workplace like a giant sandbox.

At some indefinable age, little girls and little boys begin to hear that it is time to put away their toys—it is time to be sensible and pay attention to "important things." "Don't ask such silly questions," they are told. Before long, the impulse to imagine funny pictures in clouds is squelched, the license to wile away an afternoon aimlessly building sand castles is revoked, and the very idea of sleeping under the stars fades away. That natural ability to dream, imagine, try on funny ideas, and contemplate the impossible retreats and finally goes into a deep, self-protective sleep.

One of the most magical aspects of entrepreneurship is the way an idea begins a clean, uncluttered life. Before the business plan, the employees, the product—before *anything*—there is just a bare idea. Like a picture in the mind's eye, first there is nothing, then the idea emerges, takes shape, and comes to life. The idea slowly gets dressed and takes on a life of its own. Ideas are sometimes like monsters run amok, they need money, resources, time, and more ideas. Like Audrey, the monster plant in *Little Shop of Horrors,* they whine, "Feed me, feed me!"

Anyone who has ever started a business knows what it means to cope with an idea without sufficient resources. It is the special perversity of the entrepreneur to think that coming up with those resources adds fun to the adventure. "There are so many wonderful puzzles to solve," I tell my friends. By this, I mean not just finding solutions to financing and marketing challenges, but finding ways to do more with less (in some cases nothing!) or ways to inspire a breakthrough in a problem or barrier that seems particularly impenetrable. Sometimes, *thinking* is not enough; our cerebral selves often need an added ingredient to function effectively.

FOOD, FUN, AND CREATIVITY

When I first began Odysseum, after returning from Mexico, I got permission to explore a concept. I didn't have a budget to pay people; I had no corporate legitimacy, no resources, and no visibility. I was purposely hidden in the seldom-used offices of an unused lab. I tried to maintain a low profile and keep out of the way of anyone who might want to know more about what I was doing and why. I also wanted to protect the only real resource I had—my mentor, Jerry Sudbey. I didn't need to call attention to the fact that he was aiding and abetting activity that was not only peripheral to Polaroid's business, but that many would have considered antithetical to it. I was investigating the possibilities of a service business in a company in which, the year before, the president had issued this explicit mission statement: "We are not a service company; we are a technical company."

Nevertheless, I pushed forward. Once I had completed a certain amount of research, I needed help. I needed a small team that could develop ideas and a prototype program with me. But how was I going to get talented, high-energy, busy people, who already had full-time jobs (and were more interested in protecting their corporate status than antagonizing the parent company), to work with me? Why would anyone join me if I had no power, no formal status, and was living on the edge of corporate approval every day? Who would be crazy enough to work with me? Anyone who wanted to have fun, I answered. Fun is a rare treat for adults. It is particularly rare in corporations in which "seriousness" is an earnestly pursued goal. Fun is seductive. I took a lesson from Tom Sawyer's strategy for getting the picket fence painted: I made it look like working on an "illicit," "underground" project was such an adventure and so much fun that everyone wanted to help me. This wasn't a fraudulent strategy. I really think that starting something new *is* fun. But I knew that not everyone would think so—unless, like Tom, I could make whitewashing that fence look like a mighty good time!

I used food. I enticed people to late-night brainstorming sessions by serving great meals. In grey, dingy conference rooms, under dreadful fluorescent office lights, we shared Indian feasts, pizzas, Chinese dishes, spicy Mexican meals, and garlicky pastas. Microwave popcorn and creamy cheesecakes were devoured as we filled endless sheets of easel paper, met in small groups to handle parts of bigger tasks, and argued, imagined, and dreamed a business into life.

We laughed, told stories, watched videos, and brought in photographers and artists who worked with us on a variety of imagining techniques. Sometimes, the noise level was high, and, to an outsider, chaos might have appeared to be the only thing being created—but that was the creative process at work. Out of those wild, messy, alive nights of food, fun, and work was born a prototype of a learning game that was tested first with a group of the company's officers and then with real customers.

I mention food as an integral part of fun because food is one of the vital, binding ways we relate to one another. Anthropologists have long studied the rituals of breaking bread as a means of transmitting culture and tradition, as a sign of peace and trust. I don't invite enemies to dinner. My friends gather around my table to eat, share, relate, and, for at least a moment in time, become part of something warm and larger than themselves. (It is no accident that I chose small dinner parties as the medium for the *Inc.* project; food is the fastest avenue to trust and, by extension, to communication that I know.)

The Polaroid people I recruited to work with me had full-time jobs in other parts of the company. They reported to other people. I had no titles, no raises, no security, and no rewards to offer them; I had no power over them. All I promised was that they would use their good minds and have fun creating something the rest of the corporation might benefit from, even if it did not approve of our unorthodox methods.

For a long while, that was enough. I provided space, permission, stimulation, respect, and trust. In conference rooms, which during the day were used for conventional staff and committee meetings, we behaved as though we were back in the sandbox, creating cities and castles and flying on magic carpets. Like the toys in the ballet Coppelia, when everyone else went home, we came alive.

At night and on weekends, ten women and men put their heads, hearts, and hands into the creation of an entity that had not existed before. Creativity can be madly exciting. Adrenaline pumps through the veins, and you have the feeling of being on a precipice, knowing something is about to happen. But creativity has a darker side as well. Sometimes it feels more like digging ditches. Backbreaking trials, tedious attention, and tenacious perseverance are often required to find just the right word, look, or technique. The frustration of digging for oil or gold and coming up empty can be felt in the pursuit of the right detail that you *know* will alter the shape of the dream and deliver just the right element to make a vision sing. Earlier, I said truth is the glue that keeps a business together; fun is the fuel that feeds the creative process.

Before the creativity gurus take issue with this last statement, allow me to state that of course the creative process is complex and is fed by many factors, but fun—that illusive, varied spirit—contributes to the well-being and the sustenance of true creativity.

Author Ray Bradbury has been an observer of American business for many years. He passionately believes that American business is too deadly serious for its own good. In a University of Southern California management magazine, he wrote:

> If your meeting room, your board room or your office (take your pick) isn't a nursery for ideas, a rumpus room where seals frolic, forget it. Burn the table, lock the room, fire the clerks. You will rarely come up with any solutions worth entertaining. The dull room with the heavy people trudging in with long faces to solve problems by beating them to death is very death itself.... Unless the people you meet with are funloving kids out for a romp, tossing ideas like confetti, and letting the damn bits fall where they may, no spirit will ever rouse, no notion will ever birth, no love will be mentioned, no climax reached. You must swim at your meetings, you must jump for baskets, you must take hefty swings for great and missed drives, you must run and dive, you must fall and roll, and when the fun stops get the hell out.[1]

"Let go," Bradbury urges. Let loose the impulses that tell you who you are. "Let go" he pleads. Rouse the sleeping child, and let it revisit the grown-up now and then.

"It's easy to be playful in a company where games were your business," you may protest. True. But I have learned that the product is irrelevant to the process. Whether I am organizing seminars on political or social issues, creating a not-for-profit company, or just getting games packaged (not designed or developed), I have learned that taking the time and effort to infuse the process, any process, with a playful spirit is valuable.

I do not (nor probably does Bradbury) suggest that life at the office is all belly laughs and mayhem. There is a time and place for everything. Kindergarten wasn't nonstop fun and games either, as I recall; however, there was a sufficient mix of discipline and fun— time to listen, practice, and drill, and time to explore and play—and we left Miss (sometimes Mr.) Smith's class with more knowledge and skills than we walked in with. I make the case for fun not because I lack the capacity for hard work, but because play and playfulness is a misunderstood, underappreciated resource (in the workplace at least) that can foster (quite inexpensively) innovation, energy, and creativity.

Consider, for example, the production of ice cream. Making ice cream is hard work. To make the kind of ice cream Ben and Jerry's has become famous for, employees must function for hours at a time in a large refrigerated room dressed in heavy clothes to keep warm. Ben and Jerry's ice cream is dense, packed with chunky goods, and, therefore, is very heavy. Employees lift and load, push and pack in the cold. This is not easy work. It must be very strenuous and often tedious. Yet, watching people at work in that otherwise inhospitable environment, I concluded that fun was happening there. The stereo blasted away (the day I was there they had just installed their fourth set of speakers that year), people joked with one another, someone clowned around entertaining a friend, and then it was time to switch from Cherry Garcia to Dastardly Mash. The fun that I perceived there is, in part, derived from the sense of an adventure shared, work offered up for a higher purpose and a management attitude that clearly communicates that fun is a vital, integrated, endorsed, part of work.

I have been asked if there is a danger in the "tyranny" of fun. Are there companies, for example, in which fun is the mirror image of the serious firm where everyone dresses for success and observes rigid formalities? Of course, the answer is yes. I have been in companies in which employees maintain that they work hard and play hard. Sometimes, those same employees later approach me and describe how exhausting it is to keep up with all the outings, the competitions, the hearty camaraderie of their "playful" culture. Anything carried to extremes will eventually become counterproductive. But for most companies playfulness is in short supply and in need of nurturing.

FUN AND LEARNING

When we finally moved out of the cramped cellars of Polaroid into a light, open warehouse space (don't get excited, it was $6.00 per square foot) and were operating as an independent company, we still faced the ongoing issues of limited resources in a start-up company. If you can't pay people as much as you think they are worth and you have to work long hours to complete projects, which in richer times might be finished more quickly with more hands, you have to give people a better reason to come to work than just a paycheck. I was convinced there were plenty of people ready to trade the security and fatter salaries that come with a big company (or a traditional company—a lot of small to medium size companies can be pretty conventional) for the opportunity to be a whole person, to use their brains, and to have fun. So Jane and I made a commitment to spend the time and effort necessary to build a fun, learning culture.

Movies. Game nights. Imagination sessions. We brought in a diverse collection of fun and interesting people—zany people who could set a model for letting go, using imagination, and thinking outside the usual boundaries to get things done in new and inventive ways. One afternoon we brought in a well-known storyteller for "inservice" training (although I'm sure we didn't call it that). The storyteller held the staff rapt, spinning tales of folklore and suspense. Afterward, he taught the group the basic elements of storytelling and gave each person time to tell his or her own stories. We were dazzled by the results. We were able to make connections between enhancing the sales process and storytelling, program design and storytelling, and self-expression and storytelling. Some of the shyer members of our team turned out to be the better storytellers. We could have done ordinary sales training and communication seminars, but our afternoon story session was a lot more memorable and enjoyable than most ordinary training sessions. It cost less and engaged the group more.

When employees work hard, travel a good deal and spend much energy responding to client needs, the business owner must find ways to replenish their energy and nurture their well-being—it's just good business to do so. Both staff and management bear responsibility for inventing ways to do this. A tradition emerged in our company, initiated by program managers, to send funny postcards back to the office, no matter where anyone went or what they were doing. It was a way to keep in touch with one another, a way to share experiences even when separated by time and distance.

Films were used, sometimes to provide a break in what could be a demanding schedule and sometimes as a source of inspiration. After viewing the film, we might ask, "What comes to mind now that may have relevance to our business?" This is a standard brainstorming technique: focus on something seemingly unrelated to the central topic to get a totally different perspective on your subject. It works. Sometimes the connection was related to the structure of the film—determining what about the story worked and how it might be related to the development of a new game—sometimes the connection was related to the story line itself—determining what people want and what they respond to that might have significance for our products.

One year we arranged for members of the staff to attend three different circuses. Using the circuses as our case study, we compared the different ways operations were handled and the kinds of assumptions made in each company about what their customers wanted. One of our operations specialists was a graduate of two first-rate institutions: Yale University and the Ringling Brothers/Barnum and Bailey Circus School. At Yale she learned to think. At circus school she learned discipline and attention to detail, which made her a real asset to the operations department. And her ability to switch from a highly competent program manager to a clown persona, her ability to make people laugh, was equally valuable to the atmosphere of the company.

We went to the theater and we played croquet. For my birthday one year, the staff threw a surprise birthday party. They created an event that would have been a five-year-old's delight. Everyone got presents and cupcakes and ice cream. We played pin the tail on the donkey and other childhood games. We were reacquainted with how simple something can be: "less is more" we repeated over and over. We used insights from that party with our customers, responding to their program needs with streamlined, easy-to-run and, nonthreatening programs.

Development meetings sometimes started with a round of Pictionary™ to loosen us up. At an anniversary celebration for the company, Jane and I engaged in a strawberry shortcake bake-off (employees voted on whose was the most mouthwatering). It was fun, it was freeing, it was good for business.

THE PRINCIPLES OF FUN

Some of our male colleagues have made real progress in recognizing the value of play to both a healthy company culture and a record of innovation. Women use fun in their businesses (although it is often called "enthusiasm"), too, but it's more of a secret. Wanting to be taken seriously, women do not often make a big deal about the ways they make their companies fun places to work. In part, this chapter is intended to encourage more women to come out of the closet with their ideas. In part, it is intended to show how and why fun works.

"I have never seen fun taken too far. I want no barriers to [employees'] creativity and growth," said Frank Dodge, then the founder/president of a successful software company in Massachusetts.

"If it's not fun, why do it?" Jerry Greenfield, of Ben and Jerry's asked rhetorically in discussing their business.

"The objective of our enterprise is to earn money and enjoy doing so," stated the late Bill Gore, inventor of Goretex.

"If you can't have fun at work, that's a hell of a way to spend your life," observed Marquette Electronics founder Mike Cudahy.

Several years ago, as part of my research and development responsibilities with Odysseum, I decided to pursue this business of fun seriously. (A bit of a contradiction it seemed from the beginning.) I knew it was an ingredient that made our company special (in fact, it was the very basis of the products we sold), but I wanted to better understand how it worked in other companies—or if it really worked at all. To do that, I identified companies that had been cited in the business press for environments that encouraged fun.

I identified ten companies that represented a range of industries, including medical products, robotics, ice cream, textiles, and visual scanning devices. They had been in existence from 5 to 28 years and had as few as 30 employees and as many as 5000. Their revenues were between $2 million and $80 million. I asked the leaders of these companies the following questions:

1. What is your work ethic, and how did it develop?
2. How do you explain the presence of fun in your company?
3. Does fun ever get out of hand here? How do you maintain a balance between work and play?
4. What, if any, value does fun add to your business?

Before starting the interviews I tried to get a handle on a definition of fun. I knew it when I saw it or when I felt it but wasn't sure I could define it. So, I asked our customers what they thought fun was. "Beer busts" or practical jokes were rarely mentioned. The responses I received included the following:

- Fun is stimulating activity that is provocative, mind-stretching, absorbing, and yet voluntary (as opposed to mandatory activity).
- Fun is a feeling of being totally absorbed, mentally and physically, in an activity that you enjoy.
- Fun is a release of inhibitions, stress, and energy, guided by a mind-absorbing pursuit.
- Fun is a willing suspension of self-importance in favor of active involvement with other people, things, and ideas.

The repetition of words and phrases such as "stimulating," "totally absorbed," and "active involvement" was encouraging. In just 30 minutes a child playing with a simple set of blocks can build a secret cave, a bridge, a new city, or a strange planet. While absorbed at play, children grow. Perhaps, I began to think, the value of fun that we felt at Odysseum was not a fluke. Maybe by simply reclaiming the heritage of our childhood, we can make learning and discovery spontaneous and pleasurable once again. With these thoughts in mind, I started the interviews.

After six months of talking with founders and CEOs, I came to understand four principles of the so-called fun companies:

1. *Fun is inextricably tied to satisfying work.* The founder of a successful medical electronics company put it this way:

People want to perform. They want to love their job, their boss, their company. But that happens only when you take people out of boxes.

You can't tell them what they should do, when they should do it, and who's going to get rid of them when they don't do it. You've got to give them a piece of the action and a chance to excel, and you've got to give them the *freedom to have fun.*

2.   *Playfulness and fun are linked to innovation, discovery, and openness to change.* Edward de Bono, author of *Serious Fun, Six Thinking Hats,* and *Lateral Thinking,* explains the joy of "playing around":

> You set out to move things about and to build them up, and even though you don't quite know what you are going to do, something suggests itself out of what you have already got. Far too many adults lack the ability to play around and "see what happens."[2]

Nolan Bushnell, the founder of a number of high-tech companies, including Atari, the originator of Pac-Man, was one of the owners I interviewed. He told me that he was always playing around as a kid and continued to do so as an adult. His family lived next door to what he described as a "junk heap," and his earliest memories involved scavenging for odds and ends he could "play with"—that is, things he could put together in some way that worked (like a radio or a transmitter).

3.   *Fun is integrated with the assumption that life is here and now.* People who run (or work in) fun companies are not willing to waste their lives, deferring joy to some future date. They want to live *now*. They won't compartmentalize fun to some time and place outside work, and they don't live by the old ethic of work *then* play. They have rewritten the rules to work *and* play. For creators of fun companies, the adventure doesn't begin when work is over or when the company is sold or when retirement begins. Calling on Confucius, Jerry Greenfield smiled and said, "The joy is in the journey." Fun is an imperative for his journey.

4.   *There is a connection between the size of a work group and the possibilities of a playful, fun culture.* Notice, I did not say the size of a *company.* There is an optimum size, a critical mass, beyond which people stop feeling like groups and start to feel like herds. I cannot tell you what that number is. Some seasoned company owners told me they think 500 is the most that can be organized in a division and still maintain a sense of community and informality. Others mentioned 300 as an optimum number, and some felt 1000 wasn't too large to maintain a culture of fun. Certainly, manufac-

turing plants that organize thousands of workers into large work groups under one roof, or insurance companies filled with office workers in little cubicles will require a military style bureaucracy to achieve basic production goals. Assumptions about what constitutes an optimum size work group and how to organize it need to be more aggressively challenged. I do not think that play can happen under all circumstances.

Funeral homes, nuclear energy plants, and other companies that call for a high level of alertness or sensitivity cannot tolerate the same culture of fun as a Ben and Jerry's ice cream factory. Although I would argue that nuclear plant workers and embalming technicians are probably ingenious at finding ways to "play," judgments about safety and appropriateness must be weighed against morale and motivation. My intent here is simply to stretch the current work ethic to be more open to the possibilities of fun in the workplace.

CHALLENGES TO FUN

About the same time that I was doing the interviews on fun companies, a story began to unfold in the national press. At first, it was a story so silly as not to be noteworthy, but within a week three major networks and newspapers in Boston, New York, Los Angeles, and Washington were following this tale. By then, I realized that however silly the story was, there was a larger tale to be told.

It all began a few days before Christmas in 1987. Two employees of an electrical cable plant in New Jersey donned red Santa Claus hats and wore them to work. It was a harmless enough act, perhaps a simple gesture of holiday spirit. However, a plant manager noticed the hats and called for them to be removed. They were "inappropriate for the workplace," he said. The next day, in what became a symbolic show of support, 100 co-workers of the two original hat bearers arrived at work wearing red Santa hats. Not to be outwitted, the manager suspended all the employees. It took the intervention of the union to get the hats off and the employees back to work. The case went to arbitration. The arbitrator's finding was insubordination by the employees.

This case caught the attention of the press precisely because it was so silly. These events simply would not happen in most companies. This is a tale of rigidity run amok—a tale of a control freak with too much authority and too little comfort with self or others. I followed the story with curiosity. In its very strangeness, there was a larger lesson. Not until some months later could I articulate that lesson.

The plant manager was simply acting out his work ethic—work now, play later. Hard work rewarded. Work then play. Much of the Western vision of work incorporates the Calvinist world view of earning reward through suffering. The Industrial Revolution was, in part, the successful incorporation of this view. For centuries, this mandate to work and then play was wonderfully effective in the task of controlling undisciplined workers. No one expected work to be fun. Work was toil and suffering. Fun, if it existed at all (less pain was perhaps more accurate), came after the day's labors.

To suggest that work might, indeed *should* be fun, challenges deep assumptions about the nature of work and the religious authority underlying our work ethic. In an earlier age, insisting that work could be fun might have resulted in a worker being burned as an heretic. I suppose being sent home and ordered to remove a hat was a certain kind of progress!

If you do what you care about and do it well, the reward is in the work itself. Work and play can be integrated. This shift, from compartmentalization to integration, may be the oil that helps ease us into the future. As so many of the old rules discussed in Chapter 3 fail us, the old notion that reward comes from suffering may also fall away. Watch the business journals. Listen to the dialogue on how to motivate workers. There are signs that the work ethic that guided the Industrial Revolution is being revamped. We are in transition: from a religious work ethic to a secular work ethic; from work *then* reward to work *and* play; from the industrial era to the knowledge era. However clumsy and slow the shift may occur in some quarters, a new view of work is emerging. From compartmentalizing life (work then family then play) to integrating life (work and play and family), new values are emerging.

THE THREE KINDS OF PLAY

Sometime after the Santa Claus hats story died down, I developed a model of play that helped put that incident into perspective. There are three kinds of play: instrumental, real, and illicit.

Remember the spelling bee? Anyone who has ever stood in a classroom competing in a spelling bee participated in instrumental play. The spelling bee was the teacher's attempt to get us to learn through the use of a game (as Mary Poppins would explain, "A spoonful of sugar helps the medicine go down"). Otherwise boring drills took on a little excitement, and words missed in the context of a game might be more sharply remembered later. In a way, "Sesame Street" is a sophisticated version of the spelling bee. Aware that children learn through their play, the creators of "Sesame Street" make all their learning exercises fun. When fun activities have a secondary purpose of learning, we call that *instrumental play*.

Skipping rope and playing hopscotch, tag, and toss are free-spirited activities. Unplanned (usually) by adults, the games are a form of spontaneous, self-managed fun, or *real play*. Computer hackers often engage in real play (when they aren't breaking into someone else's system!). The first wearers of the Santa hats may well have been exercising a burst of spontaneous playfulness. Real play—whether the building of a tower with a set of blocks, experimentation with a computer program, doodling at one's desk, or clowning around in a staff meeting—is the door to discovery. It is that uninhibited realm in which both children and adults try on and try out ideas that may seem inconsequential and silly and yet may hold wonderful possibilities.

Spitballs, on the other hand, are examples of *illicit play*. Throwing a spitball from the back of the room, was a way to express boredom, displeasure, anxiety, or rebellion. In a way, the 100 workers who wore Santa hats threw spitballs! They were rebelling against the tyranny of a manager intent on exercising his values regarding the proper separation of work and play, the denial of a head, heart, and hands policy.

By squelching the impulse to play—saying, in effect, "you can't bring yourselves fully into the workplace"—the manager missed an opportunity to encourage creativity and spontaneity. He also missed the chance to transform a bit of real playfulness into instrumental play and learning. He might, for example, have announced a hat competition. Instead of punishing employees, he could have praised them. This would have sent a message that initiative is valued, not considered a nuisance. Instead, the manager communicated that the workplace is not an appropriate setting for playfulness. When 100 co-workers showed up the next day, wearing red Santa hats—against the express orders of management—real play was transformed into illicit play. The workers' initial burst of spontaneity (which is at the root of creativity) grew into an act of rebellion, a proclamation of autonomy and power. Disciplinary action and union arbitration followed. Management won the battle, but everyone lost.

Not long ago, I gave a talk to a large conference audience on the topic of work, play and innovation. I started my talk by flying a dozen paper airplanes into the audience and asking for suggestions as to what could be done with a paper airplane. At first everyone sat in embarrassed silence. Finally, one brave soul offered a suggestion; then someone else had an idea. I told them I could come up with at least 25 things I could do with a paper airplane, and suddenly a flood of creativity poured forth. Later, one of the men who had been sitting in the audience, approached me. "For years," he said, "I have sat in meetings, quietly folding paper airplanes, always tempted to just throw one, but scared to death I'd be fired for being so frivolous. Next time, I'm going to go ahead and make something happen."

BALANCING WORK AND PLAY

The following diagram illustrates how the cable company (of the Santa hat example) viewed the division of work and play.

WORK/PLAY MATRIX

Work

Achievement
Maintenance
Stability
Reliability

Disorder _____ Order

Discovery
Mastery
Change
Innovation
Invention

Play

A healthy work environment provides a balance between order and disorder, work and play. Such an environment ensures both achievement of goals and openness to new ideas. What does your work environment look like?

Work and order, represented by the upper-right hand quadrant, were viewed as polarized opposites to play and disorder, represented by the lower left-hand quadrant. One of the legacies of our work ethic is to see the forces of work and play as diametrically opposed. The fear is that a little play will turn a well-ordered workplace into a state of chaos. It doesn't work like that.

The secret to effectively managing work and play and to creating a new work ethic, and a healthy work environment is not simplistic opposition; it is balance. In almost all systems, extremes lead to imbalance. All work and no play doesn't just make Jill and Jack dull, it kills the potential of discovery, mastery, and openness to change and flexibility and it hinders innovation and invention. The diagram above illustrates that when the focus is on work and order, stable, predictable environments are the result (or so managers hope; unpredictability does have a way of making itself present!). The desirability of such an outcome is understandable; in business, "no surprises" is a slogan that many executives take seriously. However, most businesses also yearn for creative, flexible, innovating employees. This is one of those rare occurrences when you can have it all—not all at once, of course, but over time. If management is willing to make room for a little playfulness in the work culture, they can create an environment that ensures both achievement of goals and openness to new ideas.

Unfortunately, too many managers and company owners are so anxious about being out of control, that if they allow play to emerge at all in their culture, it is only in the form of instrumental play. "Play will get out of hand if we don't watch out," managers will tell me. Yet Nolan Bushnell says, "I've never seen play go too far. People protect what they value, and if something does get out of hand, it's not because play is the culprit, but because there is some other problem which needs to be managed."

I often remind women to hang on to any idea that is met with the comment, "That's crazy." *Get* crazy, I encourage. My friends and I can spawn ten new businesses in the course of an evening of letting go, laughing, and encouraging one another to ever more outrageous ideas. It is deeply frustrating that I only have one life at a time and can't juggle all the ideas we generate. But I am very much aware that lots of those ideas bubble out of a place of absurdity. In some unconscious part of the brain we entertain fantasies, hopes, and possibilities that seem so unattainable that when they first present themselves to us we greet them derisively, like a strange child unwelcomed in the neighborhood. That's a terrible thing to do to our wacky ideas (as it is to the child). Wacky ideas should be grabbed and embraced; they should be examined long enough to assess them with fairness and respect.

Not all crazy ideas are worth salvaging or holding on to, of course, but even crazy ideas can force a change in perspective. In staff meetings, for instance, we often get stuck on a problem or issue, and, after a while, no matter how we try, there seems to be no good way to resolve the issue. If somebody gets silly (with boredom, fatigue, or frustration), they just might let loose with a comment that at first sounds sarcastic or just a little weird. With amused tolerance, other staff members may dismiss the idea; however, if someone else in the group feels the same desperation by this point, she or he might giggle and add an even sillier idea. Before you know it, all discipline seems to vanish and the most ridiculous thoughts are spinning around the room. Usually, the manager's first impulse is to restore order to the meeting. Things are out of control! But it is just this sort of charged free-for-all that gives birth to outrageous ideas and previously unconsidered possibilities. They might arrive in a crude, unpolished, hard to recognize form, but they arrive. With a little nurturing, these ideas may offer a way out of the problem that started the free-for-all in the first place.

Judy Rosener remarked that in her interviews with women in the International Women's Forum enthusiasm was a dominant theme. She said that enthusiasm was how they described the ways they created excitement and fun. Women's companies are often fun. We use our excitement to keep the team engaged and eager to participate. It is a way to influence others without resorting to the use of power *over* someone else.

Numerous studies explain and complain that women aren't comfortable with power. Maybe that's true, although I don't happen to believe it. I think it's more likely that women simply don't feel that the traditional use of power is either fun, efficient, or respectful and that if it doesn't get you what you want (enthused, committed employees), why use it? As Ruth Owades put it, "I can play the game as well as the next guy, but why?"

Once more, we return to the importance of relating—this time as a function of our ability to play with others. To play is to relax and feel comfortable with others. To play is to try out ideas with some sense of safety. When your guard is up, you are less likely to loosen up or to risk. Growing up in Maine in the 1950s, I remember a sporting show that was on television every Saturday night at about 6 o'clock in the evening. My father always watched it. It featured stories on fishing or hiking or boating, mostly outdoor activities set in the Maine woods. The host of the show, Bud Leavitt (rotund, balding, a jolly sort), closed every episode of the program with this line, "Remember, the family that plays together, stays together." Back then I thought that refrain had a little too much hokum in it to suit me. But I was a kid on my way to independence, and I wasn't much interested in playing with my family. Now, however, I see the power of playing together and what that has to do with relating, trusting, and feeling at ease with a group of kindred spirits.

We watch children play to assess their socialization skills and their ability to relate. We understand (usually) that play is the work of children. It is what they do to learn and master new skills. But when they grow up, I guess we assume that the kind of relating done through play—sharing, being fair, having patience, and taking turns—isn't relevant any more. As grown-ups in business, a well-socialized adult learned to "get it all," "be first," "hurry up," "be sensible." Robert Fulghum was right—everything we need to know we learned in kindergarten.

It's not really surprising to me that so many entrepreneurial companies are fun. (It's more surprising how many are not.) Entrepreneurs are frequently people who have listened to their heart and approach their work as though climbing into a sandbox each day to experiment with a set of blocks that contain endless possibilities.

Fun is a little like a great little inn: you know it when you see it. But like a great inn, there are some identifying signs. Fun companies talk to you. Walk down the halls of your business (or look around your cellar office!). Do you hear laughter? Not mean-spirited laughter, fueled by another's discomfort, but laughter that opens the heart and signals receptivity to odd, skewed, or whimsical ideas. Serious, focused, high-intensity attention does not conversely signal a dearth of inventiveness or a lack of fun, but where the whole person is present, laughter will be unsuppressed. Listen for laughter.

Look also for celebration. What events or milestones are honored and celebrated? Birthdays? Product introductions? Proposals accepted or sales made? Awards? Is there an appreciation for what has been accomplished as well as an understanding of how much more always needs to be done?

Is it more important to follow rules than to take initiative? Is control more important than autonomy? Are there prescriptions (implicit or explicit) for strict office decor or dress codes? Are "procedural" memos issued as a response to glitches in the system or other problems that arise in the firm?

Fun companies are full of alive, vital people. They have a gleam in their eyes—a sense of mischievous daring about them. The air around them is often electric. Tasks are accomplished, and products, both tangible and intangible, are shipped out the door. Industry is palpable. Just under the surface is the life force that keeps it happening. Inherent in that life force is a large element of playfulness and adventure. Isn't this fun? Isn't this grand? Aren't we lucky to be on this wonderful adventure?

DETERMINING YOUR PLAYFUL INSTINCTS

Check out your own playful instincts by taking the following quiz. Circle the number from 1 to 5 that best describes your answer to each statement. The numbers are part of a continuum—1 meaning "Never" and 5 meaning "Often."

	1	2	3	4	5
1. I propose ideas which at first seem silly or strange.	1	2	3	4	5
2. I break rules.	1	2	3	4	5
3. I play with ideas.	1	2	3	4	5
4. I start pilot projects and experiments.	1	2	3	4	5
5. I catch myself doodling.	1	2	3	4	5
6. I daydream.	1	2	3	4	5
7. I like to create.	1	2	3	4	5
8. I dare to (and sometimes do) fail.	1	2	3	4	5
9. I build on others' ideas.	1	2	3	4	5
10. I laugh.	1	2	3	4	5
11. I entertain new ways of doing things.	1	2	3	4	5
12. I explore the unfamiliar.	1	2	3	4	5

Now, total your score: if you scored 20 or less, it's been a long time since you've been in a sandbox; 21 to 34, you're willing to visit the sandbox occasionally, but it's not where you're most comfortable; 34 to 47, you're very playful—we need more of you; 48 to 60, great products, services, and discoveries are in your future!

BUILDING A PLAYFUL WORK CULTURE

What if you take stock and discover that fun and playfulness make you uncomfortable or that, despite your best attempts, they are qualities that are illusive in your company (or your one-person office)? Most of the time, companies that communicate fun start out fun. They are the spontaneous expression of people who are comfortable with themselves and enjoy what they do. However, like a small fire, fun can be kindled. With a little tending, even the most serious work cultures can lighten up and make room for fun to work its magic. The following suggestions include two principal strategies: personal change and organizational change. Whether you are thinking of starting a company, already have a company, or now work in a company, it's important to remember that change often occurs as a result of the synergy of grass-roots efforts and policy reform. And one person *can* make a difference.

1. *Examine your work ethic.* Habits are hard to change and our work ethic habits are deep in our culture. Centuries of collective agreements have reinforced our feeling that work *then* play is the right formula. If you feel guilty or uncomfortable about exploring playfulness, powerful self-censors will block all efforts to introduce the idea of an integrated spirit of work and play.

2. *Commit to fun.* Risk looking silly and feeling embarrassed. Dare to be zany. Trust your childlike whimsy. Don't give up on play or forget about it after a few weeks. Nurture it; let it grow in the garden of your company.

3. *Increase awareness.* Talk about playfulness. Circulate articles, stories, and cartoons that speak to the connections between work and play. Seek out artists, storytellers, and writers who will talk about their own experiences with the rewards of playfulness.

4. *Work with and hire fun people.* Insert a new question into your interviews (regardless of which side of the hiring fence you are on): What is the connection between work and play in your own work style? Pay attention to the answers you get to this question. Recruit from the Ringling Brothers/Barnum and Bailey Circus School.

5. *Support fun when it breaks out—or at least ignore it and let it happen.* I remember sitting in my office at Odysseum some afternoons and suddenly a fit of fun would break out in the operations area or among the sales group—anywhere people gathered. Sometimes remnants of my own Yankee work heritage (growing up on a farm instills a pretty strong sense of work *then* play!) would leap to the fore, and I'd have to hang on to my desk to keep myself planted. Sometimes, the worst thing I could have done in those moments would have been to echo the manager in the cable plant and admonish, "Get back to work!" What I had to remember was that often, they were doing work. Also, don't be a wet blanket. Nothing is more deadening than the person who ridicules or chastises someone else's fragile ideas or attempts at lightening the atmosphere. At least for a time, suspend disbelief enough to give fun a chance.

6. *Interrupt tension.* Is pressure high? Are people feeling cranky? Float a balloon into the room, hand out candy, or suggest a 15-minute dreamers break. Organize an ice cream run, and take time to eat the ice cream. Listen to the ensuing conversation.

7. *Model behavior.* Explain your desire to build a climate more inviting to a playful, energetic, and innovative spirit. Invite others to join you in the adventure, and start to sanction and model ways to do that. Remember the story of the Santa's hats. Spontaneity and initiative cannot be punished one day and expected the next. Modeling behavior requires tenacious consistency.

8. *Review company policies.* How to balance organizational controls with a tolerance for fun was explained as well as I have ever heard by Coco Montagu, the founder of General Scanning Inc. He once said to me:

> Particularly as a company grows, you need systems and rules to manage with. But that shouldn't mean sacrificing the daring, disruptive, experimenting, and challenging behavior which keeps companies adaptive and growing. To keep rules and policies from deadening an organization—killing the fun, that is—you need tolerant, parallel systems. You need rule keepers and rule breakers to accommodate both stability and change. Having both allows for the safety people need if they are going to play. You have to know the place won't fall down around you. These two forces will drive one another crazy, so it's partly up to the leader to manage both and manage the natural tension which will arise between them.

9. *Review space, light, values, and events in your offices for implicit messages of play and fun.* Workspace that restricts autonomy, lighting that depresses, and messages that consistently say, "Back to business as usual," all hinder the flowering of a culture of fun.

Achieving a shift from work *then* play to work *and* play won't happen quickly. Nor will such a shift guarantee the invention of the next light bulb. Building a successful business is far more complex than just creating a culture that incorporates the benefits of play and discovery. But it will give you an edge in the race to innovation. It will help you enjoy the journey. It will extract extraordinary feats from ordinary people. And that's not bad.

II

DREAM
BUILDERS

FIVE

Ordinary Women

> *There is nothing special about me. I didn't have any family
> member to model after, I didn't have any money, I didn't
> have any education, I didn't have any business training,
> and I certainly didn't have a genius I.Q. I had a lot of grit
> and determination, and despite the odds, I have made my
> company successful.*
>
> Mary Farrar, President, Systems Erectors, Inc.
> (before members of the U.S. Congress at the Hearings on
> New Economic Realities: The Role of Women
> Entrepreneurs, 100th Congress, 1988)

One night I gave a talk to a group of women in California. I had
been telling stories about some of the women business owners I had
met—those who had been at the *Inc.* dinners and others I know. I
didn't enhance their stories or exaggerate. But finally one woman in
the group raised her hand and asked a riveting question: "Are any of
the women you met ordinary?" This simple, elegant query stopped
me cold. Clearly I was being asked, "How could I (a mere mortal),
how could others like me, expect to find a seat at those tables?"
I stopped for just a moment and answered carefully and from the
heart, "They are *all* ordinary. They are our sisters and daughters and
partners and friends. They are you and me."

Ella Williams, founder/president of Aegir Systems in California
and a recent winner of the Avon Women of Enterprise Award, is
even more explicit on this point. She said to me:

> I'm not extraordinary, lots of women can do this [start a business]. We
> are all individual women, many of us have kids, we have responsibili-
> ties. We are full of fear: we have to make the house note and put food
> on the table. It's hard work, but so is life. I don't want other women
> to think I am extraordinary; I am just an ordinary woman, trying to
> make ends meet.

As you will hear later, Ella Williams is an African-American woman with a well of strength and faith that reaches mythic depths; her struggles and challenges to build a successful company were daunting. Yet, she is adamant: "I am not extraordinary—there are thousands and thousands of women like me."

Women are often called *extra*ordinary when they achieve— immediately creating a novelty, a special case, an exception. Lots of men run businesses, and we do not think of them as extraordinary. Men who achieve are simply thought of as men, because, after all, men are expected—indeed required—to achieve. But consider the men who belong to Rotary, Kiwanis, and the Chamber of Commerce. They are perfectly nice guys but not all giants, not extraordinary by mere virtue of having started a business. Of course, there are men like Steve Jobs and Fred Smith, and there are female equivalents like Anita Roddick and Suzanne DePasse. In every field, there are giants and leaders. But business ownership and growth is not the exclusive province of a few extraordinary women. It is, instead, a realistic option for many women, a means of economic independence, a path to self-esteem, even a potential vehicle for social change.

I had not meant to start a business. I didn't realize until well into my thirties that I had an entrepreneurial bone in my body. In spite of the fact that I grew up in a family business, it didn't occur to me that I, too, might be an entrepreneur. I was tricked into starting a company by a wise and insightful mentor. But when I finally found myself with responsibility for a company, employees, customers, and products, it all seemed perfectly natural, as though this is what I had been in training for all my life without knowing it.

It is this experience that makes me think that many women are latent entrepreneurs, late bloomers (many of the women featured in this book did not start their business until well into their thirties and forties) trained in a variety of fields, with a track record of getting things done and being reliable. They are ordinary women doing good work, making contributions, as yet unaware of their capacity and competence as entrepreneurs. Say the word "entrepreneur" and ask anyone what mental image comes to mind. Chances are a picture of a young man springs into the mind's eye of both men *and* women. It is this picture that has so many of us thinking that women who break the mold or interrupt the mental image must be extraordinary. If something is different, it is extraordinary, but that isn't the same as superhuman. Moreover, as soon as we demystify women who do run successful companies, we will make it easier for new pictures to spring to mind, enabling ordinary women—of many complexions— to contemplate life as an entrepreneur.

Women business owners are not superhuman (in most cases), rare (anymore), or strange (well, there are a few eccentrics among us!). The community of women who own businesses is wonderful in its rich variety of personalities and in the power of each woman's drive and commitment. Some women are highly charismatic; others exude quiet grace. Some are original, zany, and fun; others are more serious. A few are bold and full of fire in the belly; others are unassuming, yet they too seem to hold a clear-eyed vision. Some are very, very smart; others are full of common sense. The point is that despite studies that try to reduce entrepreneurs to types and profiles, individuality is the norm. Having the strength to hold to a vision and stay on the path, when barriers appear every few feet, may be the only common characteristic of women entrepreneurs. One woman's story is not everywoman's story.

Cattle Kate, The Bag Lady, TeleCall Inc., Peach Blossom Enterprises, Dolphin Corporation (the woman, not the animal), Tootsie Roll Industries, Systems Erectors Inc., Ace Mailing, ASK Computer, Miller Electric, Completion Bond, OwenHealthcare, The Copley Press, Minyard Food Stores, Dashe and Thompson, The Soft-Ad Group, Health Plus, Pacific Marine Yacht Charters, Turtle Wax Inc., Discovery Toys, Venus, Allison Motors, Eco-Ventures, Jenny Craig, Sew What, and Pearl Baths. What's a woman's business? Anything she wants it to be. Women start consulting companies and retail companies, they excel at service, and they are skilled at cranking out widgets. They target markets and fill niches. In short, women see opportunity and seize it. *Carpe diem.*

"Extraordinary" is a loaded word that implies being different or apart from (in the sense of extrasensory or extraterrestrial) odd or foreign. Things that are alien either are studied as something apart and weird or are not studied at all. That is why so many stereotypes exist about women's businesses: "They are all mom and pop shops" (tell that to Sandra Kurtzig); "They are all service businesses" (tell that to Suzanne de Passe, founder of de Passe Productions, and Paula Meehan, owner of Redken Laboratories); "They are not as interesting as men's businesses" (tell that to Lane Nemath, founder of Discovery Toys); and, especially, "Women's businesses aren't a good investment" (tell that to Sophia Collier, founder of Soho Cola).

Implications that women who own and run businesses are extraordinary create a double-edged sword—occasional novelty and celebrity, on the one hand, and apartness (not really being a part of the business community), on the other. As one woman put it, "In the media, when a story on a woman is covered, the implication often is, 'Isn't she cute?'" Edith Gorter, owner of Gorter Motor Express, tells this story:

> The first time I went to buy a tractor, the salesman asked me what color I wanted. I got the sense he wanted to pat me on the head and say, "Isn't that cute." He just about died when I told him I wanted a conventional tractor, single axle, with a 238 Detroit Diesel Allison and a 5 and 2 transmission.

Women who own businesses are wonderful, exciting, diverse, and full of life, but they are not necessarily extraordinary and certainly not cute.

"Cute," like "extraordinary," is a functional word. It is used for a purpose—often to trivialize. Women's work has always been trivialized. On my bedroom wall is a piece of lacework made by my grandmother. It is framed against a blue matte, which causes it to look quite elegant and dramatic. Not long ago, a friend of mine, an artist, happened to see the piece and gasped, "How beautiful, I have lots of work like that from my grandmother, but I never thought of framing it. I never thought of it as art." Of course not. It was "busy work," "handiwork" (odd that tying flies for fishing is seen as an aesthetic endeavor). Alarms go off in my head when the word "cute" enters the conversation and there is no five-year-old in sight. "Cute" is that wonderful double entendre used so effectively to put a woman in her place. Women's work, whether caring for children, cleaning a house, creating lace tablecloths, baking bread, running an office, or running a business is nice, cute, even necessary perhaps, but not important.

Do I mean to say that women who run successful businesses aren't pretty special? Of course not. Everyone who starts something new and makes it work has reason to be very proud of themselves. And I don't mean to imply the business owners I write about are ordinary in the sense of common or unremarkable. Some of the women described in this book are, indeed, extraordinary—but extraordinary by virtue of the extra distance they have gone in creating noteworthy businesses, not extraordinary simply because they had the audacity to start a business. Assuming one has desire, a good idea, and the ability to execute the idea, the business of starting a business should be no more farfetched a notion for a woman than being a teacher, a social worker, a doctor, or a lawyer. With any luck (and our collective effort), our daughters, nieces, and sisters will not be saddled with the patronizing idea that one must be extraordinary to start a business. They will see that owning a business is *not* beyond their wildest dreams.

My experience with the dinners I hosted for *Inc.* magazine, as well as with all the other women I met in the course of putting the dinners together, was exhilarating. The women were diverse and life-affirming; they were solid and remarkable. My life is part of a constellation of women friends who own businesses, work for women-owned businesses, and consult to and invest in businesses. Sometimes I feel quite giddy with the pleasure of being in the midst of such a community of leaders and doers. In quieter moments, I am humbly grateful for the wealth of relationships I have with women who so actively engage with the world, who work to make a difference, and who dare to become themselves. Yet, women owners are still invisible, so, there is mystery about them and real curiosity.

When I am asked about women business owners, I am struck by how often the same questions are asked. The questions seem to fall into four broad categories. The first set of questions concerns the source or the beginning of the business. Where did the idea come from? How did they get started? The second curiosity, quite naturally, focuses on money. Where did it come from? How did they get it? How much did they need? A third area of interest has to do with life balance. In Chapter 1, I described "striving for balance" as a quality that many women work to incorporate into their lives. Still, I am intrigued by the question. Not because I don't understand it, but because the question itself is so consistent. Women seem to assume it is something one reasonably strives for, not that it is unquestioningly sacrificed for the sake of the business. It is a different starting point than that of most men. The final category is hardship. What are the risks, the costs, the hardships of business ownership for women? I'm not sure why this question is so persistent. Perhaps the aura exists that starting a business is *so* hard that only the toughest among us could take the heat. Or maybe the fallout from the notion that only *extra*ordinary women can own a business raises normal curiosity about the kind of Herculean challenges these women face. The challenges are pretty daunting sometimes, but over five million women have found themselves up to the task. And many more will.

WHERE DID THAT BUSINESS COME FROM?

Stories of who started what and why bring women entrepreneurs to life. They take women out of the anonymous realm of women entrepreneurs and make them individuals again. Every woman comes to her business in her own way. Often, when you ask an owner, "How did you get your start?" there is a chuckle and a smile of remembrance that indicates what a surprise the whole adventure has been. So few women were raised to consider business ownership as a serious option that when it happens it may feel like an accident.

Having said that, there seem to be three general ways women (and their male counterparts, I suspect) come to a particular business:

1. They follow a dream or simply get inspired.
2. They adopt a business. Some women inherit, buy, or otherwise take over an existing business. Sometimes a business gets adopted because, in the quest to survive, it is the *only* opportunity that presents itself.
3. They respond to perceived needs and market opportunities.

I want to be careful that I don't suggest that finding a business is a nice, neat process: one can get inspired, buy a business, and respond to market opportunities all at once. Life is rarely as orderly as a book chapter, but dividing the various ways to think about starting a business in this manner may be helpful to those still considering the possibility. For those of you who have already created a business (or two), it might also prove useful to consider your own starting process in light of these three categories.

Following a Dream

Some women are truly inspired or simply "follow their bliss," pursuing dreams and passions that give shape and substance to the whole of their lives. Ultimately, those dreams may place them at the head of a business they may or may not have understood they were destined to start. Odysseum was an inspiration that came to me while gazing out over the blue Pacific. Kathy Bressler stayed true to her spirit and created Cattle Kate. Marti McMahon followed her heart and today owns a fleet of ships that sail the San Francisco Bay. But before telling their stories, let me remind the reader that an inspiration is not quite like a bolt of lightning. As I described in Chapter 1, Odysseum was the culmination of many events that finally synthesized and gave me access to my own desires. In like manner, Bressler and McMahon stayed true to what they deeply cared about for many years. Sometimes we work on our dreams or inspirations for a long time before recognition of what we have been creating all along sets in. Many readers may have dreams and businesses fulminating now. Owning and taking responsibility for your dreams is often the door that opens just before the business.

Cattle Kate is a mail-order business through which owner Kathy Bressler sells clothes that have the look and feel of the Old West. Bressler lived for a time in Atlantic City, Wyoming. Home was a cabin, without electricity, heated with wood she chopped herself. The town of Atlantic City boasted a population of 15 inhabitants. Kathy, who grew up in Pasadena, California, says of Atlantic City, "There was magic there. I found my place, my home." The place Kathy Bressler found was populated by an independent group of individuals who worked for their daily bread, depended on each other, shared resources and talents, and supported each other's dreams. For the residents of Atlantic City, this was a place out of time—a town with values more reminiscent of an earlier era—made almost "Twilight Zone" real at a little bar called the Mercantile. The Mercantile is like a set from a mid-1800s Western movie. Kathy and her friends frequented the Mercantile, the center of social life in the little town. Bressler, a spirited and talented woman, began to design clothes to go dancing in—first she designed them for herself and then for friends. As she put it, "We'd play dress up with petticoats that went swish, swish; we loved the era and we loved to dress up."

Bressler did a number of jobs during that time to earn her living. Friends helped her build a cabin in Atlantic City, but to pay for the cabin she sometimes had to leave town to get work. She worked as a miner, as a camp cook, and on a ranch. "I needed a job, I didn't mind hard work," she says. The old-timers in the town remembered an earlier Kate, another hard-working, independent woman who had been a homesteader there in the 1800s. Because Kathy reminded them of the original Kate, she soon became known about town as Cattle Kate. Kathy explains about herself, "The jobs I took just made sense then. To be a laborer was easier for me than to be a bookkeeper."

Eventually, on one of her working trips away from the town of Atlantic City, Kathy met a soulmate, fell in love, got married, sold her cabin, and left the Mercantile and life in Atlantic City behind. But she did not leave her memories or her feeling that there had been something very special about that life. Says Kathy Bressler today, "There was joy and a special experience living some of the old ways—close to the earth, helping people. There was more to my pleasure in that place than just making clothes for people. This was a way to share a way of life."

In Jackson Hole, married and with a little girl, Jenny, Cattle Kate cast around for ways to make money and to channel her energy. With a $300 loan from her husband, she began making silk scarves that are worn by cowboys. These became so popular that both individuals and retail stores started to place orders with her. Next, she expanded into a full line of clothing. There was a real demand for her western clothes. She decided to take a serious plunge and publish a high-quality catalog featuring her designs. Kathy explains the start of her company this way:

> I had no business experience, just Atlantic City and a love for the West. It was an experiment. When I put dance cards and "yoo hoo tootaloo" hankies in the catalog, I didn't know if anyone would get it. When people started ordering those, in addition to the clothes, I knew they had gotten it. They shared my love for the West—the era and the values represented by my clothes. When people "got it," that was worth everything to me.

Cattle Kate has followed her heart for a long time. She dropped out of college and registered in the National Outdoor Leadership School in Wyoming, where she learned serious mountaineering. She found her way to the mines of Wyoming and the dance halls of the Mercantile Bar; yet, all the time Kathy Bressler has been attending to the things that really matter to her, trusting that somehow if she paid attention to those things that moved her—the beauty of the West, community values, relationships of mutual care and respect—she would not be led in wrong directions.

Today Cattle Kate sells clothes all over the world. Her buyers feel they are wearing a little of the frontier spirit—identifying with another era or another way of life. Kathy Bressler is an especially independent woman; it would be hard to imagine her fitting into someone else's dream. She was driven to pursue her own.

Marti McMahon owns and charters boats. She designs the boats, builds them, and fills them with people and events. Marti is the owner/operator of Pacific Marine Yacht Charter, a fleet of boats that sail San Francisco Bay catering to the dreams and demands of brides and executives, media moguls, and royalty. She told the women sitting at a dinner table in San Francisco:

> The business started in my kitchen and in my garage with a phone. I used to entertain close friends on my boats. I have an eye for decorating so I used to paint and varnish the deck, make tablecloths, cook, and do everything. I think I've refurbished eight or nine boats. We purchased vessels in need of help. And I would go at them with my rubber gloves and lovingly redo them. But my dream was that one day I was going to design a boat from scratch and not have to start by pulling out mildewed carpet: I'd order carpet. And eventually it happened. I took something that I loved and did for friends and made a living out of it.

Marti did not grow up amid sailboats and yacht clubs. Her family moved to the United States from San Salvador when she was young. She grew up in Chicago in a small apartment with her family. Her father sold auto parts; her mother spoke no English when she arrived in this country. But the family worked hard, and, as Marti grew up, she always had some kind of business going. At one point, she and her mother joined together to design and make dresses. Using the "Tupperware™ model," they did "shows" in people's houses, fitting the women right there. Marti's mother, a seamstress, made the dresses; Marti purchased the fabrics and designed the fashions.

Marti bought her first boat with her former husband 25 years ago and began to enjoy the pleasures of boating and entertaining friends on Lake Michigan. Boats and entertaining became inextricably paired for Marti. A gourmet cook and a natural hostess, her eye for design eventually led her to see the entrepreneurial possibilities in giving people what they love—good food and entertainment on the water. In 1976, Marti, her husband, and three children moved to San Francisco. They purchased a boat, a 60-foot, 49-passenger vessel, that Marti, accompanied by a crew, tutor, and three children, brought from Fort Lauderdale, Florida to San Francisco through the Panama Canal. She docked it behind her waterfront house. With help from family and friends, she refurbished the rundown boat herself. *The Pacific Adventurer* became a gleaming yacht. Marti put an ad in *The Wall Street Journal* and got her first client; Pacific Marine Yacht Charters was born.

> I started doing the cooking in my kitchen and rounded up the neighborhood children. I had 11-year-olds stuffing mushrooms and making hors d'oeuvres. And I recruited neighbors—women who lived in

Tiburon and were supporters of my venture—they thought this was a great adventure. I took them on cruises as hostesses. That's how I got started.

She had a business, and now she wanted a fleet. In 1980 she bought an 83-foot, 97-passenger motor yacht. Once again, she refurbished the rundown boat herself. But Marti still had a dream—to design her own yacht from scratch. Unfortunately, financiers didn't share her vision. It was two years and thirteen bank turndowns later before McMahon found a company that would loan her money to build the 100-foot, 149-passenger, *California Spirit*.

In June 1991 Marti took delivery of another boat that she didn't have to "tear mildewed carpet out of." The *San Francisco Spirit* is a chic, luxurious yacht that is big enough to accommodate 700 guests. It was delivered to her new berth, the popular Pier 39 in San Francisco, where it sits like a glorious emblem of the best of the bay. This time around getting financing was not a major problem. Marti has realized her dream. But she has had problems. Holding on to a dream is not an easy task. She explains:

> I went through a very difficult divorce and was hanging on by my fingernails, trying to keep the business together and—as a single parent—trying to keep my family together. Had it not been for friends who really believed in me, I would have lost the business. But that's behind me now, and the business has grown tremendously in just the last two years.

Adopting a Business

Not all women come to their businesses by following a dream. Some end up adopting businesses through inheritance or by purchasing a business started by someone else. Sometimes women get started on a path that results in business ownership when they "do what they have to do" to keep food on the table and a roof over their heads. And in some cases a business is plunked in your lap, wanted or not.

Lonear Heard was a mother with four daughters (including young twins) when her 38-year-old husband, James, was diagnosed as having cancer. At the time that he became ill, this African-American couple owned four McDonald's franchises in southern California. Before his death, which came just eight months later, they spent time discussing the family's future. Should she sell the business or take it over and run it? Although she had shared responsibilities for the company with her husband, sole ownership was another matter. But her oldest daughter, Lonjeana, was just 16 and was already being groomed to take over the business. Lonear decided to go for it. She wouldn't abandon the business they had worked so hard to build.

Lonear Heard grew up on a farm in Mississippi; she was no stranger to hard work. "Slopping pigs and picking cotton was plenty of motivation to get an education and do something else," she explained with a smile. She and her husband met in college. After graduation they worked for a couple of years, saved money, and, with full scholarships, entered Atlanta University. In a year and a half, they had both earned master's degrees—his in American history and hers in business administration.

After they graduated, James Heard went to work for Olivetti Underwood in Chicago. A manager at Olivetti owned several McDonald's restaurants in California and needed someone to manage them. He was impressed by Jim Heard's abilities and talked him into moving to California. A few months after giving birth to twins, Lonear joined him. "I was 23 years old. I had a 5-year-old who had to go to kindergarten every day and new twins. We had one car, and times were tough."

While James ran the restaurant, Lonear handled the bookkeeping, held down second and third jobs teaching part time, and cared for the children. Within a year, they bought the restaurant from the Olivetti manager who had gotten them started. Over the next ten years, they constantly reinvested in their restaurant and purchased three more McDonald's franchises. When her husband died in 1981, she had four children and four restaurants. To qualify as a full owner with McDonald's, you must pass rigorous courses in operations, finance, and service at Hamburger University. Lonear had attended Hamburger University as a spouse with James. Now she had to take more courses on her own. Each time Lonear went off to Chicago to take the required courses, her sister stayed with the children. In July 1984 Lonear Heard graduated from Hamburger University with full owner status.

She continued to grow the business. By 1983 she had added a fifth restaurant to the chain, and in 1984 she built McDonald's number six. Over the next few years, she enlarged the chain to eight restaurants. Recently, she sold one of the restaurants to a young man who had worked for the company since he was a teenager. "He really had grown; it was time for him to be on his own," she remarked with pride.

After her husband died, Lonear continued to groom her oldest daughter for the business. Lonjeana is almost ready to buy her own restaurant. She went to college and took courses at Hamburger University and each summer she came home to work with her mother. By the time she graduated from college, she also had her "degree" from Hamburger University!

Lonear did not start her business in the classic sense of having an idea and creating it from scratch, but she has made it her own in the way she has grown it (yearly revenues are over $17 million now), managed it, and prepared her daughter to carry it on. When she earned her MBA, her assumption was that she would work for someone else. "Did you ever think you would have your own business?" I asked. "Never," she answered.

Shellee Davis didn't inherit a business, she started one using someone else's products. Davis was the first black woman business owner authorized by the Xerox Corporation to sell their equipment in the United States. Shellee Davis didn't start out as an entrepreneur. She graduated from Rutgers with a degree in criminal justice. Unable to find a job in her field, she went to work for People Express Airline, where, she says, she learned about customer relations. She had been located in the Columbus, Ohio office of People Express. By the time that company decided to consolidate its operation in New Jersey, Shellee was married and expecting her first child. Rather than move to New Jersey, she left the company.

At first she was unsure of what she would do next, but a good friend was also looking for work after the birth of her first child. Kathie Cole, a talented interior designer, and Shellee decided to pool their skills and open a commercial interior design firm—Britt Company. Shellee handled the marketing and customer relations end of the business and Kathie handled design. As Shellee puts it, "The business worked for us because businesses using our services worked a more regular 8-to-5 schedule; residential design puts you at the mercy of homeowners who can only meet with you in the evening or on weekends. We both had families and a more regular life was important to us."

Shellee credits her hometown with providing programs supportive of women's businesses.

> There were a number of outreach programs in Columbus, and we signed up for everything. People knew we were constantly looking for opportunities. That's how we came to the attention of Xerox. They were looking for a dealership in the area, and our company was identified; we were asked to apply. We did but didn't think we had a chance. We didn't have the typical dealer's profile—neither of us had experience with equipment and we didn't have any real financial backing. We did have a good reputation in the town. We also had the support of a Xerox vice-president. However, when we first met our dealer sales manager (whose job evaluation is based on our performance) he was shocked, to say the least, to see his new dealers—two enthusiastic, inexperienced, pregnant women. Kathie was eight months pregnant and I was seven months pregnant!
>
> We must have been convincing that day because we were awarded the dealership. Ultimately, Kathie elected to stay with Britt Company. She really did prefer the interior design work. But in January 1988, I incorporated Britt Business Systems, and, with a $50,000 loan from an aunt (who has always encouraged me), I made my first purchase of $25,000 worth of Xerox facsimiles and typewriters. On February 10, 1988, I sold my first fax machine from my hospital bed, just hours after the birth of my second child.

She was forthright, "Britt Business Systems is not a result of past experience or special skills relating to the marketing of office equipment. An opportunity presented itself which demanded that I draw from my family upbringing, my past educational experiences, and the will to succeed." The Xerox vice-president who took a risk on two pregnant women—with no experience in office equipment—deserves credit; not a lot of officers would have taken such a chance. But the gamble has paid off for Xerox. Britt Business Systems has ranked among the top revenue-producing dealerships nationwide every year. And in 1990 they were the top revenue producer in the Midwest region.

Some women come to their businesses via the sheer drive to survive. For 13 years, Ella Williams worked as an accounting assistant for

Hughes Aircraft Company. But she had always felt a strong sense of inner confidence and wanted someday to be a lawyer. With the support of her manager at Hughes, she began taking courses at a local junior college. She graduated with honors, still working at the aircraft company, and then decided to enroll at UCLA. At this point, she decided to take a leave of absence from her job in order to finish her education and have time to spend with her two daughters. But as she was nearing graduation, her marriage deteriorated. In despair, she filed for divorce. Suddenly she was without income and struggling through a painful divorce. Continuing her education at that point was out of the question. The divorce was a painful, enraging experience. Although she had a sympathetic lawyer, she found herself in front of a judge who had little concern for black women. Fortunately, when her lawyer asked: "What are you not willing to give up?" She responded, "I'll give up anything, but I must have the house." She said to me, "I realized that the house was my avenue to freedom—it was an asset. Even if I wasn't working, it was still an asset." She got the house.

Still, she needed a way to support the house payments, her two daughters, and herself.

During this time I read an article in the *L.A. Times* that described a new program offered by the Small Business Administration which was meant to help women and minorities start nontraditional businesses. I thought, well if Hughes can make proposals for government contracts, so can I. I went to the local SBA office to apply for the program I had read about, and they sent me away with a huge stack of papers. It was just awful to get through. I know that they think if you make it through those papers, you must really want to go ahead.

I had talked with engineers I knew from Hughes Aircraft, and they let me include their résumés in my application. Then I got the help of the former marketing manager in field service and support at Hughes, Chips Sawyer. Chips was retired. So he spent his time teaching me how to market. Here I was trying to get military contracts, and I didn't even know how to get on the bases. We started with a real shot-gun approach. We visited every military base within a 500-mile radius: Sacramento, McLellan Air Force Base, Point Mugu, Fort Huachuca, Norton. . . . I didn't care what they gave us, I just wanted work. I assumed that whatever the contract happened to be, I'd find a way to deliver.

It took three years to get my first contract. Whenever I got a nibble, I would call the engineers who had agreed to help me and arrange to meet them at 6:00 a.m. at a cafe on Pacific Coast Highway. I'd drive them to the presentation at 8:00, and they would have to be back on their jobs by 1:00 p.m. And we did it! One of them still works for me. Of course, just to make ends meet, I had to take other jobs while I was also marketing and learning from Chips. For two years, I worked as an assistant to the plant manager at an oil company; I did filing in an insurance agency; I worked for Computax.

I was under a lot of pressure. Because once I had submitted my application to the SBA program, they told me I had to capitalize the company. I took out a $65,000 second mortgage on my house—that was at the height of the high interest rates in the 1980s, and I had an interest rate of 21 percent. It was all I could get. This was the only way I could do it. I stepped up to the plate and hit the ball. But it was terribly frightening. I thought I was going to lose the house and my kids would be out on the street. Every night I would cry, and every morning I would pick myself up and dust myself off and get right back out there. I gained 50 pounds over those three years. The stress was awful.

Then one morning as I was driving Chips home, after one of our presentations, he said to me, "You know Ella, you can do this on your own now." Well, I didn't want to hear it. At first when we visited the bases, I would go and just sit beside him, watching, trying to take in as much as I could as fast as I could. I was the president of this company, and eventually I was going to have to open my mouth! But he said to me, "Yes, you can." Just a few weeks after that, he died. I was in shock.

But not long after his death, I got my first contract. I had been marketing to this one man for three years. I left loaves of bread or cheesecake as a calling card. I needed to do something that would distinguish myself. Week after week I would go back and meet with him, just keeping up the vigil. And he'd ask, "Well, do you have anything yet, Ella?" And I'd say, "Well no, not yet, but I am very hopeful"— trying to put on a positive face. Finally, one morning when I stopped in, he said, "I'm going to give you a contract." Well, I sat down, and he started with we need this and we need that and it just kept building. By the time he was done, I had a contract for $8 million. After that contract was finalized, some of the people in the office said to me, "You know, we thought you were a little crazy, Ella. We didn't know how you could stay at this for so long without work."

That was in 1980. Eleven years later, Aegir Systems has won many more contracts. Her company analyzes the reliability and safety of equipment in defense transportation systems. Recently, Aegir Systems also has been winning contracts in the civilian sector, servicing mass transit in Los Angeles and environmental projects in Washington, D.C. Ella explains her drive, "I had to succeed. If I had failed, I would have lost my home, the only asset I had."

Responding to Needs

If you haven't got a dream; if there seems to be no reason to think an inheritance will turn you into an entrepreneur; if you aren't sure about buying a business, or if life hasn't yet forced you on a path toward a business, what else can give you direction? Sometimes the answer is simply to look around and search for pressing needs not yet being filled.

Nancy Alexander owns Peach Blossom Enterprises. She is a Yale School of Management graduate. Prior to graduate school, Nancy worked in several large companies that had given her opportunities to be involved in start-up projects and turnaround operations. Although she developed a taste for the entrepreneurial life, she didn't yet have a burning desire to begin anything in particular; she felt a need for more experience. Wanting to earn her stripes and credibility, she took a corporate job at the Bank of America in San Francisco. After three years there, Nancy felt sure that her next experience would be to set up her own company. However, she still didn't have a vision of what kind of company it would be.

In the late 1980s, Bank of America went through hard times; to cut costs, they offered a voluntary layoff program to employees. Nancy chose this time to leave the bank. Fatefully, the day she left the bank, she also got pregnant. She and her husband spent time traveling in Europe, knowing they wouldn't have many more chances to travel for a while. By now, although she wasn't yet aware of it, her business had started "coming at her."

Nancy gave birth to Alyssa and was confronted with the issue of choosing diapers. By 1988, in California the cloth versus paper diaper controversy was just beginning. As she (and some of her friends) began to do research on the best choice for diapers, she started "getting into trash" and, as she puts it, "slowly got hooked." Nancy became well aware of the various environmental trade-offs associated with cloth and paper diapers and began to observe who used what kind of diapers and why. In San Francisco there were a number of diaper services available. But when her family moved to Connecticut five months after the baby was born, Nancy found there was only one diaper service in all of Connecticut.

Suddenly, a need was obvious. Nancy was aware that many of the nation's trends start in California and move east. In San Francisco she had been involved in a community that took environmental responsibility seriously and, as a result, had a number of businesses responding to the growing environmental consciousness. In Connecticut, on the other hand, although the demographic profile (according to her analysis) for her market was right, the level of environmental awareness (at that time) was significantly lower. Nancy saw this as her opportunity to get into the market ahead of everyone else. Confident that the pressure to be more environmentally sensitive was heading east and aware that several local landfills were projected to fill within the next few years, Nancy decided to open Peach Blossom Enterprises. She planned to be ready to meet the demand.

Nancy Alexander did not start out with a love of diapers or even a clear understanding of what her passions were. She knew that making a contribution of some kind was important to her; she wanted her own business, and she knew that there were some businesses she didn't want to do. She employed an active mind, an ability to be in tune with current and long-term needs, and a willingness to do her homework to ferret out a business opportunity. Today, Peach Blossom Enterprises is in the black and growing. The early start helped her to get out in front of several competitors, thereby giving her a stronger financial foundation. Continuing to assess needs and opportunities, Nancy Alexander is growing her business by staying close to her customers and listening to their needs. Owner Alexander explains, "I am a mother helping other mothers make a better world for our babies."

Originally, Alexander's business strategy had been to perfect her business locally and then expand nationally, perhaps franchising her operation. But as the business grew, new opportunities became apparent. In the course of building her business, Nancy's relationships with her customers led her to see that they were all working on "building a better world for our babies." This realization has given her an entirely different perspective on her business.

> I'm creating depth in my market rather than trying to build the biggest diaper service. Peach Blossom Enterprises' slogan now is "caring for our children, caring for their world." Strategically, this idea has opened up a number of new opportunities for my business. Building the biggest diaper service isn't necessarily the way to build a better world for our children. But building a company which seeks a range of opportunities to "build a better world" is. Every week someone calls me and, in one way or another, says, "I just love your business." That's quite a relationship to have going with my customers and I want to build on it.

And building on it she is. Peach Blossom delivery trucks now pick up plastic bottles for recycling when they drop off diapers. The plastic is sold to a recycling company (owned by another woman) that uses the melted plastic to make compost bins. The bins are then sold through Peachums, the Peach Blossom catalog of baby and environmental products. "I feel like I'm planting seeds with this business," she says. "Not everyone gets what I am trying to do, but those who do are steadfastly loyal. They get infected by ideas inspired by my company, and will take them to their friends. In that way we really do build a "better world for our babies."

Is this a woman's business? Absolutely. It is a well-conceived business that was able to shift strategy as new information, feelings, and experience came in. Nancy has not stuck blindly to a business plan that originally intended to grow a bigger business. Instead, she listened to her market, understood the importance of the relationships she was building, and shifted her business accordingly.

Coming to a Business

Kathy, Marti, Lonear, Shellee, Ella, and Nancy each came to their business in their own way. Businesses evolve from passion, life circumstances, and the simple accidents of the fight for survival. But coming to a business is not a matter of sitting around and waiting for it to happen to you. Coming to a business is an active sport. The activity is in the "coming to." I see this "coming to" as a somewhat mysterious two-way process. Who knows what takes us down certain paths, bumps us into people and opportunities that seem coincidentally right or in alignment with our needs at a particular moment. Who knows what magic force is at work that switches on the light bulb in our brains. Am I suggesting that magical, mystical forces bring us to our destined businesses? No. I am simply open to all possibilities, as you must be to see a business "coming at you," whether it's a yacht for entertaining, a cowgirl dress designed for dancing, or a fax machine for communicating.

I let the magical, mysterious stuff take care of itself, assuming that if I do my part the business will meet me halfway. That's the two-way process I mentioned. My part, the active part, involves looking, reading, discussing, seeing, and questioning. Active curiosity, in league with the mysteries, will bring you face to face with your business. You may choose to turn away from it ("Glad to meet you; thanks anyway"), but at least you will meet the opportunity.

Women are always meeting other people's needs (Marketing 101, aka "Meeting Other People's Needs"): friends, children, partners, volunteer organizations, bosses. Some women even seem to have a kind of sixth sense about other people's needs. They hardly have to ask, "What do you need, dear?" They just know. It's a well-socialized talent, a strength, an asset. (Okay, so sometimes it gets a little neurotic, and sometimes it replaces caring for one's own needs. If you channel that ability into a business, it won't look so neurotic!) That ability to sense and to be responsive to other people's needs can be used to assess business needs. Read magazines and papers. What problems are out there to be solved? (Don't tell me you can't find a problem to solve. The world is rife with them!) Read magazines in fields you know nothing about. There is nothing like a completely fresh eye on a subject to make a light bulb go on. A perfectly naive—and brilliant—query from an innocent may have totally escaped people who are immersed in their field.

So you know nothing about flying? Buy *Aviation News* for six months. What do you observe, hear, or notice that is an unfulfilled need in this area? Talk to pilots, plane owners, and mechanics. What are you hearing that needs to be solved, cared about, responded to, invented? I use flying as an example, but choose any field you have curiosity about and delve into it. "Coming to" the subject fresh can actually be an advantage. Much has been done and accomplished by people who didn't know something couldn't be done.

Pay attention to your own needs. Karen Smiley started Womanswork, a glove manufacturing business based in Maine, when she couldn't find comfortable, well-fitting work gloves for women that she could use on her own farm. Karen didn't want those cute little white things with flowers that didn't last through a single season of hoeing and weeding vegetables. So she sat down, sketched her hand on a piece of paper, and began to fiddle with some designs. If no one else would take care of her needs, she would do it herself! The result is Womanswork, a mail-order company that sells well-fitting, attractive, sturdy, leather gloves to women all over the country. Smith and Hawken sells Womanswork gloves now, and women who work in the trades, in the U.S. Park Service, on construction—anywhere women do work using their hands—are buyers, grateful that Karen sat down and met her own needs.

What do your kids need that would make life easier for them or you? Donna Caliere watched her sister set her daughter's hair in rag curls one night.

Watching her, I thought, that could be refined. I went to work on a design that would recreate the effect of Scarlett O'Hara-like curls but that would be easier to sleep on than the old-fashioned rag curls made from cotton. I spent almost a year working out the first design, but I wasn't happy with it. I'd lay in bed, trying to visualize it in my head. I kept thinking about a spiral, a fat spiral, like a curl. I saw a Slinky in my mind, but you can't sleep with a head full of Slinkys! Finally, one night I thought, what if I took a biology slice down the center of a spiral, what would I have? A fish spine! I've now worked out a prototype I think will work and have submitted it to the patent office.

It's too early to predict the success of Donna's invention. But her process is instructive. First, she observed something that everyone takes for granted—curling little girls' hair. Then she asked herself, could this be done better? What do your friends complain about that no one has given much thought? Read, watch, see, ask. Ella Williams turned to the only thing she had been exposed to—defense contracting. Seeing herself as an owner rather than as the payroll clerk was a simple (although still difficult) matter of reframing possibility. Why *not* own a contracting company? Explore—and don't forget to get crazy. Fun is a door to creativity. Do you remember getting in a completely nutty mood with friends? Someone comes out with a perfectly ridiculous idea and you all howl! Sometimes it is those completely crazy ideas that, when mined or pushed a little further, have real value. Don't be afraid to embarrass yourself with an idea that may be hooted at—consider that a mark of distinction, a seal of originality. We are all afraid to be laughed at, but those are the risks required to break through barriers and start something new.

Of course, some ideas are simply crazy, but our tendency to dismiss crazy ideas too quickly wastes originality. Although it is important to separate wheat from chaff, dismissing a crazy idea may mean you are failing to see a business "coming at you." So the next time you are in a group and someone says, "What a crazy idea," write it down! Remember, the car was first considered a crazy idea ("a rich man's toy," it was called), flying was thought to be impossible as well as crazy, and sending packages overnight was an idea hardly worth considering until the tenacity of Fred Smith made that crazy idea a reality.

Some women fail to see a business coming at them because they devalue what they know and can do. "Anyone can do that," you may say to yourself. "That's not really important" is another often-used phrase. After all, anyone can make chocolate chip cookies, but when Debbie Field did it it turned into a huge company (Mrs. Field's

Cookies). This business of devaluing what we know and what we do is dangerous, and it keeps women from taking advantage of financial opportunities. Despite decades of feminist consciousness-raising, the presence of significant role models, and countless books and articles on the subject, some of the most successful and powerful women in this country still talk in whispers about their own lack of value: "Why does anyone listen to me?" they say. Here we encounter the long-term effects of trivializing women and their work: "If I know it, do it, think it, it must not be important." Another way to look for a business coming at you is to turn this thinking to your advantage: "If I know it, do it, think it, maybe it's a business!"

MONEY

There are two things to be said about getting money to start a business: it's hard, and it can be done. The story of women and business capital is the story of women and money in general. We don't get as much as men. Lots of folks will say that it's really hard for men to raise capital for a business, too. That's true; however, it's fool-hardy not to acknowledge that it is harder for a woman to be taken seriously or be trusted with "other people's money."

Where do women get money to start their businesses? Anywhere they can. Cattle Kate borrowed $300 from her husband. Frances Lear used money from a divorce settlement to start her magazine. One woman used 15 credit cards, each with a limit of $5000, to raise $75,000 in start-up capital (odd how banks are willing to give women credit cards but still find it a leap to give them a business loan). Another woman told me she sold her house to get business capital, and Ella Williams took a second mortgage on her house. The owner of The Soft-Ad Group, Paula George, said:

> About six years ago I decided I could no longer work for other people—I am such a strong individual—so I went out on my own with $5000, a Mac with one disk drive and a 128K memory, and a telephone. Today I have a multi-million-dollar company with almost 50 employees. I have headquarters in San Francisco, Chicago, New York, and London. Our client list reads like the *Fortune* 50. I invented a new form of advertising—a kind of electronic brochure that can be delivered on a computer disk and mailed to your target market.

Shellee Davis borrowed $50,000 from an aunt. Marilyn Dashe and Jean Thomson, who you will meet in the next chapter, each put up $200 to start what is now a multi-million-dollar international business. Some women who leave corporate America after years of playing that game use pension funds and cash in stock options to get their start. A woman in Minnesota is building her business on sales:

> I still don't have a bank after nine years.... I'm in my second bank, and I feel like I have no bank. It's been pay as you go because I could never get the working capital I needed to finance the business. Fortunately, sales were good, and now I don't really need a bank.

Start-up capital for women's businesses comes from a variety of sources: loans from friends and family, savings, deals made with vital suppliers, and private investors (some of whom invest specifically in women-owned businesses). Occasionally, government agencies (state and federal) and nonprofit organizations have funds available for specific kinds of companies. For example, since its founding, WOMENVENTURE, one of the country's most successful economic development funds for women, has helped create over 700 businesses owned by women in Minnesota.

Expansion capital—that is, money necessary to grow a company already established—is quite another story. As Kathryn Keeley, president of WOMENVENTURE, puts it:

> Women have proved they can start and run businesses. But we haven't yet invented the support mechanisms—that is, capital access—which will allow us to grow those businesses. We need women-controlled capital. [Women-controlled capital—now that's a change in the social order!] We keep trying to legislate access to capital, and we keep trying to get the banks to help us, but once again we are going to have to pioneer.

What that means exactly, and what will be pioneered, is not yet clear. What is clear is that women are finding ways to start and grow their businesses. Between 1972 and 1985, against all odds, the number of women-owned businesses in the United States grew from 5 percent to 30 percent. In the next two decades, I predict we will not have a simple linear progression of more businesses that resemble those started since 1972. Instead, we will have both a growth in the percentage of women-owned businesses and a dramatic growth in the size and impact of those that already exist.

I often rail against the difficulties women face in raising capital, both for start-up and expansion. The injustice—that is, the ongoing tedium of bankers and investors who feign gender-blindness while, with stonelike passivity, they work, more or less consciously, to keep women away from capital needed to build their businesses and achieve economic independence—is exhausting. In the course of raising capital for our company, Jane and I met with a vast array of people curious to meet us, interested in our story, and nervous about putting large amounts of money in the hands of women. Not everyone was sexist, of course. There were some very wise and helpful professionals with whom we spent time—some of whom did invest in our company; however, on several occasions, we encountered patronizing, even overtly rude, behavior. Enormous amounts of energy are required in the normal course of starting up a business. Encounters required to confront sexism and racism drain you of energy you would rather put into your business. It is these tiny offensive indignities—reminders of sexism and racism—that, while hardly worthy of note in the specific, become cumulative and corrosive with time. They exert the most tiring toll. It is painful to read the testimonies and listen to the stories of women who have been denied credit or capital simply because of gender or race.

Still, there is a paradox that confronts us. Women have had lesser access to conventional sources of capital, which prompted them to search for alternative funding. Forced to subvert the traditional world of lending and investing, women have maintained control of their businesses and their visions. They have been able to hold on to the values and goals that drove the start-up of their businesses and, in the process, make money.

Marti McMahon, owner of Pacific Marine Yacht Charters, relates a conversation between herself and a competitor:

> One of the principals [of a competing charter company] came to see me and found me setting the table for a charter. They have a lot of investors in their company and a big fleet of boats. He told me, "You know Marti, we grossed about $20 million last year, but we didn't make any money." And I said, "Well Sam, I wish I could say I have all the boats you do, but I did make money." I really did. I'm sole owner of the vessels, and I'm proud to say I own them!

Marti's story is not unusual. Since women often are not able to attract debt or equity investors, they wholly own their businesses and have the freedom and autonomy to play by the rules they devise. This is the paradox. Lack of access to capital has forced women to go it alone, often resulting in slower growth and the appearance of less aggressive business visions; yet going it alone also creates both license and opportunity to reinvent the rules of business. If I own the ballpark, so goes the thinking, then I can make up the rules. "Owning the ballpark," no matter how small the "stadium," has enabled women to create businesses that may be healthier for the planet, better for the lives of women (and the people they care about), more amenable to the integration of meaning into our work, and better as a model for business generally.

In part, because of the very conditions of the antagonistic environment that I deplore, women are emerging as leaders. They are redefining and transforming the nature of business and the nature of work. That is a powerful contribution to be made by women at the end of the twentieth century. But there is a dilemma. If women suddenly had access to money as well as the means to grow fast and reward investors in the style to which they have become accustomed, would we simply join the game as it is played? Would we give up on the new game we have struggled so hard to create?

It's tempting to try to get into the game as it is traditionally played. We want to be taken seriously, after all. We want to be seen as equals, as people running businesses that matter. If you get venture capital, you must matter. Historically, money has told us what we are worth. But it's not just money. It's a matter of self-esteem. Women are often accused of being afraid of risk. Many of us don't believe that we're afraid to take risks. Yet, all the studies that say it's so wear on us, after a time. Obviously, it's easier for young men to risk *Other People's Money*. If they were risking their own, as women must do (for lack of access to other people's money), it would be interesting to observe how their own risk-taking behavior might alter! In the meantime, women are stuck with pejorative labels, including the "conservative" label. Imagine how quickly the term "reckless" would surface if women played it any other way.

There is also the factor of legitimacy. Too often I have heard someone (an investor or a business reporter) say, "Well of course, she started that business with her husband's (or her father's) money" — as if that is somehow not legitimate money, as if that disqualifies her from claiming it as her business. (Isn't it a great American tradition that fathers help sons get started in business? What's the difference?) When Frances Lear took a generous divorce settlement and turned it into a magazine, much was written in the gossipy press about how she didn't have a clue what she was doing and would just "waste" the money. Oddly, no one seemed to think that it was illegitimate for Donald Trump to take money from his dad to get started in real estate. There were no similarly gossipy articles (then) about the likelihood that he would simply "waste" the money. Likewise, the legendary stories of the Morgans, the Rockefellers, and the Watsons are simply stories about dad getting junior started in business.

Women who take money from dad, a spouse, or a government program, however, are seen as not having proved themselves. Women can't get money from traditional lenders and investors because they don't have a track record for growing businesses aggressively, and they don't grow businesses aggressively because they don't have access to capital. If they get capital from anyone they know or are related to, it "doesn't count." So they can't really prove themselves that way. Is there something wrong with this picture? Of course, there is. Where money is concerned, women are systematically shut out. The double standard is a little too obvious to ignore.

To change the system is a goal women have been engaged in from the time of the suffragettes. We got the vote; now we want to get into commerce. Pushy I know, but there it is. As we get closer to our goal, we face choices we will have to assess carefully. Will we enter the game and play by the rules that currently exist? Will we relinquish our transformative drive, as so many women in the large corporations were forced to do, doing anything to fit in and, in effect, becoming equal opportunity entrepreneurs? Or will we hang on to our values and discoveries and actually change the rules while insisting on a place in the game?

The seduction to be in the game as it is played is huge. I fall prey to it as well as anyone. Tell me I can't do something, go somewhere, be part of anything and I will do almost anything to open doors that are barred shut. However, I am convinced that unless we continue to play by our own rules we will lose the edge we have developed in the adaptations to business we have made.

Why has it continued to be so hard for women to get capital for their businesses? Jennifer Wilson, founder of Sky Venture Capital Fund, calculates that 95 percent of all businesses owned by women are self-capitalized—that is, women rely on savings, family loans, sales, and business-generated capital to fund their businesses. I asked Jennifer what she thought the single biggest barrier was to women's access to business capital.

> The system is structured in accordance with men's lives, not in accordance with women's lives. When a banker or investor looks at the pattern of a woman's life, he may see unrealized career goals [they were cut off from access to the top] and a career path impacted by family obligations and view this as a sign of instability. Over the last 20 years, women tried to dress, talk, and learn to be like men so they

could fit into the structures established by men, thereby gaining access to capital. But that wasn't enough, and it hasn't really worked.

Investors look at more than that, they ask, is there value here? Will I get the rate of return I want if I invest in businesses owned by women? Women's businesses have grown steadily and are stable, but when we look back over the record of the last five years we will probably see that women's businesses didn't grow as aggressively as investors like. You can't grow a business aggressively without access to capital. So women are placed in an impossible bind. They must prove themselves in the marketplace before being "worthy" of capital but must prove themselves without the capital needed to show aggressive growth.

This is a little like asking a woman to prove she is as good a swimmer as the man in the lane next to her, but telling her she can only stroke with one arm. Then when she doesn't win, the judge says, "See? She just isn't up to the race." Is there something wrong with this picture?

In 1985 Jennifer Wilson went to a national venture capital conference in Boston with a business associate. Two to three weeks after the conference was over, follow-up material began to arrive from those who had attended the conference. Most of the mail was addressed to her associate. Finally, her secretary observed astutely, "Harry is getting four times the follow-up contacts that you are." Jennifer mulled this over. Harry had left the conference after the opening session. She had stayed throughout, meeting and talking with movers and shakers in the field of venture capital. Jennifer adroitly intercepted the next call that came in for Harry. It was from another man who had been at the same conference. "Why did you ask for Harry and not for me?" she asked forthrightly. To her surprise he answered her honestly, "There aren't many women in venture capital. It's a rough-and-tumble business, and the women who are in it are highly visible. I figured since I didn't recognize your name, you weren't important."

Taken aback, fuming, but grateful for his candor, Jennifer realized that this experience had implications for women in business. This was the catalyst that got her to leave her job as investment manager of the Iowa Product Development Corporation, where she managed an investment portfolio of 16 companies. She opened an office in Des Moines and started to work full time to establish a venture capital fund designed specifically to invest in women entrepreneurs.

When she first started her odyssey, some people were taken aback. Such an idea had simply not occurred to them. An investment fund just for women? But she has gotten support from otherwise conservative businessmen who have daughters in the work force. Says Jennifer, "They have raised their daughters to be competitive and ambitious, yet they are becoming aware that opportunities for women are still limited."

Wilson is still a distance from her $20 million capitalization goal. There are complex dynamics woven among women, men, money, and intimacy, she maintains. If men and women are equal in business and on the battlefield, as well as in the business of child care and relationships, how will men define themselves? Jennifer believes the answers to this question are relevant to the challenge she faces in putting together the venture fund, as well as to the problem of women's access to capital.

Kathryn Keeley explains:

> We are talking about sharing power, we're talking about sharing money, and we're talking about something that goes even deeper than that. Women's business ownership represents redefining work, the nature of work. We are not just talking about money and power, we're talking about identity. It is safer for the traditional business institutions to ignore the whole movement of women's business ownership and continue to pretend that women have no greater difficulties gaining access to capital than men. It's safer because the ways women go about their businesses, the values they bring to it, the way they talk about it, what they try to create in their work environments, adds up to redefining the whole traditional male corporate system. Women haven't talked about what they are doing, they've just done it. Women-owned businesses are growing by leaps and bounds, and we're getting more secure and self-confident. And now we are talking about our values and our views of money, power, and business.

Wilson, Keeley, and I share the same goal for women and their businesses — that is, to see that women have the resources they need to build their businesses and to see that women's businesses are valued properly to attain those resources. Jennifer is taking on the financial establishment, attempting to bring money, a life-giving fluid, to thirsty businesses owned by women. She is particularly interested in creating a fund that will provide growth funds rather than start-up capital to women's businesses. Keeley's organization is involved in funding start-ups, and Keeley herself is involved in the political process of supporting the evolution of women-owned businesses. Keeley is a familiar figure on Capitol Hill. Both women (and scores more not mentioned here) are opening doors for other women. They are pushing for social, legal, and financial changes that will enable businesswomen to realize the potential of their businesses and make an even greater contribution to the U.S. economy.

In a letter to me in 1991, Jennifer Wilson made this point: "Past performance of women-owned businesses cannot be used to assess future potential because too much has changed too quickly." Clearly, how women get money and what they do with it is the riddle of the future. I'm betting on the values and innovations of women business owners to solve the riddle in a way that will resolve the paradox of capital access and growth. In other words, women will pioneer ways to attain women-controlled capital *and* play by their own rules. With increasing self-confidence, women will decide for themselves what constitutes growth and aggressive growth.

I don't believe that women should have to suffer in order to play their own game. Women have suffered enough. One woman involved with raising capital for businesses said to me, "We were raising money for some tech-related companies owned and operated by men. They raised a million dollars in a couple of months to start a company. And they didn't even have a prototype. Women have to have the company half done before they'd raise the first $100,000."

I don't mean to imply that men have an easy time raising money for their businesses. Every entrepreneur has her or his own kind of suffering, their own kind of difficulties. It is true, however, that some men have a network they can tap with somewhat greater ease than women. Women who are ready to start looking for capital should follow these suggestions offered by some of the women mentioned earlier in this chapter.

1. *Start small, use your own savings.* One night I listened to a woman describe how she had started at swap meets and built a $5 million business. "Men's shirts," she explained. "I sold one product—off the ground—until I could afford to buy larger quantities of shirts. Then I rented more spaces at swap meets all over southern California. Eventually I had trucks going to swap meets at 18 locations all over the state." Her husband had bankrupted three businesses. This UCLA-educated teacher started with nothing but a small savings account, a piece of ground, and a pile of men's shirts. She has just retired, and her son, trained as a CPA, decided to take over her business.

2. *Borrow money from friends and family members.* Sure that's risky, but think how careful you will be with that money. Think how carefully you will consider decisions if the stakes include

the well-being of someone you care about. Keep it businesslike, make sure they understand your business plan and draw up documents that specify the responsibilities of all parties.

3. *Be resourceful.* Credit cards, second mortgages, and stock options are all sources of capital that most people are taught not to use for cash. But we're not talking about getting your hair done. We're talking about finding a way to raise capital to fund a business.

4. *Find a partner.* Marilyn Dashe and Jean Thomson each threw $200 into the pot to begin. Other partners are able to pool somewhat more. A partnership, if it is with the right person, can expand resources way beyond mere capital. A partner can contribute energy, credibility, and talent to your effort.

5. *Create innovative alliances.* Let's say you want to sell boxes to retailers. You have a great distribution system and good alliances with the buyers in six of the nation's biggest retail chains. (Okay, so I'm building a dream situation; pay attention to the point!). But you don't manufacture boxes. You have to buy them from a company that does. Interview three such companies and give them the option of providing an advance against sales or of providing credit that will enable you to get and deliver the first shipment. You may have to pay them a premium for a year or two, or perhaps you can give them an equity position in your company. But it's a start. Look at forming an alliance with companies to which you will add value. Although I generally encourage women to walk their own path, a partnership with a company is not always an unholy alliance.

Robin Wolaner had no money, no MBA, no track record. But in 1984 she decided to start a magazine for new parents. She quit her job as the publisher of *Mother Jones* to work full time at the business of realizing her dream. Between January and July of 1985 she raised $175,000 to start *Parenting* magazine. Her first investor, a venture capitalist, said of her, "My theory is you invest in people...I was persuaded of her capability and motivation." Robin eventually raised enough money to test her idea. With a positive response from a direct mailing that was strong enough to convince other investors, Robin approached *Time* magazine. A key executive in the group, Christopher Meigher, remembers, "This very confident young woman; I thought, my God, she's younger than I thought. Are we going to trust this money to a woman we know nothing about? She was confident enough without being cocky, she pushed it to the right degree."[1] She certainly did. In January 1987, the first issue of

Parenting magazine hit the stands. At the time, Robin retained 51 percent ownership. By all accounts, Robin's relationship with *Time* has gone well. The magazine has made money, *Time* is happy, and no one will be surprised if Robin comes up with yet another idea and does it all again.

6. *Pursue private investors.* Talk to anyone you know who might be interested in your idea. Ask them to give you names of people they know. Reaching private investors is a little like looking for needles in haystacks. Private investors often keep a low profile. It takes real tenacity to find someone who knows someone who will introduce you to someone who is a private investor.

Judy George, an experienced entrepreneur and owner of Domain, a chain of retail furniture stores, suggests asking a successful friend to host a breakfast to which potential investors can be invited. You can present your business plan, field questions, and begin the process of connecting with potential investors. Most investors will not sign on the spot. They are very careful and will wait to see how you go about the business of making your case. The investor must be sold on your business and also feel comfortable with you. Private investors play with their own money, not some faceless institution's. But a savvy private investor can be a great help in the process of starting and growing a business.

7. *Investigate state and federal programs.* Although many women report frustration and discouragement with funding programs designed for women, some do get money; therefore, it's a source you can't afford to overlook. Both Ella Williams and Lonear Heard were able to start their businesses with the help of the SBA; tenacity will be a real asset if you go this route. Local chambers of commerce and small business development centers sponsored by the SBA may be able to put you in touch with programs appropriate for your business. Small business investment companies (SBICs) licensed by the SBA to provide capital to small business are also worth contacting. Your local SBA office should have a list of such companies in your area.

8. *Find a bank.* You will need a relationship with a bank anyway, so interview several to get a sense of how competitive they are and how open to a woman owner they might be. Banks demand collateral. One woman, a talented African-American who graduated from graduate school with only $5000 in student loans still to pay (she had been a top scholarship student throughout) wanted to borrow $100,000 to open her business. The North Carolina bank she

went to demanded that her parents (who owned their house) cosign for her. With that, she got her loan. Four years later, much of that first loan paid off, she went back to the bank to borrow $250,000 to expand her business. This time, the bank wanted the mortgage on her house (valued as much as the loan), her life insurance policy, her accounts receivable, *and* her parents' signatures. It's not a pretty picture, but she gave them what they wanted and got her loan. She is a determined and smart businesswoman. She'll find another bank, and that first bank will lose what might otherwise have been a long-term, lucrative customer.

9. *Venture capital.* Venture capital has worked well for some women. There are some terrific venture capitalists out there (okay, so I can't name a dozen; trust me, there are some) who understand how to work with women entrepreneurs and why it is a good idea. For purposes of expansion and growth, venture capital can provide the necessary funds; however, a word to the wise: venture capitalists will insist on doing aggressive "due diligence" on you and your company before they commit any dollars. Insist on the same right. Do your homework on their track record before accepting any dollars. Talk with other entrepreneurs to whom they have committed capital; talk with bankers, lawyers, and others who have had reason to do business with them. Yes, it is an old boys' network and sure they will protect one another, but you will pick up some information and may save yourself a lot of needless grief.

10. *An invention.* Women-controlled capital, investment clubs started and run by groups of women entrepreneurs, new loan models like those created by WomenVenture, and other loan structures that may look more like FHA loans than high-risk/high-return venture capital investments are all inventions that need to be created as ways of funding and growing women's businesses. Other cultures have actually created models of resource pooling that could be adapted by women entrepreneurs.

BALANCE

The third most frequently asked question about women and their businesses is "How do they find balance in their lives?"—not "Do they?" but "How do they?" Men more rarely ask this question. Many men do not expect to achieve balance the way women do.

My candle burns at both ends,
It will not last the night.
But ah my foes, and oh, my friends,
It sheds a lovely light.[2]

This self-knowing poem by Edna St. Vincent Millay rings true for many women who own businesses. Women are busy burning a bright light and loving every minute of it. Can you burn your candle at both ends and find balance?

What is balance? Equal amounts of work, family, and amusement? I for one do not want life parceled out in neat equal parts. I want some time for friends, time for travel, creativity, and reflection, time to do Saturday morning errands, time to read the Sunday *Times,* and lots of time for business. Others want lots of time with children, some time to read a book, and plenty of time for their business. The formula changes with the person.

There are not enough hours in the day for the lives we lead. If you are a single parent with a limited support system you know there aren't enough hours in the day. But where balance is concerned we are often our own worst enemies—making choices in our own worst interest, saying "yes" too often, being unwilling to make choices, or getting stuck with a set of "shoulds" about what we "have" to do. When I was a kid, the yearning for balance was never discussed. Parents worked during the week, on Saturday the family did chores, and on Sunday we took those interminable Sunday drives. For better or worse, life was less complex. By Monday morning we were willing and eager to return to the business of school or work.

There is an elegantly simple connection between complexity and balance. The more complex your life is, the less balance you may experience. But the notion of balance may be misleading us. The word "balance," overused of late by the press in the increasing coverage of the impact of work on family life, is not often precisely defined. Women who own businesses learn pretty quickly that they cannot have it all. "Life is a series of trade-offs," my business partner reminds me. When women owners talk about finding balance, they really mean they have made conscious choices about what they can and will take on—they have pared back to those things that matter most. Sometimes when business owners plead for more balance they mean they want to find time to do everything. But women business owners know that isn't possible. They have to make choices, and they do—in ways that are integral to their values. As one entrepreneur put it, "Women who try to have it all are killing themselves. You have to make compromises."

Trying to have it all or do it all is a terrible trap, particularly in the context of lives as demanding as those of the women who own businesses. A business owner from Michigan was only half kidding when she said, "The only friends I have are other women business owners. They are the only people who understand if you don't call them for two months."

Does this mean that women who own businesses are no better off than their corporate sisters or than men struggling to start a business and relate to a family? No, it just means that what we call "balance" is perhaps more appropriately called "healthy choices." As a woman from Boston explained:

> When you are the owner, your time is precious, and, more importantly, your energy is precious. I find myself focusing on fewer things, weeding out people and events. But it's not a question of becoming narrow, I think it's a matter of becoming selective and being very choosy about who to surround myself with and what to allow in.

The ability to sort out what's really important is one of the strengths that women often bring to their businesses. To many men, money and power are what's important—sometimes they're all that's important—so their choices are integrated with those goals. Women willing to contemplate goals that reach beyond money and power will make trade-offs that may sacrifice the conventions of success— fast growth and fast money—without sacrificing the health of their companies. They may gain parts of life they feel to be important: time with children, spouse, and/or friends, time spent alone, and time for community and learning apart from the business. Their conscious choices about what is important and what they have to do to get or keep what is important to them is what gives them a sense of that elusive golden egg we call "balance." Three different women who attended the *Inc.* dinners put it this way:

> I'm a daughter of the Betty Friedan generation. The messages I got were "get the education, get the business, have the kids." Be this "super" kind of thing. Then you get exhausted, pull back, and say you can't do that.

> I've been very fortunate. I've had steady growth. One year the business doubled. But I would caution anyone going into business, don't go too fast...that was the same year the business ran me. Then I decided, that's never going to happen again.

You're going to work 50 or 60 years. So you spend 10, focusing on your kids. It's not like the world is over if you spend some time raising your kids.

These women have attained balance in their attitudes about time, speed, growth, and what's important to them. Obviously it's not easy for all women to find time for the things that matter most to them. All of us have days, weeks, even months when life seems very much out of control and we despair over the to-do list in our heads that never seems to get any shorter. However, the fact that women talk about choices and balance and strive for integration of work and "other"—indeed, they expect life to have room for relationships as well as business—is the sign that something profound is happening in their businesses. Those women who ask, "How do women business owners achieve balance?" auger a sea change. Where no questioning occurs, where no expectation of life outside work exists, no change will occur. As more men start asking other men how they attain balance in their lives, we'll know they are paying attention.

HARDSHIP

I am aware that I often downplay the hardships women endure in the process of creating their companies. In part, I suppose that's because I am always prone to see what people *can* do, not what they *can't* do. It's also because women do not dwell on these hardships, although they are real and certainly not trivial. Whatever difficulties women face are simply challenges to be met, outwitted, and overcome. Indeed, many of us dress our difficulties in the guise of opportunities. ("There must be a pony in here somewhere," we mutter as we dig through the steaming heap.)

But hardship and difficulty are part of the story of women and their businesses—financial loss, relationships that come unglued, encounters with sexism, and, for some women, racism as well. Hardship is felt in the night, when, alone at last, you face the fear of missing a payroll, losing an investor's money, harming a client, or firing an employee. Some days, hardship comes in the irritating form of a tennis game you have to miss or a birthday party that must be postponed. Other days, it comes in the frightening form of losing a client, plummeting sales, or losing a contract proposal because of your gender or the color of your skin.

When Marti McMahon talks about the struggle to hang on to her business in the middle of a painful divorce, as Ella Williams remembers redeeming aluminum cans at the supermarket to get enough money to buy her children milk, as I recount the story of having to lay off employees, or as other women relate the exhausting effort of working through a bankruptcy or difficulties with investors, you can bet we are sharing hurts that cut deep.

At the *Inc.* dinners, two women described desperate trials to hold a business together while caring for a seriously ill child. Both women were single mothers. Both survived the ordeal, as did the children and businesses. I suspect the outcome of similar trials, endured by other women, are not always so positive. Even when serious illness is not part of the equation, the most basic requirements of dependent care—for children or elderly parents—can place burdens on the shoulders of women. Simple fatigue is a frequent enemy for some women. Particularly in the start-up phase of a company, a mother trying to oversee her children's education and nurturing, while nurturing a company into life at the same time, may fight what feels like an ongoing battle for sleep. Illness is one of our most feared enemies. Health is as important to us as a long-term investor.

In hearings held before the 100th Congress on "The Role Of Women Entrepreneurs," women told shocking stories of treatment at the hands of bank officials who stubbornly maintain they treat all entrepreneurs alike, regardless of race or gender. The 1989 *Avon Report on Successful Women Entrepreneurs* reported that respondents maintained that "having to convince the business world of their skills and abilities, rather than a true lack of business skills, was their greatest obstacle." One-third of the women who participated in that survey said their greatest professional obstacle was "not being taken seriously," this most frequently in the so-called nontraditional fields of manufacturing, engineering, construction, etc.[3]

Some women struggle for years to start a new company, only to find that the money is not available, the market has changed, or a competitor has gotten too big a head start to make catching up feasible. At the risk of sounding like the Yankee I am, hardship is the fire that forges the steel found in so many women who own companies. Women are strong (popular perceptions to the contrary), and the odds they face, the difficulties they surmount, make them more so. Lots of women do not know just how strong they are until, wrestling with a bear of a problem, they subdue the beast. Gaining confidence through the steady resolution of one challenge after another is one of the dividends that come to women over the course of business ownership. I may be criticized for not detailing personal stories of hardship and pain. So be it. Pain is everywhere, and there is plenty to learn from. My purpose is not to entertain the reader with "Little Nell" stories, but to show how women use and transcend their trials to grow, learn, and create.

Some years before starting my business, I attended an Outward Bound expedition off the coast of Maine. It was an important experience for me — not because I value a macha self of "woman against the elements" — but because it was a powerful setting in which to push myself, learn something about leadership, and get in touch with just how much I really can handle. Not all women need an Outward Bound experience to prepare them for the rigors of business. Surviving life in a large corporation, raising kids, outwitting poverty, enduring and growing through a painful divorce or the death of a significant other, even the loss of a job, qualify as personal "Outward Bound" experiences that test your mettle and teach you something about your personal strengths and limits.

One woman's hardship is another's inspiration. What feels hard to some women may be no big deal to others. However, we know that there are some common problems: obtaining access to capital is a problem. Insufficient support systems make life very hard for many women. Myths and stereotypes get in their way. ("Isn't she cute?" "It's not a real business." "Women aren't serious about their businesses." "Women's businesses are temporary; they don't outlast the founder.") Culture and race may add another layer of difficulty. (The flip side of this is that the support and comfort race and culture can provide may be a tremendous source of strength and aid.) Acts of God (illness or earthquake) and events outside our control (war or a stock market crash) may jeopardize the best business plan and undermine the strongest woman. But we cope.

How women cope is more important than an inventory of troubles.

1. *Mutual support and friendship.* According to one woman at an *Inc.* dinner: "Women are most powerful when they admit weakness and get support from friends." Said another, "I use my friends a lot. I don't know what I would do without them. That is one of the things that has helped me through."

When you own a company, there are some things that you bear alone — fear in the middle of the night, the buck when it stops at your desk — but most of the women I know running successful businesses have strong (if sometimes small) friendship circles. They may not see some friends for long stretches of time, but they know they are only a phone call away and will pick up the phone to be in touch. Reflecting on the impact of technology on our ways of doing business, a woman in Boston told how she used an electronic network that connects her with colleagues internationally: "I feel I have this extended web of people around me who I can tap. There's a tremendous sense of buoyancy I get from that."

2.   *Advisory boards.* Lillian Handy, the owner of TRESP Associates, a military subcontracting company in Virginia, uses an advisory board to transcend and break through the barriers of the old boys' network, which might otherwise keep her from winning contracts. Handy's board consists of high-ranking retired military officers, finance specialists, marketing pros, and a federal contract expert. *Black Enterprise* described the value of her board to overcoming formidable obstacles. Handy once assembled an ad hoc committee of her board members to review an Army logistics contract. Included in her advisory group was General Arthur J. Gregg, the man who had once run the army's logistic command—"the consulting equivalent of having James Brown critique your newest R&B act." The bid was successful.

In Boston, another woman described her advisory group: "We have breakfast once a quarter. I hate them," she said affectionately. "They are absolutely honest. Because they are not investors in the company they tend to have more distance on issues and come at things with a high degree of common sense." Another woman described her own advisory board: "Only someone who has a very deep commitment to you will take the risk to say whatever is true." (Are we back to relating again?!)

3.   *Time out.* Seek balance through exercise, meditation, weekends away, time alone, a skiing trip. Anything that helps women gain perspective, gain a little distance on their business—and stay healthy—contributes to the business of coping.

4.   *Experts.* Women who get lost while driving stop and ask for directions instead of driving around aimlessly refusing to ask for help. Similarly, they seek advice from experts. Sometimes this is made more difficult by the limitations of their financial resources, but barter arrangements, delayed payment plans, even free advice is available and is used to buttress their own knowledge and experience.

5.   *Invention.* Taking kids to the office or on business trips is still hard for corporate women to do, but when mom is the boss she

can invent new norms about what is appropriate. One means of coping with conflicts between work and family is to invent new rules. In like manner, inventions about flexible hours, job sharing, quality control methods, customer service practices, and anything else associated with the operation of a business are made to accommodate the multiple needs of employer, employees, and customers.

6. *Professional memberships.* The National Association of Women Business Owners (NAWBO) may be the largest organization representing women business owners now in existence. With at least 37 chapters in the United States and affiliations with 22 countries overseas, it has a domestic and international reach that makes it visible and potentially very powerful. NAWBO is one of the main sources Congress turns to for expert witnesses, NAWBO officers are often contacted to respond to bills and policies that may have an impact on their membership. NAWBO provides a network that gives women who own businesses a national voice and access to information, training, and other resources. Other organizations provide similar services on state and local levels. Women are increasingly involved in their local chambers of commerce and have a growing presence in the ubiquitous Rotary, Kiwanis, and Lion's clubs. The Committee of 200 and the International Women's Forum are composed of women with sufficient financial clout and stature that they, too, are called on as experts and representatives of women entrepreneurs.

CONCLUSION

Ultimately, the answers to the four questions I am most often asked about women and their businesses are individual and personal. Each woman comes to her business in her own way, just as men come to their businesses in their own ways. They get capital however they can. They struggle with working out a life that has meaning and some modicum of balance within the confines of their own particular circumstances, and they cope with adversity with strength born of their own special heritage and experience. More than five million plus women have started businesses and found ways to do all these things—ordinary women building extraordinary businesses.

SIX

Voices

Seven women business owners are profiled in this chapter. They do not represent all women business owners, but they are each right-stuff women who run their businesses by new rules fashioned with each new day and each new challenge. The women are from all over the United States and reflect the diversity of our changing society. They represent a span in culture, generation, education, industry, and experience. But that is all they represent. They do not reflect all white women, all minority women, or, indeed, anyone but themselves. They are individual women who are at once ordinary and special; they are human, approachable, smart, and resourceful, and they have a great zest for living, giving, and making a difference. These seven women dare to dream and are brave and committed enough to make their dreams reality.

I have featured these particular women because I like their stories and respect their efforts. I do not offer them as the "Best-Managed Companies Owned By Women," although I think that each woman manages her enterprise very well. Rather, I offer them as a sampler of companies—a collage of products, experiences, values, and ways of managing worthy of note and attention. Women's stories are too seldom documented, and women's own views of their businesses are rarely heard. To truly learn about women and their businesses, we must first abandon preconceived judgments and just listen. My intent in this chapter is to give these women a voice, so that we may begin to do that.

The stories included here are not like films, with neat plots and tidy endings, nor are they biographies in which many witnesses are interviewed to pin down fact and reality. Instead, this chapter is a collection of oral reports, as women share their experiences and views on the life of their businesses. Follow the transformation of

Ruth Owades from a corporate marketing director, a woman whose highest dream was a safe corporate job, to a celebrated entrepreneur. Listen to Terrie Williams as she reveals the practical realities associated with running a business in which celebrities and stars are the "product." Reflect on a relationship that will probably outlast many marriages, as Jean Thomson and Marilyn Dashe discuss the pleasures and challenges of growing a business and managing their business partnership. Meet the incredibly energetic founder of the San Francisco *Hispanic Yellow Pages,* Sonia Melara. Experience the at-ease-with-herself persona of Edith Gorter, who took over a moribund family business and fashioned a force in one of the country's most male-dominated industries—freight trucking. Finally, pay attention to Leeann Chin, who shares with us the experience of growing a business when all of life—family, history, and culture—reinforce messages of "can't do, can't do" instead of the "can do, can do" message so necessary to entrepreneurial success.

Ruth Owades said to me, "I never had the female mentor I would like to have had." That's a statement many women will nod "Amen" to. Happily, by our sheer numbers, we can change that for the next generation of young women. For the reader, perhaps the stories, insights, and hard-won wisdom of the women you meet here will provide sustenance for your own journey and your own dreams.

RUTH M. OWADES
Calyx and Corolla

Ruth Owades is gracious, poised, and comfortable to be around. Although her business is a daily buzz of deadlines and nationwide deliveries of flowers, everything surrounding her seems tranquil and under control.

Ruth is the founder/owner of Calyx and Corolla, an upscale fresh flower mail-order business. For less than the price you would pay your local florist for the standard fare of carnations and azaleas, you can have fresh, unusual flowers delivered directly to your spouse, lover, sister, brother, mother, and friends. And with the cooperation of Federal Express and growers in the United States, Europe, Central America, and Asia, flowers from the finest gardens in the world can be delivered overnight. Because there is no middle person involved—no retailer or flower mart—the flowers from Calyx and Corolla last five to ten days longer than those purchased from a local florist. Higher-quality, longer-lasting flowers and hassle-free ordering and delivery have made Calyx and Corolla the florist of choice for busy people.

In the fall of 1990, Calyx and Corolla made the transition from a young start-up company to an exciting, nationally recognized firm. This transformation can be attributed in part to a genuine human impulse to make a contribution. Thousands of U.S. soldiers had been sent to the Middle East as part of Operation Desert Shield, the allied response to Iraq's invasion of Kuwait. Like so many Americans at that time, employees of Calyx and Corolla were feeling very low about the impending war. Wanting to alleviate their own feelings of powerlessness regarding the inevitability of war, Ruth and her staff sent Calyx and Corolla catalogs to the troops in Saudi Arabia, enabling soldiers to send flowers at a discount (and at domestic rates rather than higher international rates) to family members for Christmas. Some months later, the international business press learned of what Calyx and Corolla had done and began to give the company a good deal of media coverage. National awareness of Ruth's company increased dramatically, and sales increased as well. Ruth tells the rest of the story:

> The idea to send catalogs came out of the distress that everyone felt. We started in the fall, before war had broken out. At that time it was Operation Desert Shield. But already people were feeling sad, seeing mothers and fathers sent off to war. Here in the office, we sat around, as so many others did at that time, asking ourselves what we could do. Of course, we always want to increase sales, but in large part this effort was altruistic. Wanting to do something for the troops was a response to the kind of sadness and lethargy that was coming over the workplace—not just at Calyx and Corolla, but everywhere. The *Wall Street Journal* reported that in companies all over the country people were standing around watercoolers and coffeepots talking about how awful things were. I think we were simply inspired to try to do something which might make ourselves and the troops feel better.
>
> What is wonderful about my own business is that no matter how I feel emotionally or physically, when I get to the office, I love being here. But during the Gulf crisis, being here did not make me feel better,

it didn't help. Everywhere one went—in the car, at home, in the office—there was just this awful news. The motivation to do something positive was strong, and finally taking action did have a tremendous impact on us. Just putting together the idea, writing the letter to the troops, and having discussions about what we were doing made everyone here feel better. Even figuring out how and where to send catalogs was a challenge that got everyone involved and acting, doing something. Where could we send them, to whom, to what address?

I belong to the International Women's Forum, and some months previously we had had a meeting in New Orleans. I had met a woman there who is a retired brigadier general. I called her and reminded her we had met at the dinner. She was very nice, knew of the catalog, and responded positively to our idea. She didn't know immediately how we should proceed or who we might contact, but she promised to find out and get back to me. And she delivered. Through the Pentagon, we got what, months later, turned out to be the address that was printed in all the newspapers for people who wanted to write to soldiers stationed in the desert.

Finally we wrote a letter, offered a 15 percent discount, and sent a packet of catalogs. At first we had no response, so we wrote again and sent more catalogs. Then, all of a sudden, we started to get orders. Not for Christmas—Christmas had come and gone—but for Valentine's Day. By then, war had broken out, so we increased the discount—with the increase in tension, we felt even more empathy with the soldiers—and mailed a larger packet of catalogs. I think the impact of actually being at war and away from home, combined with the sentiments attached to Valentine's Day, all came together. Because then we had a very big response.

And what happened here in the company was unbelievable. Every time an order came in, we all became very excited. There it was, on paper. They didn't use the fax, they just mailed in order forms. Their stories were so poignant. Men who missed their anniversaries would write messages saying, "Don't worry, I'll be home. I'll make this up to you." There were heartfelt messages to kids and mothers. And, of course, there was the guy who sent a dozen roses to five different women, all with the same message, "I think of you always!" Never in our wildest dreams did we anticipate the kind of press we ended up getting. It was a very positive by-product of our impulse to respond to the troops—but a real surprise.

The day I visited Ruth she had begun her day at 6:00 A.M. I was with her at noon when she welcomed a key supplier into her office to review the success of their Mother's Day sales and look ahead to their goals for the rest of the year: arrangements with growers, improved flower packing techniques, inventory solutions, and pricing. Ruth is one of the supplier's key customers—someone he wants to retain because he knows that as she grows so will his company grow. In the old world of power business negotiations, Ruth might be considered, by virtue of her buying power, the party in control. The meeting I observed might traditionally have been one in which the customer, feeling entitled, made demands, offered ultimatums, and maneuvered to gain advantage in pricing and stock quality. But there was no sense of power politics in the meeting I observed.

Ruth sat in her modest yet elegant office, her back to a grand view of San Francisco and the Bay. Rick Cahill, the supplier, could see the city and the Bay over her shoulder. He had a breathtaking, calming window on the world. Rare orchids, sunset-colored calla lilies, and dewy yellow roses in simple vases gave the reclaimed warehouse office a feeling of beauty and warm sophistication. Sitting across from one another at a mahogany table, Ruth and Rick exchanged news on mutual friends and colleagues and chatted about his recent travels. Ruth asked about his golf game and later also queried, "Are you learning from your meetings with Peter?" For his part, Rick talked about what he was learning and where he had traveled of late.

Once they established a link—a relationship—they moved on to the agenda. Each had a notepad in front of them, and an air of mutual respect seemed to fill the space in the table between them. Ruth began by asking Rick how he felt about the just-completed Mother's Day activity. At first he didn't seem to know what she meant. She restated her question, "What did you think about how it went? Is there anything we might do differently next time?" Finally, he understood that she was searching for a qualitative, as well as a specific, assessment of the whole operation and responded that he had a general feeling of satisfaction about their success. Then he mentioned a specific flower that hadn't sold as well as they both had hoped it would, resulting in excess inventory and an oversupply of boxes that were taking up valuable warehouse space. Ruth and Rick spent time exploring various solutions to these issues. At no time did the customer (Ruth) communicate to the supplier (Rick), "That's your problem, you're the seller." This was a partnership, a relationship.

Ruth's goal is to keep her supplier attuned to her needs and her business. She wants him to care about Calyx and Corolla enough to go the extra distance for her. She wants him to feel that her success is his success and that she is concerned about the well-being of his company. Their conversation was a true dialogue. At one point, Rick mentioned that he had an oversupply of dried statice. "We can help

you with that," she offered, perhaps thinking about how to include
it in a catalog offering.

Later, the conversation turned to a quote he had given her for
flowers she buys from another grower. "You were very high," she said.
"How far off was I?" he asked. Checking her notes, she told him what
she paid the other supplier and compared it with the number he had
quoted. They were substantially far apart. Crestfallen, but realizing
she would be crazy to switch to him at this point, he agreed she should
continue to buy from the other grower for the time being. "I'll get
back to you when I can do better," he promised. She offered to meet
him halfway on price, essentially agreeing to pay a little more than she
was currently paying. Each seemed to feel they had been fairly treated,
and they moved on to the next item on their agenda.

As the meeting continued, time was used efficiently and
there was no hint of jockeying for best advantage, withholding
information, or manipulation. There were no power plays, no silly
games. These two people had met to discuss their business and their
business relationship. They shared information, views, and goals.
They shared a solid business relationship.

Contrast this with a description of Liar's Poker, a game detailed
by Michael Lewis (in his book of the same name), which he likened
to the job of a bond trader:

> The game has some of the feel of trading, just as jousting has some of
> the feel of war. The questions a Liar's Poker player asks himself are,
> up to a point, the same questions a bond trader asks himself. Is this
> a smart risk? Do I feel lucky? How cunning is my opponent? Does
> he have any idea what he is doing, and if not, how do I exploit his
> ignorance? If he bids high, is he bluffing, or does he actually hold a
> strong hand? Is he trying to induce me to make a foolish bid, or does
> he actually have four of a kind himself? Each player seeks weakness,
> predictability and pattern in the other and seeks to avoid it himself.[1]

Granted, the trading floors of Wall Street firms are not representative of all large companies. But isn't there something uncom-
fortably familiar about this description of an American business
"game?" This is *not* the game played at Calyx and Corolla.

Rick and Ruth finished their meeting and her associate took
him off to a business lunch. Ruth gave me a tour of the operational center of her company. On the floor below her office, the
heart of the organization beats. This is the order center. When a
customer calls to place an order, it comes to a person sitting in front
of a computer terminal in this relatively small but pleasant room.
The day I was there, about 20 customer contact people were working

at the computers. At peak holidays, there may be as many as 100.

Vases stand on display against one wall. Computer terminals are arranged against two walls that have large windows overlooking the same scene one views from the owner's office upstairs. Bouquets of lavender, lilies, and more roses grace tabletops. A bonsai tree holds court near the front of the room. The person with the highest sales during the week will take that home. Mark, the assistant supervisor in charge of customer relations, is also an accomplished pastry chef. Birthdays and special events are celebrated with cheesecakes and tarts he prepares for the honoree himself.

I have seen other such computer terminal centers—airline companies that sell meeting services via a central group of computer operators tied to phone lines; consumer product companies that attach people to computers and phones and call them customer service reps; travel agencies; and financial services operations. Most of these other centers have no windows, little space, and little freedom. The people are extensions of their machines; timed and monitored, efficiency is the goal.

Efficiency is important at Calyx and Corolla, too. A company poised to grow to a $25 million company by the mid-1990s cannot afford to be careless or cavalier about sales. Attention and accuracy are also critical. Customers have very little sense of humor if wedding or funeral flowers arrive late; they get downright crabby if their anniversary flowers are sent to the wrong address; and they are occasionally nasty if their white tulips arrive at a party in shades of red. But Ruth is confident that the Calyx and Corolla way will ensure that the company meets its goals, both financial and service. She believes that if people feel good about their product and are treated respectfully, not as extensions of machines hired to put in a certain number of hours a day, everyone (customers, employees, investors, and Ruth) will benefit.

Calyx and Corolla was started in 1988. It is the second business for Ruth Owades. Her first, Gardener's Eden, was a catalog business that sold upscale gardening accessories that Ruth started from scratch and later sold to Williams-Sonoma. Although Gardener's Eden was a great success for Ruth, it was also a surprise. During her two years at the Harvard Business School, when her classmates waxed dreamily about their plans to start a business, Ruth made it clear that her idea of happiness was a nice, safe corporate job. Having a business of her own was not the slightest bit attractive to her. As she explains:

My father owned a bookstore. My whole family loved books, but the bookstore was not very successful financially. My introduction to the life of the entrepreneur was very negative. I watched my parents struggle to make ends meet and the store work. And it never did. My father eventually became very ill and finally had to sell the store at a big loss. I saw what he went through and what it did to him psychologically. Having a business of my own was the last thing I wanted.

Ruth got her nice, safe corporate job. She graduated from the Harvard Business School in 1975 and for the next three years was head of marketing at CML Group, a mail-order conglomerate outside Boston, Massachusetts. Asked if she had been happy having attained her dream (the safe corporate job), she quickly responded:

No, of course not. It was a particularly boring corporate job, as many corporate jobs are, and if the job isn't, the politics usually are. Until you are there, you don't appreciate how frustrating it can be. The tasks are so trivial. Some mornings I'd be watching the clock by 9:30. But for a long while I wondered what was wrong with me. I was being paid a lot of money. There was this great contradiction: if they are paying me this much money, it must be a good job! It took a tremendous force of events to get me to look at the possibility of leaving and starting a company of my own.

What did trigger her change in attitude was an idea. As director of marketing for CML, she had done a good deal of research and had come to believe that the market for gardening accessories was ripe.

I put together a proposal for the chairman and president, and they thought it was great. They gave me the go-ahead to proceed. I worked on it for six months, along with my other duties, and was having a great time. But I began to sense a change in attitude as I got further into it. The presidents of existing divisions began to undermine the concept and my ability to execute it. Finally, the chairman reversed himself and rejected the idea. He said it was too big a risk and inappropriate for corporate to start something new. Was it the politics or the organization? Was it because I was the only female manager? Was it a combination of all these things? I'm not sure.

Regardless, in 1978 Ruth left her safe corporate job to begin life as an entrepreneur. She started Gardener's Eden and spent the next four years pioneering a new mail-order market. Her company gave those who loved to garden access to tools and materials that made their weekend sowing and reaping more enjoyable. In 1982, wanting additional capital to expand the business, she sold Gardener's Eden to Williams-Sonoma. For the next five years, she ran the company for Williams-Sonoma, growing it to a $15 million division before deciding again to leave the world of the corporation. Explaining why she left a safe corporate job a second time, she says:

> When I owned Gardener's Eden, I spent the whole day moving the business forward. As part of the larger corporation, I spent half my day moving the business forward and the other half just playing the game. It just didn't seem very productive. I can play the game as well as the next guy, but why?

She decided there wasn't a good reason to go on playing the game and left Williams-Sonoma. She left on good terms and with the knowledge that they might be interested in investing in her next venture. But she did not know exactly what she wanted to do next. Needing time out to reflect and integrate the lessons gleaned from the Gardener's Eden experience, Ruth spent the next year indulging her love of gardening at her home in Sonoma, California. She described that year as a vital time-out.

> I'd never really had time off, not since I was eight or something! It was important to have a total change of pace. In Sonoma there is a real difference in the weather, and, after all those years of getting up and dressing for the office in the foggy San Francisco mornings, to throw on a pair of jeans and go outside on the sunny patio was wonderful. Everything was different—the weather, where I woke up, what I wore, how I spent my days. I was busy. I played tennis, swam, worked in the garden, read novels I'd not had time to read, saw friends, learned about wine. It was very pleasant, especially Sunday nights. I could have another glass of wine, watch the sun go down and not think, "Oh god, it's almost Monday, I've got to get organized, go to bed, head into the city, get some work done," or any of those things which used to characterize Sunday nights. Friends came to dinner and by 10:30 would have to leave saying, "Gotta be at work tomorrow." And I'd think, "Not me!" That was wonderful. I don't want that all the time, but it's important to have it sometime.
>
> A lot of people around me said, "Oh, you'll never last two weeks. You'll get bored and need to get back to work." Well, I didn't know if I would or wouldn't, but I was doing just fine relaxing, unwinding, recharging, being outside. Understanding just how tired I was and peeling away the layers of fatigue, took months. And I was "lasting" a lot

longer than people had expected I would. So then the questions began, "Was I going to retire? What was I going to do next? Did I have any ideas?" I think a lot of people were uncomfortable because my behavior seemed so different to them; they knew me as such a hard worker, what did this mean? And after a while, I wanted to say, "Enough!" I was very comfortable with what I was doing. My discomfort didn't grow until I started to think about business number two—the flower catalog.

But that didn't come for a while. Three or four months into this time-out, I got a big job offer from a large company based in Chicago. It was history making—"first woman in charge of" and that sort of thing—and significant enough that I felt I had to consider it. So I met with the company executives a number of times, went back and forth on it, getting excited and then thinking, commuting? Between Chicago and San Francisco? Really. I struggled with whether or not I wanted the job. Finally, I turned it down and went back to enjoying myself.

Ultimately that experience made me think about what I did want. By now I had begun to think about the catalog, I was getting excited about it and working it out in my head. It just happened that after leaving Gardener's Eden I took an office near the wholesale flower mart. I have always loved flowers, and, now that I had time and was entertaining again, I stopped frequently at the mart to get flowers. By my fifth dinner party, I began to notice how busy it was there. *Something happened* to me. I went to the library and began to research the flower industry. By now I was begrudgingly pursuing the flicker of an idea. Finally, six or seven months after leaving Gardener's Eden, I began to think, "I really ought to decide if I am going to do this or not." Three months later I had written the business plan, talked to growers, and started to raise money. By July, I had the money and began to put a team of people together. A year had passed.

As Ruth said, "*Something happened.*" Ruth's successes seem to arise out of some inner well that she intermittently taps and then acts on. Trying to understand the nature of that well, her feelings of confidence, and her willingness to act on an instinct, I asked her to talk about significant people in her life.

I never had the female mentor I would like to have had. But I did have a wonderful collection of professors and teachers who encouraged me. My brother was very smart and preceded me everywhere. But one of my grade school teachers took me aside and said, "You are Ruth, and you are very smart and capable," implying that I did not have to live in my brother's shadow. I think that had an enormous impact on me, though then I had no idea what she was talking about. Though my father was very proud of me, in our house the male child was much more important. When my father was alive, he would tell me "You can be anything you want to be." It sounds so simple. But my mother didn't tell me that, and my brother told me the opposite. There was, of course, that one grammar school teacher. Still we don't hear often enough that we can be anything we want to be. I heard that I could be a teacher or a writer—those were the options.

The other important person has been my husband, whom I didn't meet until I was an adult. He was already a success in his career and has been this solid force who believed, unquestioningly, with such intensity, in my ability to do whatever I wanted to do. And he has given me so much support. When I finally decided to go to business school, he happily lived through those incredibly difficult two years with me. He went to cooking school at night while I was in business school, so I didn't have to worry about making all the meals. And when I finally started Gardener's Eden, he was actively enthusiastic about my plans. I didn't have that kind of support growing up, and, if I hadn't had it at some point, I don't think I would have done any of the things that I have.

The well I referred to earlier—the source of inspiration, power, and confidence that Ruth seems able to draw upon—may not come from the encouragement she received from others, but clearly such support helped her to realize her own potential. Her strength and power have been augmented by her own ability to reflect and learn.

A key turning point for me was when I stopped fighting those things which felt characteristically female—when I said it's okay to listen to my intuition. For years I denied that. When I realized that it was a valuable thing, I made better and better decisions. I gained a real strength of conviction and realized I had a marvelous tool. My body told me whether a decision I made was good or bad and gave me reliable reactions to people we were considering hiring or working with—is this someone we can do business with on a handshake? When I accepted my strengths, that made an enormous difference in my ability to lead.

When I talk about this among a group of women, they know what I mean. Understanding my own power has been slow. It has grown over time. It is only in the last few years that I have come to realize the potential that one person—in this case, me—has to make things happen, to really make a difference.

TERRIE WILLIAMS
The Terrie Williams Agency

We were whizzing down Pacific Coast Highway 1. The wide Pacific spread grandly to our right, the disconcerting blue of an October day in New England. My passenger had been absorbing the views with the kind of quiet appreciation only a woman who spends much of her time in Manhattan can. Suddenly, she took her phone (which appears to accompany her everywhere) from her bag and punched in a number. "Hi, Erin? This is Terrie Williams. How you doing? I just passed your house." Terrie had a brief conversation with Erin

Davis, son of her client, Miles (now the late Miles Davis), let him know she was thinking about him and his family, put her phone back in her bag, and turned to admire the vista on her right again. Her business is people, and she doesn't miss an opportunity to check in, show attention, connect.

Terrie Williams is the founder/owner of The Terrie Williams Agency. Her company has offices in New York and Los Angeles. Her client list is a virtual who's who of stars and corporations: Anita Baker, Eddie Murphy, Coca Cola, Ortho Pharmaceuticals, and Essence Communications. She was in Los Angeles to pick up yet another award. In 1991 she received the prestigious Matrix Award presented by New York Women in Communications in recognition of her distinguished achievement. Terrie was the first African-American woman in 25 years to be so honored. Her office holds an impressive collection of statues and plaques, including the New York Urban League Building Brick Award and the D. Parke Gibson Award from the Public Relations Society of America. The awards Williams has collected over the last few years tell us something about the way her colleagues in the world of public relations view her. But Terrie Williams is a lot more than the sum of her awards.

Sandra Kurtzig, founder of ASK Computer, is concerned with (among other things) staying on the leading edge of technology; Lane Nemath of Discovery Toys is concerned with creating safe, appealing playthings for children; and Frieda Caplan, founder of Frida's Finest (and the new owner, daughter Karen), concentrates on getting fresh, healthy produce to her customers. Every business is concerned with its own set of critical issues. Terrie Williams's focus is people. And public relations is about just that—relations and relating. Terrie gives the same kind of obsessive attention to quality relationships that a manufacturing entrepreneur gives to creating well-engineered widgets or that a product entrepreneur gives to quality and service. She lavishes the same (or maybe more) attention to detail on her clients that *Fortune* 500 marketing executives give to their product lines. She skims six or seven papers a day to stay abreast of current news and trends that may affect her clients' lives and fortunes. She also is sincere—the "love-ya-let's-do-lunch" lingo, often overheard in restaurants in Hollywood and New York, is a foreign language to this professional.

Terrie is grounded. She seems solid, reliable, rock steady; there is a steady-state hum about her that may be the whir of her brain. It is always spinning, always attending to what else can be done to position the client or to get attention for the film, act, record, or product. Terrie and her bicoastal staff of account executives and specialists run an operation that supports some very big names in business and entertainment and helps create recognition for names heretofore unknown. To do that in the crowded world of celebrities vying for a place in *People* magazine, is a feat that has eaten a lot of wannabees.

It was Brenda Trotter, Terrie's assistant, who had helped me spirit Terrie away from her Los Angeles office to the quieter world of Ojai, California. I wanted us to be able to meet and talk in a more leisurely fashion about life and business than we might have done in L.A., with phones ringing and people poking their heads in to ask a question or say hello. I would not have gotten her out of the office had it not been for Brenda and her colleague, Tony Wafford.

Brenda and Tony seem to typify the team Terrie has assembled around her to grow the Terrie Williams Agency. It is a team of professionals who, according to Terrie, "want this as much as I do." "This," of course, being the thrill of building something from scratch—the reputation, the client list, and the financial rewards that accompany their achievements.

To an outsider, Terrie's company may look pretty glamorous—relationships with celebrities, film premieres, backstage privileges, and a constant round of parties and events. However, it is a high-pressure, fast-paced business filled with the tedium of countless details and the endless quest for the new "hook"—that is, another way to get the media to pay attention to a client. Keeping a team energized, excited, and motivated is never an easy task. In an industry that can burn out staff fast, Terrie has energized her people and created a group intent on sticking together. Her key people have been with her from the beginning—perhaps because she gives people opportunities to learn and then lets them loose. She is quick to say, however, that it is her name on the door, and although she is managing more and handling fewer clients personally now, she continues to feed ideas to account execs and support their needs to provide services to their clients.

I admit that I harbor an extra ration of cynicism about the world of public relations. Politicians and corporate executives have used public relations and "spin control" to cover a lot of dubious activity with a veneer of respectability. But Williams raises the standard; her own integrity is palpable. Terrie related directly to me—no hype, no cover, no untruths. What sets her apart in the field of public relations is that she pays attention, relates to her clients, and works with what is real, not with what her clients want to be real. Two stories make the point: helping Willie Stargell claim a second career and getting newcomer, writer, director, producer, Matty Rich, press attention to bolster his success with his film *Straight Out of Brooklyn*.

Terrie met baseball great Willie Stargell through mutual friends. He was not looking for a public relations agency. When she suggested her agency could be helpful to him, he wasn't interested. But Terrie is nothing if not persistent. She kept pushing. "What do you do for fun?" she asked him. "Fun?" he wanted to know. "Yeah, fun," she prodded. "What are you interested in, what do you care about?" "Well," she relates, "finally I found out he was a gourmet cook, a member of Les Mis du Vin, the international wine society, and extremely knowledgeable about wine." Click. Terrie remarked, "He didn't appreciate that what he knew and cared about had value. But I knew we could help him become a respected spokesperson in the wine industry and start him on a second career."

Starting from scratch with a reluctant client, she approached the food critic of the *New York Times* and suggested they do a story called, "Eating Out With Willie Stargell." Stargell was featured as an expert on food and wine. This led to other stories about the multidimensional (there *is* life after baseball) athlete. Thanks to the work of the Terrie Williams Agency (and his own ability), Stargell is now on the board of directors for the Culinary Institute of America, writes a column on wine for an industry publication, and hosts celebrity cooking seminars. Because Terrie persisted and paid attention to what's just beneath the surface, she garnered informtion that got her a new client and a new career for that client.

Terrie and her staff have learned how to listen to their clients, knowing that within the client lies valuable raw material. The best public relations firms don't look for things to make up about their clients; they look for the strengths their clients already have and help build on those. The story of Matty Rich illustrates that ability to listen and act on information that might otherwise be lost, ignored, or untapped. In contrast to Stargell, Rich, at 19, is just starting his career. He has produced a film, *Straight Out of Brooklyn*, that received sufficient critical praise and audience response to make it a success on many counts. Matty Rich has opened a lot of doors on his own, but Terrie has helped expand his audience and gain attention for him in the mainstream media.

Terrie described one opportunity she orchestrated for Rich after the premiere of his film.

In every interview he talked about *The Brady Bunch*. That show was, in a way, the inspiration for his film. He told every interviewer that watching *The Brady Bunch* was a powerful contrast to the life he lived in Red Hook [a tough section of New York]. Matty would relate to the interviewer, "Whenever there was a problem [on the show], everyone got together and discussed it as a family. Or if an ice cream fell on the floor his father would say, 'No problem, Bobby, go get another one out of the refrigerator.' If I had dropped an ice cream on the floor, my father would have slapped me and yelled, 'That's $1.50 you just put on the floor.' I made *Straight Out of Brooklyn* because I wanted to make a film about a real black family." I heard him refer to *The Brady Bunch* and tell this story over and over. Finally, I thought, wouldn't it be something to get him together with *The Brady Bunch* [cast].

Terrie called her contacts at the *Arsenio Hall Show* and suggested they invite Matty Rich and a cast member from *The Brady Bunch* to be on the show. She described what happened.

He and Florence Henderson were asked to do Arsenio's show. The experience of meeting Florence Henderson, who had played *The Brady Bunch* mother—and was able to talk about the show with him—just blew him away. It was very, very emotional because it took him back to the very beginning of his odyssey. Not only was this an important experience for Matty, but he was also introduced to a huge audience that might not otherwise have known about his film. That's what my business is about—listening to my clients and finding those parts of their experience that we can focus on which will help them tell their own stories.

Terrie's listening skills are no accident. After graduating from Brandeis University, she earned a degree in social work from Columbia University. For three years, Terrie was a medical social worker at New York Hospital, but she found her role too restrictive and left that job. She took with her the skills she had acquired that enabled her to hear the music that rests under the words people say aloud. Social work training also gave her an understanding of the patience required to work with clients who are sometimes their own worst enemies. Although she makes it clear that she doesn't take on clients whose work reinforces stereotypes and she won't work with clients who are on drugs or are playing on the edges of the law, she will go the extra distance for a good client who happens to be a pain in the neck. "There are times when I am no day at the beach, and friends stick by me and love me anyway. I feel I have to give my clients at least that. Social work taught me understanding, to look beneath the surface and try to see what causes behavior that may drive me crazy."

The Terrie Williams Agency is just four years old—by some standards still in the start-up phase of development. Williams developed the public relations department at *Essence* and became the youngest vice-president there. Her company was started (with the blessing of Ed Lewis, publisher of *Essence*) six months before she left her job.

During those last six months I saved the income I received from my first two clients—not much more than 10 or 12 grand. When it was time to leave *Essence*, I didn't know what I was going to do. I started looking for space to open the business and fell into a really great situation. I met a guy who was moving his p.r. firm to Washington, D.C. but had nine months left on his lease. He wanted to be able to use the office four or five days a month, so I walked into an office all set up—phone, fax, mail room, files, the works. I paid a share of the rent and a portion of the equipment lease. There was no way I could have started a business without such a situation. I didn't own a home, I was a first-time business owner, I had no credit, and no other source of funds.

But she did have clients—impressive clients. She left *Essence* with an agreement to handle their public relations and with Miles Davis as a client. I asked her how she landed someone as high profile as Davis right at the start of her business. Her response once again emphasizes the importance of her ability to build relationships and take risks.

I met Miles when I was a social worker at New York Hospital. I had heard he was in the hospital, and, though I didn't know much about him, I knew he was a legend of some kind. I found his room and dropped in on him. I wasn't the social worker on that floor, but I walked in and introduced myself. We established a friendly vibe. I guess I was bold! And I visited him a few times after that. We stayed in touch off and on, but then I didn't see him for a couple of years. Later he was honored at an event which I attended, and I approached him again. By that time I was pretty serious about starting my own company. I convinced him to let me handle his public relations free-lance. His needs were pretty standard: getting releases out when he performed, handling the publicity for his autobiography when it came out. That was a little tricky. We held a book party for him and arranged a press conference, and he didn't show up. Usually, that's a tough thing to handle. Fortunately, Miles had been performing with his back to audiences for years, so all you could say was "Miles is Miles!" We were friends for a long time.

The story of how she developed Miles as a client tells something about her ability to build on relationships. But the story of her business relationship with Eddie Murphy tells legions about her character and the hard decisions she is sometimes called on to make when integrity and business revenue face off.

Eddie Murphy was the first client to officially sign with the Terrie Williams Agency. Terrie met him in 1985 at a surprise birthday party held for Miles Davis in Malibu, California. She heard then that Eddie was looking for a new agency; however, given her status as a newcomer to the field of public relations, she didn't think seriously about approaching him. Some months later, through friends, she heard the same information again. Still she didn't act. She should have been in baseball—the third time she heard the news she decided to go for the home run. Terrie put together a proposal and sent copies to both his home and his office. Two months later they talked on the phone. He wanted her agency to represent him. With Murphy on her client list, she had broken through the toughest barriers. Her company was on its way.

For the next two years, all went well; the relationship was mutually beneficial. As far as Terrie knew, Eddie Murphy and his company were pleased with the exclusive representation. Then she got a call from one of his managers. It seemed that the folks in Eddie's camp felt he needed two public relations firms: one that would handle general and black media (Terrie's agency) and another to handle the general market and film-oriented media. To Terrie this was a direct challenge, because one of her most important achievements has been to represent clients in both mainstream and specialty media. Murphy's managers were implying that she and her agency couldn't cut it in the mainstream press. She resigned the account. She was dignified, gracious, and clear: she wouldn't send a message to her other clients, her employees, or other professionals in the field that her agency wasn't skilled, experienced, or professional enough to do the job with the mainstream media—that is, the white media. There had been no contact between her and Murphy; this had all been the very "businesslike" work of his managers. Deeply disappointed (and knowing she would have to work extra hard to make up those lost revenues), but sure she had made the right decision, she got back to work.

Three months later, she and Eddie Murphy were both at his brother's wedding in New York. Murphy pulled her aside and asked why she had resigned his account. Surprised and not a little indignant, she explained that she was disappointed he had not discussed with her why or when he felt the need to hire a second agency to handle his public relations. Patiently, she tried to communicate that "as one of the most powerful entertainers in the business he was sending a message that my company could not do the job exclusively for him." She went on to explain that it didn't look good for either of them to participate in something that so undermined her as a professional. He agreed on the spot and one week later had fired the new firm. The Terrie Williams Agency was brought back to handle all his public relations matters.

To start any business is hard work. To start and succeed is often even harder for women of color than for their white sisters. They may have more difficulty accumulating capital and acquiring mentors, people who will advise, guide, and act as rainmakers in the early, fragile stages of a business. Terrie was able to save a small amount of money before leaving her position at *Essence,* and that was a terrific advantage. She also credits a number of people with being helpful: *Essence* publisher Ed Lewis supported her dream to own a business and continues to be available when she needs to talk something out with someone she respects; Miles Davis introduced her to Eddie Murphy; and Bill Cosby calls with advice and support from time to time. But a mentor—someone in her field who could really open doors and be a support throughout the process of building and growing a business—is a luxury she and many of her African-American colleagues have made do without.

As an African-American, Williams is a pioneer in the field of public relations. Issues of race still challenge her business. "When we get awarded business to publicize a film," she says, "or when a company wants to do a product introduction, sometimes we get the whole project. But sometimes we just get that portion of the project involved with the black media."

Williams owns one of the hottest agencies in the country. She has access to all the mainstream media as well as the minority media. It is a powerful combination, one that many so-called general market agencies cannot claim. Still, she is often called on to convince clients that her account execs have a direct line into the newspapers, magazines, and broadcast media that the clients want. Observes Terrie, "Whatever else you want to say about what people of color do, I think black folks are pretty extraordinary to achieve what we do in the light of all the barriers we have to work against."

Among some of her colleagues, there is a sense that her company may be as important to the future of blacks in public relations as to her own clients. In an article published in *Crisis* (August/September 1990), the magazine of the NAACP, one of her competitors stated that, "Terrie's representation of Eddie Murphy has put a lot of black celebrities on notice. It says this man trusts that this woman knows what she is doing." This, she suspects, will give other black stars the confidence to sign on with black-owned agencies. Given Terrie's success to date, it may also give other blacks in public relations the self-confidence to follow in her footsteps.

I asked Terrie to describe the "stuff" of her business—the kinds of routines she and her staff deal with regularly.

We handle film premieres. We make invitations to the press, and, once you get press people there, you have to make sure their needs are accommodated. It's a lot of little things: you have to rope off an area for them, sometimes you have to get them stanchions to stand behind so they can get the shots they want when the stars walk into the theater. When celebrities get out of cars, you have to announce to the press who is approaching so they get the right shots. Then you set up interviews and help them get sound bites they can use. Inside the theater, you have to make sure the mike and other equipment needed is actually there and that the program flows the way it is supposed to.

Sometimes our company has responsibility for putting on big events which press people get invited to. Then there are a million details to worry about. We handled all Mandela's press when he was in New York. There was a press conference at the *New York Times* and two at Gracie Mansion [the official residence of the mayor of New York]. There were supposed to be interviews for him with the black press, but he was exhausted and had to cancel those interviews. I shuttled between his team and the press folks and tried to ease the situation. I had to deal with damage control and how it would look for him to cancel that press conference.

This business requires a constant stream of creative ideas. You can't stop thinking for a minute. The staff gets together for brainstorming sessions to develop ideas on how to position a client or to come up with an event or story line for our clients. But brainstorming goes on outside the office, too. I can't go to a concert or a play without thinking, "How do we sign this group or this individual?" "How can I get the entertainer on stage to introduce the client who is sitting here beside me?" I can't just go to an event or concert and enjoy it. I'm on. My account execs and I are working, no matter what else we are doing. Not long ago I attended a performance in the Beacon Theater with a client. As we were sitting there, it hit me that it would be ideal if the performing act on stage would acknowledge that my client (whose new film was just opening) was in the audience. I spent the next hour shuttling back and forth between backstage and my seat. First I had to talk my way into their dressing room, then I had to tell them about my client and convince them to introduce him. It worked, they had heard of him. They put the lights on my client, gave him a great endorsement. That effort gave the client a little extra recognition. I couldn't just sit there and enjoy the concert.

This kind of nonstop attention is part of what has made the Terrie Williams Agency grow and attract an enviable list of clients. But if she and her staff are always giving attention to others, how does she take care of her own life?

In the beginning, I could not have handled both the business and a relationship. I couldn't have accomplished what I have if Mr. Right had been in my life at the start. There were times I would get off a plane and think to myself, "I am so glad I am not hooked up with someone, because I want to be in the office *now*. I've been in L.A. for a week, I've got a load of stuff on my desk, I want to go to the office, and I don't want to feel guilty that someone is waiting for me at home."

Terrie now sets limits on her days at the office (although what she and I consider "limits" is a relative concept!) and is involved in a relationship she consciously makes time for. "Is it a sign of success that you are now able to cope with both a relationship and your business?" I asked her.

I am not sure if it's success or just different priorities. When I come home I still want to do work, make calls, look over things for the next day. But now some of those calls wait. I don't always like that. But having a relationship matters to me. It's a challenge to have both—the business and the relationship. And in the long run, I don't want to be alone. Growing and diversifying the company, so I can be just a little less hands on, is one of the ways I am developing the business to accommodate my long-term goals.

The names in her contract file are impressive, but the achievements she speaks of with pride are the people who have entered the field of public relations after spending time with her company.

I'm not sure if I want to have kids. But if having children means passing on knowledge and something good about yourself, I've already done that. A lot of young people have come through the agency, either as interns or part-timers, to learn the business. Many of those people are now involved in many different aspects of the public relations business.

Terrie Williams has plenty to be proud of: as a role model and teacher, as well as a manager, professional, and company builder.

DASHE AND THOMSON, INC.

MARILYN DASHE   **JEAN THOMSON**

The house at 322 Groveland is large, red brick, and three stories; its backyard is small, and it sits on a quiet elm-lined street. One can imagine that the house once held a family with children who grew up happily here. From the outside, there is an appearance of tranquility that is appealing. Inside, the house is now alive with the friendly hustle and bustle of a growing business. All three floors are jam-packed with people and equipment. A large oak table, in what was probably once the former family's dining room, functions as the heart of the company. Staff meetings are held there on Thursday mornings; department meetings, informal talks, and lunch are also shared at the table. The morning I was there I noticed a stack of crossword puzzles copied from the morning's newspaper in the middle of the table. "You have a few crossword fanatics here?" I asked. Richard Trest, the office manager, grinned and nodded. "What a good idea," I thought. A crossword nut myself, I know how aggravating it can be to open a newspaper and find someone else has already done the silly thing. In this company, everyone had their own puzzle without having to buy their own paper! Although the business housed there is a high-pressure one, 322 Groveland has a comfortable, open ambiance.

Jean Thomson and Marilyn Dashe own the building together. They have been here for six years, ever since they moved out of Marilyn Dashe's third floor where they started Dashe and Thomson. Now, the company has grown. Six years ago Dashe and Thomson was a small, local company offering business writing seminars and technical documentation in the greater Minneapolis area. Revenues were near $400,000. Now it is a technical documentation firm with clients all over the world, partnerships with companies in both Japan and Brussels, and revenues of $2 million a year. Dashe and Thomson, Inc. has now outgrown its 322 Groveland headquarters. Once Jean and Marilyn sell this building, they will lease larger office space.

I met Jean Thomson and Marilyn Dashe at one of the *Inc.* dinners. I was intrigued by their business and by them individually. But it is their partnership—a business relationship that has lasted and grown in the course of growing their business—that really caught my attention. Maybe that's because it reminds me of my own relationship with my business partner. The blending of different personas to create an effective team was a challenge I enjoyed. I was curious to meet with the partners together, to watch them interact, and to try to get a handle on what it is that makes their partnership successful.

To give the reader a sense of how their partnership works, I have retained their conversation in dialogue form. In this way, you may get a feeling for the ways they attend to, encourage, and support one another. I was struck by how very patient they are with one another, giving each other room and time to speak and nodding encouragingly. As I read the transcript of our interview, I sometimes felt that if I took the two names away I might think that I had met with just one person. This is not to say that they agree on everything—they don't—but the rhythm of conversation flows and is integrated in a way that gives that illusion. Occasionally, they ended a sentence together with the same words; often one would quietly agree "yes, yes, that's right," as the other spoke. I have sometimes been with couples who talk at once, each calling for your attention and putting you in the awkward spot of trying to be responsive to both, so you are unable to do well with either. Jean and Marilyn give each other plenty of room to say what's on their minds, and they really do listen to one another. I asked them how they are different from one another.

Marilyn: Our personalities are completely different.
Jean: That's true, it's probably why we get along so well.

Marilyn: It's like a marriage, I don't think you can have two people who are exactly alike working together.

Jean: I think we are both extroverted. I don't mean we have these big personalities all over town. I mean we go outside ourselves for help and decision making. Neither of us is solitary. We both need other people. We need to check things out, and we go to each other for input.

Marilyn: I make decisions really fast. That doesn't mean my decisions are always right, but if I see a problem, I can't stand it. I have to fix it. Whereas, Jean can take a problem, think about it, get more data, and research it before she tries to solve it.

Jean: I do need more data. I also need more time; I trust time to help. Maybe I take too much sometimes, but I think we balance one another.

Marilyn: The situation with the realtor is a good example. We had a real turkey. This guy drove me out of my mind. The real estate market is slow, and I knew that wasn't his fault, but I just didn't like doing business with him. I kept saying to Jean, "We've got to change realtors." And she would say, "He's not that bad, wait until I get back from Hong Kong." But I told her, "I've got to get rid of him." So I went ahead and got a new realtor. I think that was the right decision. But it is an example of how very differently we operate. I can't stand to wait; though I can see that when we do take time to be more deliberate, there may be a benefit. I think a lot has to do with the way I live my life. I have so many things I have to do. Between the business and three kids who have to be in three places at the same time, I have to make a lot of quick decisions.

Jean: The counterbalance we lend each other is good. And we understand each other. Part of our deal is acceptance. If you don't accept one another's differences they will drive you crazy. You have to say, "That's part of the total package. I'll take it because the other parts are so great." And setting time limits is important, and that's what Marilyn gets to do.

I resonated with this conversation on differences and acceptance. It is the great luxury of my own business partnership. Jane and I are very different, but we value our differences and defend each other's rights to individuality. No doubt, partnerships—business and personal—succeed or die on this very issue.

Jean and Marilyn first met in graduate school at the University of Minnesota in Minneapolis. They had assessed their career options, decided the likelihood of making it to the tenure track was pretty slight, and struck out on their own. I asked the two women to describe how they got started.

Jean: We were graduate students in English, working on our master's degrees. We both specialized in writing, with an emphasis on technical writing for business. One night we had pizza with a couple of guys who were colleagues in our department. We came up with the idea then that we could take what we were doing and package it for business. Marilyn and I were the ones who finally went ahead and did it.

Marilyn: The two men weren't committed. They didn't really want to do a business. Of course, neither did we in the beginning; we kind of fell into it. I didn't really know Jean. And the conversation that night over pizza was like hundreds of conversations you have where you say, "I really should do such and such idea." Ninety-nine of them never get off the ground, but one works. Every now and then, one of the guys would wander into the office and say, "You know we really should get out of here and just go out and make some money." And I'd say, "Yeah, that's a good idea." It was very casual; we weren't really serious about it. But when we were finished with school, we needed a job and going out on our own started to sound like a good way to have a job. Technical writing was just starting to come into its own. I had a part-time writing contract with a company then, and it looked like a field we might be able to do something with. But there was no big plan initially. Probably, what finally drove us to start the company was the need to run our own show. I had worked for an employer. You had, too [she said, turning to Jean]. I hated being told when to be there. I wanted to do it when I wanted to do it. It was very appealing to go out on our own.

Jean: There was a man who started with us. But we came to blows early on. He dictated to us and critiqued our teaching styles. He wanted to run the show. But we began to ask each other, "Why do we need this guy telling us what to do?" But it took us a while to act on our feelings. Our whole process of growth has been about gaining confidence to act on our own knowledge and feelings. We've gained a lot of self-esteem in the last ten years.

Marilyn: Particularly in the beginning, there was always somebody coming to us and saying, "Just give me a piece of the action, and I'll help you do it." Early on, we bought into that. Everyone seemed like they knew more than we did. They knew marketing, they knew finance, they knew whatever. And, of course, we did need to know how to market better. It was very attractive when someone came along and offered help.

Jean: Many of those early "helpers" did have knowledge that was good, but they turned out not to have anything magical.

I asked them how they finally got rid of the guy.

Jean: We paid him for a piece of work he claimed was his, and he finally left.

Marilyn: That was it. We never heard from him again.

I wanted to know how they decided to run the business after that.

Marilyn: There wasn't much of a business then. Keep in mind, we were working out of my third floor in the beginning, and we both held other jobs for awhile. I was still teaching.

Jean: That was 1981.

Marilyn: At that time, we were just teaching seminars. All we had to do was decide who would teach which seminar. We did some marketing and had various appointments, but that was about it at first.

Jean: And we hardly had revenues you could count!

Marilyn: I remember we were getting paid $1000 for one contract, and I thought that was wonderful.

Jean: Then we got a contract with Sterns Computer Systems around Christmas in 1981.

Marilyn: '81? It was that early?

Jean: Yes, that early. They introduced the Stearns Computer in April of 1982.

Marilyn: So it was that second year of the business that it began to feel a little more real.

Jean: The seminar business really got us going. That first year we made $7000.

Marilyn: I thought it was $16,000.
   Jean: That was '82. [The two of them laughed.] The next year we went up to $28,000; then we went to $72,000. The business kept doubling.
Marilyn: And in the process, the business changed.
   Jean: We have changed a lot from the first three to five years. It took us that long to figure out who we were and what we were doing.

They began by providing writing seminars in business and technical writing to companies in the greater Minneapolis area. They still offer 14 different seminars, ranging from "How to Write and Produce Effective User Documentation" to "Product Liability: How It Affects the Writing and Design of Labels and Instruction Manuals" to "How to Write Better Technical Memos, Reports, Proposals, and Papers." But now those seminars are held in London, Tokyo, and other major business centers all over the world, as well as in Chicago and Minneapolis. The firm also offers technical documentation, translation, and training. Their technical writing services include computer software documentation and equipment manuals. They write training manuals, user guides, and systems documentation. The day I visited I watched a young woman working on a complex set of instructions for a new machine that would be used by operators at the Malt-O-Meal Company. Her job was to design instructions that were clear and easy to use. Sophisticated, expensive machinery is undermined if the operators can't understand how to use it properly. The Dashe and Thomson people are proficient at turning the often-convoluted language of engineers into user-friendly language that the rest of us can handle.

As the world has gone global, Dashe and Thomson have gone with it. In partnership with a Japanese company, Toin (also owned by a woman), and a company in Brussels, they provide technical translation services worldwide. The partnership with Toin provides the Japanese company (which is 25 years old and has revenues of almost $25 million) with an added service and Dashe and Thomson with additional revenue. For example, once Toin translates from Japanese to English, Dashe and Thomson Americanize it—that is, they will recognize in context that a "sealed instrument" is not a legal document with the Japanese hankyu seal affixed, but instead a device on a machine. This part of the business is likely to grow. As more and more European and Japanese companies import goods to America, they are finding that the translation and writing services provided by

Dashe and Thomson can give them a competitive edge. Consumers are increasingly cranky about buying VCRs with instructions they can't understand, and both American and overseas companies are finally realizing that clear, easy-to-understand instructions do make a difference to their sales revenues.

Jean and Marilyn have attracted an impressive list of clients: Pillsbury, Honeywell, Toro, Motorola, Hitachi, Fujitsu, 3M, and Unisys. It's quite a distance to have come from that first conversation in the pizza parlor. I mentioned in an earlier chapter George Gendron's observation that it often takes a good ten years for a company to hit its stride and understand its market. I asked the two women to comment on that.

Marilyn: I think that's right. We did a lot of wrong things in the beginning. And we learned tremendously from our mistakes—both with people and products.

Jean: And we gained experience. You learn and do things better the second time.

Marilyn: Or drop them. We really...

Jean: ...winnowed down and perfected a lot of areas that we hadn't done well for lack of experience. You just have to do this stuff for awhile. That's how you get good at it.

Marilyn is married and has three kids; Jean is single. I asked how the work/family issues were handled.

Marilyn: Not well!

Jean: There's a disagreement here. I always cite Marilyn as someone who fits the two worlds together as well as I can imagine it being done.

Marilyn: I have felt guilt on both sides [with the business and with the family]. The kids are now 18, 14, and 11. The youngest was an infant when we started. I think owning a business works really well though, when it comes to handling personal issues. You can leave in the day, do your work at night, or whatever you need to do. It works very well for me—I can get to their games, I can get to the school plays, I can do what I need to do, and I can juggle my time accordingly. I've always felt very lucky to have the business. I've watched other women, who have a regular job, struggle. I would go crazy without the flexibility this gives me.

Jean: In a more structured organization, that kind of flexibility is often forbidden.

Marilyn: Of course, we give the same kind of flexibility to the employees.

Jean: Many of whom also have children, and they also have the freedom to go to their kids' plays and games. Everyone's on flextime here. There are not "set times"—you just do your work and get the job done. How, is up to you.

Marilyn: There is an issue with the world out there though, where you deal as a mother. You are not taken seriously. My friends on the soccer field still say, "Do you go to work everyday?" What they are asking is, "Is it a real job?" I am taken seriously when I am here, doing it—with these people or with clients—but out of this environment, I often feel I am still not taken seriously as a business owner.

Jean: Sometimes at a party, someone will ask, "How's your business doing?" And when you respond, you might get, "Oh, isn't that wonderful, isn't that nice? Aren't you thrilled?" You'd hardly put it that way to the CEO of Pillsbury. You might ask a few pointed questions and inquire about what plans he had for the company...

Marilyn: And you'd not ask a man who owned a business if it supported him. It's often assumed that my efforts are just a supplement to my husband, who must support me.

(Later Jean told me that Marilyn's husband, Dr. Charles Dashe, has arranged his work schedule at a medical clinic so that he works four long days a week plus on-call time. That leaves him free one day a week to handle the errands and the groceries. Clearly, Marilyn's husband now sees her contribution as more than just a nice supplement. But it wasn't always that way. Marilyn said, "I remember the days when what I was doing was not taken seriously by anyone. Nothing changed in our family until the money from the company became crucial and really mattered. That was about five years ago.")

Marilyn: My favorite question is still, "Do you go to work every day?" [The three of us chuckle.]

Jean: As though the business just sort of runs itself!! That's why it's still one of the greatest pleasures to talk with other women who own businesses. They never ask questions like that; they know what it's like to own a business.

Returning to the subject of her family, I asked Marilyn how her kids feel about the fact that mom owns a business?

Marilyn: I've never had any trouble with that. No one ever made me feel bad by saying, "Wish you were home baking cookies" or anything like that. The kids are very much in this business. They talk about it; they know who's hired and fired. They've grown up with the business, and they consider Jean part of our family. They sometimes come and answer the phone. They think it's fun. And they know all about the move, they've been with us to look at some of the properties we've considered.

Jean: You share the business with them.

This seems very different from the work/family separation that has traditionally characterized family interactions. If balance is a function of integrating one's life, Marilyn has achieved that by integrating her family into the business, which is not the same as creating a family business, wherein Mom, Dad, and children all work in the business. In Marilyn's case, bridges between work and family have been created without completely absorbing the whole family into the business. Children and spouse have the freedom to pursue their own lives and interests, yet there is a way to stay abreast of and in touch with Marilyn and her business. As the business grows, so does the family.

Changing the subject, I asked the partners how they stay in touch with one another in a way that keeps them in sync.

Marilyn: We try meeting regularly, but that's hard. It's better to go out to dinner when we can.

Jean: Now that we have different areas of the company reporting to us, we're both in meetings 80 percent of the time. We do have a weekly financial stocktaking with our accountant, Suzannah Martin. That takes an hour or two every week, and it's a good touchstone. Beyond that, there are the dinners. How often do we do those?

Marilyn: Not often enough. Once, twice a month?

Jean: And about once a year we manage some kind of trip together.

Marilyn: Except for this year.

Jean: No, we had Florida.

Marilyn: That's right! That was really fun.

Jean: It was a retreat, just for five days. But it was great.

Marilyn: We had never done it before, I had never been away by myself like that. That was really fun.

Jean: We went to Sanibel Island, Florida. It was our first annual retreat. We just sat on the beach and walked and ate...

Marilyn: It was lovely. We needed a break. We decided to do this at the last minute. We both had a lot going on and were at the end of our ropes.

Jean: It turned out to be so lovely because not only did we get more relaxed—each individually—we also got to do a lot of talking.

Marilyn: It was very good.

Jean: Actually it's worked out that we've had a major trip together every year.

Marilyn: Usually business trips.

Jean: We were in London together last year and had a wonderful trip to New Zealand and Australia before that. And we went to Japan...

Marilyn: But this was the best, because it wasn't business. We weren't feeling the exhaustion that comes at the end of the day when doing business abroad.

Returning to the earlier question of differences, I asked them how they handle tensions.

Marilyn: [Laughing and looking at Jean] I don't yell at you as much as I yell at Charlie, I can tell you that! I work things out differently at home! [Then, reflectively] It's a process. You have a meeting, you come out somewhere, you have another one, and someone has moved a little...it's a series of events.

Jean: Yes, I think each of us can express frustration, and the other will say, "I hear you," in so many words. Maybe there isn't agreement right away—I think of the Japan issue—but it becomes clear to me over time.

(The "Japan issue" Jean refers to is the challenge they faced when the partnership with Toin, their Japanese counterpart, stopped producing income and began to be a serious drain on profits. Marilyn pushed to close the operation, but Jean, the partner responsible for getting that part of the business up and running, was reluctant to do so. Jean was able to say, "I felt Marilyn's anguish, and I could understand, too—I'm very bottom line–oriented—that if something didn't change it could do our whole business in. It's more important that the whole structure remain, not just one area, because then everyone would be out of a job, not just that one section. But it was very hard for me." Finally, they agreed to issue a deadline for changes to occur that would turn that operation around. Happily, that proved effective, and the business relationship with Toin is once again profitable.)

Marilyn: It's back to being clear on priorities. There are a lot of issues I am not ready to kill myself over. [She chuckles.] I may disagree on some things with Jean, but I trust her decisions.

Jean: We have a lot of the same values. And I think we are both committed. Even when there is tension, we can look at each other and feel the commitment to keep the company going.

Marilyn: Alive, yes.

Jean: There is something that lives beyond us. There is the corporation, it is an entity; it should live. I think we are committed to that. Neither of us wants to see the company die on our death or retirement.

I asked them if there are times when one person has to win.

Jean: I don't feel that.

Marilyn: No, I don't feel that either. We each get what we want about half the time.

Jean: I think we try to integrate ourselves into the partnership and into the greater good of the operation. In terms of business decision making, we put the business first.

Marilyn: We both need this business. For all sorts of reasons— financial and psychological.

Jean: It would be sad not to have the business.

Marilyn: We need it to survive. That's it. I can't imagine myself looking for a traditional job.

Jean: There is tremendous psychological advantage to owning one's own business . . .

Marilyn: That's the push—above and beyond anything else. Wining is less important than keeping this company healthy.

Turning away from their relationship for a moment, I asked about the way the operation worked and how decisions are made within the organization. Marilyn responded quickly and with a laugh.

Marilyn: With a lot of input from the people, I'll tell you that! This is not a quiet group. We encouraged it, so we get what we encouraged.

Jean: Right. We might be bottom line, but everyone's always got more than their two cents worth!

Marilyn: And everybody knows everything. When we were having trouble last fall [with the Japan issue], we shared the financial picture with everybody. We have tended to do that throughout. So there is no big mystery. They can really understand what a profit is and why, after you pay the salaries, there's a whole lot more to pay, and what it really means to run a company. We've kept everyone involved, including the office manager. We give out monthly financial statements to everyone. I think it works.

Jean: It means involvement, commitment on the part of employees. They feel part of the picture, part of the reason for the results.

Marilyn: And the problem, when there is a problem. We also have each account manager run their own profit center. They are responsible. They see that commission is based on profits, so they know exactly why their commission is whatever it is. There is a lot of power distributed among the people.

Jean: And a lot of autonomy. They are paid on their net. They watch their expenses, so they are responsible through and through, for both income and outflow.

I knew both women had meetings stacked up that they needed to get to, so I asked my last question: "What have you gotten out of the last ten years?"

Jean: I trust myself a lot more. I think my own intuition and knowledge are strong enough, are good enough. That's a huge change. I wish women could jump right from being 11 years old to 40—40 is a wonderful age because you come into your own. There is great potential when you realize your own ability.

Marilyn: This business has done for us—at about the speed we have been able to assimilate—everything I have wanted.

Jean: Yes.

In a working paper for the Stone Center called "What Do We Mean By Relationship?" Jean Baker-Miller relates a conversation between two women, Beth and Ann. The two are discussing the news that Ann's friend, Emily, has just learned she has a serious illness. Ann feels terrible. Beth doesn't know Emily but is able to be supportive of Ann anyway. Baker-Miller describes their conversation as "a moment in a relationship between two people." She used their conversation to illustrate how "good things" are produced in a relationship. She described the "good things" this way:

1. Each person feels a greater sense of zest (vitality or energy).
2. Each person feels more able to act and does act.
3. Each person has a more accurate picture of her/himself and the other person(s).
4. Each person feels a greater sense of worth.
5. Each person feels more connected to the other person(s) and a greater motivation for connections with other people, beyond those in the specific relationship.[2]

It is from the thousands of such interchanges, the thousands of moments, that people have in the course of a relationship, that the good things (and the bad things) emerge. In her paper, Baker-Miller analyzed the conversation between Beth and Ann in detail. She found that there was a way of being with another person (or persons) that actually encouraged the experience of the good things. She described them as empathy, connection, and movement. Empathy is the ability to be in touch with another's feelings. When Jean says, "I could feel Marilyn's anguish" — relative to the Japan dilemma — she exhibits empathy, even in the presence of her own pain. Connection is the ability to fully hear and be responsive (which you hear when Jean and Marilyn echo one another), and movement is an interchange that goes back and forth and enables both parties to feel a sense of flow in the relationship.[3]

The interview with Jean and Marilyn was but "a moment in the relationship" between the two. But throughout the time spent with them, I felt their connection. They don't just *say* they hear one another, they actively *listen* to one another. I expect there are plenty of "good things" in their relationship that no doubt make themselves felt in their business!

SONIA MELARA
CommuniQue World Marketing, Inc.

The first time I met Sonia Melara we went to the horse races. I had been invited to join Sonia and five other San Franciscan entrepreneurs for a night at the races "with the women." It was an evening of female bonding. I don't think anyone won or lost more than $10 or $20 that night, but we consumed a lot of french fries and popcorn, speculated on the various names of the horses, laughed a lot, and generally had a great time.

I had met two of the other women previously, but did not know Sonia. Among my friends, I have something of a reputation for my high energy, but that night I encountered the embodiment of high energy. Sonia is a woman who doesn't have a moment to waste; she has mountains to climb and the intelligence to choose the best trail. I remember thinking what a terrific business partner she would make—smart, high powered, with the energy and ability to juggle many issues and responsibilities at once.

Now here she was six months later, appearing quite tranquil and still managing to accomplish three things at once. It was a Saturday morning, and Sonia had agreed to meet with me to talk about the *Hispanic Yellow Pages,* which she founded in 1984. "I know people say you must focus on one thing," she said as she made coffee, heated a fresh apricot pie in the microwave, and helped me settle into her kitchen with my tape recorder and questions. "I never learned that. I did learn that if you are running several things at once you learn to handle them."

The old saying, "If you want something done, ask a busy person," holds a kernel of truth. In addition to having been publisher of the *Hispanic Yellow Pages* and *El Mensajero,* a Spanish newspaper for northern California, she has served as the president of the San Francisco Parking and Traffic Commission, a director of the San Francisco Chamber of Commerce, the president of the San Francisco Hispanic Chamber of Commerce, and a director of Invest in America, an organization that encourages young people to learn about and consider ways to be involved with business as a career. And oh, by the way, she also has started a new company called CommuniQue World Marketing, Inc., a full-service firm providing strategic planning services to reach ethnic markets. Of course, she must also respond to the many requests and queries that are the privilege and burden of active, high-profile people. Sonia is a dynamo, and I wanted to understand the source of her drive.

I had spent time looking at several issues of the *Hispanic Yellow Pages.* It's a fun, practical publication. Well designed and easy to use, it seems less cluttered and busy than the *Yellow Pages* I am used to. Sonia's feelings for the importance of community are reflected in her publication. The cover of one edition of the *Hispanic Yellow Pages,* for example, is a child's drawing of North America and South America. Children appear on both continents, engaged in environmental clean-up activities. The drawing was the result of art competitions held among third- to sixth-grade students in the regions covered by the 16 editions of the *Yellow Pages.* Each region has its own cover. One theme of the competition was "My Environment—How Can I Contribute to Its Improvement?" Sonia is absolutely committed to community. In part, that is because she deeply cares about people in her community. But, in a kind of hard-nosed, practical way, she also is convinced that businesses that are a true part of the community they serve are more successful over the long term than those companies that give only cursory attention to their host communities.

It's not surprising then that inside the publication, in addition to the business listings (which are its main purpose), there is a section on community services. Here the reader can learn how to vote and apply for citizenship, find out about public transportation, and look up information on immigration resources. There are short health bulletins from the Red Cross, the American Cancer Society, and the American Diabetes Association. There is advice on earthquake preparation and response and a well-organized listing of community services, including everything from language classes, to child care to job services. Sonia described still another aspect of the *Yellow Pages* that I had missed.

In the front of the *Yellow Pages*, I placed a questionnaire people can fill out and send back. It provides the company with demographic information, but it also gives the user an opportunity to talk about what they like and don't like and provides a way to communicate. I got a letter from a mother who told me she uses the book as a magazine which she reads every night. [Not surprising in light of all the good information Sonia packed into it.] She lives in the Central Valley of California and works in the fields. She wrote "like a good Mexican mother I come home every night to prepare meals for my children and my husband. Afterwards it is so nice to sit quietly with a cup of coffee and the *Hispanic Yellow Pages* to read." Now I read a letter like that, and I know that if I have done nothing else in this world I have created something that has made a difference in someone's life.

Therein lies the power of Sonia Melara's drive. She is a woman with a mission: she is driven to make a difference and a contribution. She was trained as a social worker and had an entrepreneurial flair for solving social problems early on.

I always had a sense of responsibility for helping those who needed help, not one on one, but in a global sense. I joined groups and organizations which made a difference. In 1974 I was one of the founders of La Casa De Las Madres in San Francisco, a shelter for battered women. My mother hadn't been abused, and I didn't, at that time, know anyone who had been abused, but it was something that was needed. We needed to do it. I feel that whatever you do, there has to be a meaning to it. Money alone is not enough. I want money to be a by-product of what I do, but not the reason for what I do—that is clear to me.

To explain her own values, Sonia told me a story about another entrepreneur, Gwen Kaplan, founder of Ace Mailing, which is also based in San Francisco. Gwen, like Sonia, is a former recipient of the San Francisco Chamber of Commerce Entrepreneur of the Year Award.

Gwen was also a social worker, and she makes a point of hiring people who might not otherwise find employment—people with handicaps and language problems. Gwen and I both believe it is important to give opportunities to people who wouldn't make it if they didn't have jobs. What I usually hear from business owners is, "Hire the handicapped, it's cheap labor." My view is very different. I think, "We'll train them, and, as opportunity comes along, we move them along." I don't hire people to exploit them.

People as partners, not as instruments, is a keystone of Sonia's philosophy, both as a business owner and as a citizen. It is this philosophy that provides a foundation for so much of what Sonia achieves.

From 1982 to 1984 Sonia served as the National Director for Leadership for the Mexican-American Legal Defense and Education Fund. During that time, she traveled extensively and became aware of the interest among businesses to reach the growing Hispanic market. In Texas she saw a *Yellow Pages* and started to think about the feasibility of starting something similar in California. She had begun to have conversations with various people about her idea (including the Texas company) when, while riding a bus one day, she noticed a billboard proclaiming, "500,000 PEOPLE WANT YOU." It was an ad to businesses interested in reaching the Asian market. After meeting the founder of that company, she started the *Hispanic Yellow Pages* and joined with the *Asian Yellow Pages* to form Direct Language Inc., the largest second-language communications and publishing company in the United States. The *Hispanic Yellow Pages* eventually grew to include 100 employees; it covers 16 territories and has a circulation of over one million. Three primary markets rely on the *Hispanic Yellow Pages:* (1) people who only read Spanish, (2) people who are bilingual but prefer to read in Spanish, and (3) people who politically and sociologically identify themselves as Hispanic and use the *Yellow Pages* to reinforce that identity.

Mensajero, the newspaper Sonia helped establish, is another Spanish language publication. It serves northern California and provides Hispanics with news from their home countries. Quite simply, the mission of the *Hispanic Yellow Pages* and *Mensajero* is to reach the largest second-language market in the United States. It is fair to say that one of Sonia's goals is also to provide Hispanic people with a feeling of critical mass—an identity that emerges from connections people make to one another when they experience a shared culture.

Part of the reason I was able to catch Sonia at home on a Saturday morning was that she was in a brief lull between leaving one business and starting another. After seven years growing the *Hispanic Yellow Pages,* she is moving on and setting up another firm, CommuniQue. Involved as she has been with the business community, she came to understand the profound lack of knowledge most companies have about ethnic cultural markets as well as the needs of those cultures that are trying to sell products into broader markets. CommuniQue is, in a way, a bridge between cultures. By analyzing demographics, language, perceptions, and preferences, the new firm helps create appropriate and ethical marketing strategies for companies.

Even before the new census data started to come out, I could see that there was not a good market consulting company who knew how to look at different ethnic groups. Businesses which use the *Yellow Pages* publications to reach Hispanic and Asian markets too often just pull ethnic people out of human relations departments and put them in marketing. The assumption is if you can speak Spanish, or Chinese, or whatever you must be an expert on that culture and everyone in it. That kind of "attention" to ethnic markets is irresponsible, not to mention not very useful.

That's the problem with segmenting people; you begin to think of certain people as experts just because they look the part or speak the language. I got called to sit on a panel exploring the problems of Central American children a while ago. I asked why they had called me. I have no children. I have not studied the problems of Central American children. I have many skills, but I know very little about this subject. "You were recommended because you are Central American," I was told.

There are many frustrations for women who have been pegged in one way or another. Pushing back the boundaries of the boxes people try to put them in is, I suppose, a kind of exercise that keeps women aware of the dangers of labeling. Hopefully, such vigilance also reminds us not to box in others. Sonia's businesses are fueled with a desire to expand horizons and a determination to help others break out.

Sonia Melara grew up in El Salvador. She was 15 when she came to the United States. The firstborn in her family, I have a feeling that Sonia was a precocious and self-confident child. A high school teacher lives just up the street from her in the Sunset district of San Francisco. "She still thinks I'm one of the best students she had," says Sonia. And probably so. Her parents were divorced when she was an adolescent, and Sonia's response was to take on a leadership role in the family. "I always feel responsible for everything I do; if I create something, I must continue with it for better or worse."

As a publisher, Sonia has created products that help give Hispanics voice and identity. Sonia draws from her culture to feed her businesses. And her heritage, like Ruth Owades's roots in her father's bookstore, certainly influenced the path she has taken. About her drive, Sonia says:

> Remember I am from a Latin American country, a developing country where if people don't work, they don't eat. There is no such thing as welfare. Everyone has to strive for the next meal. Coming from that environment, you learn that nothing is backing you; you have to take care of yourself. You always have a sense of no backdrop. You can't fail. That survivalist instinct is always there. My mother reinforced traditional values—you have to get married, you have to have children—but she also stressed that you have to be able to take care of yourself.

For the most part, Sonia listened to her mother. She is married, has no kids, and does take care of herself!

> I grew emotionally in the course of starting the *Hispanic Yellow Pages*. I was experiencing so much joy that I often felt nothing could stand in my way. My self-esteem grew. I have always felt pretty confident, but, when my husband looks back, he tells me I am more positive, happier, more fun to be around. He has been very supportive. But, I think this all came from within me in the process of the business.

Sonia's businesses have been directly connected to her culture. The fact that she is a Hispanic woman is significant to her products, to her ways of managing, and to her persona. But I also became aware of how much American culture we share: education, feminism, urban sophistication, and the excitement of being in the heart of change at an important moment in history. Sonia and I have friends, history, and values in common. These things lend a sense of shared experience and excitement to the camaraderie I feel with her.

Around San Francisco, Sonia is known as "a shaker and a mover," not as a Hispanic woman—although she is absolutely that, too. She has found ways to integrate her cultures—Central American and American—her languages—Spanish and English—and her family, friends, and business colleagues. Her comfort with the two cultures gives her confidence as well as access to knowledge, perspective, and opportunity. Not everyone is able to do that. Many entrepreneurs submerge their culture and heritage altogether; others simply ignore the diversity of our society and in that way limit themselves and their businesses. Sonia succeeds in integrating her work and her culture, and this is part of what gives her texture, strength, and a particular edge in her businesses.

EDITH GORTER
Thomas C. Gorter Motor Express

Two men stood on the warehouse dock. It was early. One grumbled to the other, "I don't know what we are here for. These truckers are always late." The man beside him looked at his watch and said, "Oh, no, Gorter's got this one, it'll be early." "No way," the first one insisted. "Okay, I'll bet you a dollar a minute," said the the other. The bet was accepted. At 8.45 A.M., 15 minutes early, the Gorter Express truck pulled up. "I told you so!" said the man who had been willing to gamble on Gorter. Smiling, he collected his $15.

Edith Cole Gorter was trained as a dress designer at the University of Chicago. Her grandmother had been a French seamstress, and her mother taught Edith to sew before she could read. "I was always getting into trouble for taking quilt pieces; I made dolls' clothes with anything I could get my hands on." She never envisioned herself as the head of a trucking company.

Edith became the owner of Gorter Motor Express, located in Grand Rapids, Michigan, pretty much by default. Ben Gorter started his company in 1910 with a horse and wagon. It is a company with a proud tradition. Early on, he showed himself to be a man on the cutting edge of transportation. He had a fondness for motorcycles and bought one of the first to come out. Later, he was also one of the first to purchase a two-piece truck—a 1936 Studebaker, the upscale model of the times. A photo of that fancy truck hangs on the wall in Edith's office. Ben Gorter ran the company until 1958 when he sold the operation to his sons, Robert and Tom, Edith's husband.

Robert ran the company, and Tom drove trucks. In 1972 when Robert suffered a heart attack and died, there was no one who could run the company. Tom had been a truck driver and had little understanding of, and no interest in, the business operation. He was a driver, a good one, and assumed he would close the company and get a job driving for another company.

Money was tight. Robert Gorter had not been well for some years prior to his death. Under his management, the business had declined and when he died, the company was serving just one client. Edith could see that the situation was perilous; financially, the company (and her family's income) was in jeopardy. Edith loved her house and didn't want to lose it. She was determined that her three daughters would be able to go to college. She decided to take over the business. "I had to do it. I didn't know what else to do. Everyone told me I couldn't run a trucking company, but I thought, 'You just watch me!'"

As soon as I arrived at the Gorter Express Company, Edith offered me a cup of coffee. I went with her to the lunchroom, and we came upon one of the truck drivers washing dishes and cleaning up the small kitchen. The room was immaculate. The driver was good-natured and welcoming, and for a minute I forgot I was in a company that is part of the male-dominated trucking industry. The atmosphere was comfortable and informal, yet an air of respectfulness prevailed. I was pretty sure I would see no calendar girl pictures hanging on the garage walls and that I wouldn't overhear any jokes I might find offensive.

We drank coffee, and I listened to Edith and the driver, Garry Prins, share stories and joke about his time with the company. Then she gave me a tour of the truck yard. First, we went to the garage where the tractors are kept. She invited me to climb into their newest—a huge, satiny, red machine with a 425 horsepower Caterpillar engine that is expected to last for more than one million miles (our cars should be so good!). The cab was a driver's delight. It is completely padded to muffle noise and fitted with a control panel and stereo equipment that makes it seem like a cross between a recording studio and an airplane cockpit. The cab itself was as shipshape as any well-cared-for yacht. Behind the driver's seat was a twin-sized sleeping area that looked inviting. Garry opened the hood and showed me the gleaming chrome fittings of the engine. I could see how, sitting up in the cab, you would feel a tremendous sense of power. I'm pretty sure I wouldn't want to drive for three million miles (the distance two of Edith's drivers have achieved), but I could imagine, for a moment, the pleasure of being (with apologies to Roger Miller) "Queen of the Road" for just a little while.

Garry has had 14 years of accident-free driving while working for Edith. They obviously respect and admire one another. "The drivers represent me. I often tell them that without them I would be nothing," she said. "And I tell others the same. I can sell snow to an Eskimo, but if we don't have someone to deliver it, it doesn't matter." Edith's rapport with her drivers is a key element of her success with the trucking company. "The drivers are professional and a joy to watch at work," she mused. "They make it look so easy."

She may be dependent on the drivers, but she knows her business.

> I can't fix the engines [having seen them, I imagine only a well-educated engineer could], but, when someone calls and has a problem, I can usually diagnose what's wrong. One time, a driver called in with a problem, and I asked, "What's it doing?" "It's not running," he said. "What do you mean, 'It's not running?'" I pressed. I asked a few more questions. Because it was a 5 and 2 transmission, you go from the low side to the high side. But, because of the way they are engineered, in cold weather they sometimes ice up and you can't shift from one side to the other. You just have to be patient. So when he said he couldn't shift out of low gear, and I knew how cold it was there, I had a pretty good idea what was wrong. "You have ice in the transmission," I told him. "If you just drive it slowly, it will melt." "Oh no, no," he said, "it's something terrible." "Okay," I said, and handed the phone to the mechanic who told him that he had ice in the transmission and explained, just as I had, how to thaw it.

Gorter Express delivered bus seats to General Motors from 1936 to 1987, until GM stopped manufacturing buses. For the most part, Gorter Express now services the Michigan furniture industry. From the one client, two trucks, one tractor, and two trailers she had when she took over the business, Edith has grown the company to include many hundreds of clients and $1.8 million worth of rolling stock. Her trucks carry office furniture (and a few other commodities) from Michigan factories to businesses all over America. Westinghouse Office Systems, Irwin Seating Company, and Fleetwood Furniture, for example, all ship their products across the country via Gorter Express. With 72 units in operation—some trucks being loaded, others being unloaded, some enroute—she is dependent on her drivers to deliver those goods on time (if not early!), safely, and with respect and courtesy for the customers.

When Edith took over the trucking company, she wasn't exactly a newcomer to business. For the previous six years, she had managed a fabric shop in Grand Rapids.

I loved that—all those beautiful fabrics. But business is business; you're supposed to make money. For about a year and a half, I managed the fabric shop and ran the trucking business. And though it was difficult, I discovered that I had been around the trucking company so long I had absorbed a lot of knowledge about the business. And I had learned to be good with customers. Customers from the fabric shop continued to call me for two or three years after I left, asking me advice. That's what you do for people—you respond to them and maintain relationships because that's what makes them come back, whether it's silk or freight. When I finally left the fabric shop, I missed it—all those beautiful colors and fabrics: silks, camel's hair, lamb's wool, and cashmere. But I knew that I had to focus, to concentrate on learning and growing the trucking business if I was going to have any chance of saving it.

By May of 1974 I had contract bids out to three companies. I won two of the bids. Then I had to figure out how to deliver on my promises. I didn't have any money, and I needed equipment desperately. But even with the contracts in my hand, banks were reluctant to loan money to me. Finally, I got a loan for $5000 with my house as collateral. Still, they required my husband's signature before they would grant the loan. A while later, I needed more equipment and went back to the bank requesting $50,000. They were no help then. The banker I dealt with said, "Edith, we'll give you money for a tractor, but we don't see why you need all those trailers." Well, of course, you need at least three trailers per tractor. Trailers are constantly being loaded and unloaded, some are holding cargo and are ready to go, while others are on the road. A conservative ratio for even a small company to do business properly is three trailers to one tractor. They didn't understand my business and were not helping me. Finally, a friend of mine, a farmer who had retired and started a second, very successful business, loaned me the money to buy more equipment. And later, the man who owned a local General Motors dealership helped me buy a tractor when the banks once more refused to loan me money. Without the help of good people like that, I don't know what I would have done.

I have a feeling she would have figured out something. Edith Gorter is a resourceful and determined woman. While she was growing a trucking company, she was also growing a family. Edith has three daughters, Deborah, Lori, and Leslie.

I went to work [in the fabric store] as soon as Leslie, the youngest, was in kindergarten. I gave them my presence and stability for the first five years. One of my girls once said to me, "You were never a normal mother." I laughed, because she was probably right. I really didn't like cooking and cleaning, though my home was always spotless. All my housework was done by 8:00 in the morning, and, from then on, I did what I wanted to do.

I asked Lori, who works with her mother, how life changed when her mother took over the business.

It didn't change. I was 16 when my mother took over the trucking company, and Leslie is eight years younger than I. I had started cooking and cleaning and taking care of Leslie when Mom started at the fabric store. Deborah was already in college. When she went to work at the fabric store, times were tough. That's a stronger memory than the first few years of the business. And what I remember most of all are the Christmases. She always went all out at Christmas.

From a distance, at least, Edith Gorter's daughters appear to be smart, feisty, independent women. Edith explained:

My girls were allowed to do anything they wanted to do, as long as it didn't cause permanent damage. You see, I wanted these things for them: self-confidence, self-reliance, and a sense of humor. I had secretaries who remarked on how often the girls called me. I think they thought it was strange that I always made time for those calls. But no matter how busy I was, I did always have time for them...all this talk about quality time...that's silly. As long as you love your kids and listen to them—you have to listen to them—they'll be okay.

When they were in their teens, we had many arguments. They'd ask me, "What should I do about this or that?" And I'd look at their options with them and then push them to make their own choices. They didn't always like that, but I trusted them.

I checked back with Lori to see if she thought her mother's ways had worked. I asked her if her life was different from or harder than her friends' lives.

My best friend's mother was a doctor. And Alice had five little kids under her to take care of, while I only had Leslie. Alice and I mothered and cleaned house. The majority of my friends' mothers worked. So it didn't seem odd. And Mom has always been there for us. Whether she was physically home during the day or not, we always knew we could count on her.

Lori has worked with her mother in the trucking company for 11 years. After graduating from high school, she trained to be a nurse and worked in that profession for several years until she burned out. "I used to work 15 or 16 days in a row at the hospital and then would have 2 days off. I worked overtime every night—there were no eight-hour days. In one two-year period, I had two real weekends off." She eventually left the hospital and went to work part-time for a doctor. I asked her what got her started in the trucking company. "She needed help," was the reply.

At first I only came on Wednesday and Thursday mornings and continued to work at the doctor's office one day a week. My son, Robbie, was two years old then. But soon, that wasn't enough because the company was growing and Mom did everything—the phone, the scheduling, the freight bills, the customers. It got to the point that it was too much for her to do alone. So I quit the doctor's office and worked here full-time. Before too long, we needed more help. I called my sister, Leslie (who was working at a company on the other side of town), and urged her to talk to Mom about coming to work with me. For five years the three of us worked together.

I asked Lori if she thought she could run the business. She would only say, "In the last six months I have learned the most about this business." But, while we were talking, one of the drivers interrupted us to ask her a question. I noticed that her voice changed as she spoke with him. She answered his questions with assurance and authority. Whatever her own doubts, I suspect Lori has her mother's ability to rise to the occasion.

Leslie is no longer working in the business. She lives in North Carolina with her husband, an engineer for the NASCAR Winston

Cup Racing Team. She is a scorekeeper for another racing team. Edith says of Leslie, "She always knew what she wanted to do." Leslie was interested in cars and racing from an early age. Her father taught her about engines, and when she was 15 she bought her first car. Edith laughs when she remembers that. "She went to my suppliers [for the trucks] and got a new battery and a radiator and put those in the car herself. Then she wired it for stereo."

The oldest daughter, Deborah, lives in Washington State on a 42-foot sailboat. Trained in agricultural management, she worked for a time on a ranch in Colorado (a ranch with half a million head of cattle, that is). There she taught bovine artificial insemination to farmers. Her mother remembers that "before starting that job she returned home to appropriate a pair of her father's old coveralls—they had holes and old stains. Deborah knew she couldn't go there wearing new ones." In addition to the classes she taught, Deborah "dehorned and branded cattle, vaccinated, and delivered calves." Deborah said to me, "I grew up with a mother who told me I could do anything I wanted to, so I did!" Later, this grounding in the real work of agricultural management gained her a job with Farm Credit Services of Mid-Michigan, and, after several promotions, she eventually landed in their internal audit division in St. Paul, Minnesota. But she got tired of the excessive travel associated with that job and left. Now she is a financial analyst in the Development Loan Fund of the Business Finance Unit of the Washington State Department of Community Development. In this role, Deborah Gorter oversees loan programs for start-up businesses and economic development. But plans are in the works to take time out for an around-the-world cruise in the boat she now lives on.

I commented on the obvious to Edith. She has a team of daughters with a good mix of talents to take over the business. Would they? Edith was unsure, but, when I asked Lori, she said she'd probably give it a shot. And Edith clearly does hope her other daughters will want to be involved. "Debbie has the financial background that would be great to have here, and Leslie has mentioned that she'd like to open a branch of Gorter's in North Carolina." And Deborah herself said, "I'm well aware of the blood, sweat, and tears my mother has put into the business and my grandfather before her. I'm not sure when or how, but I'm not willing to give up the family legacy." But Edith is still young and vital. As Lori remarked, "You have to understand, that by the time she is ready to retire, her daughters will be old—we may just have to pass the company on to the fourth generation," who happen to be Lori's daughter and son. Edith, in fact, told me about the day she walked around the property with her grandson, Robbie. He wanted her to explain everything that she was doing. Finally, he said, "Well, Gram, if that's really what you want me to do, I'll do it, but I really wanted to be a policeman." Maybe Julie, her ten-year-old granddaughter will take over the reins in time. No doubt she will at least have the option.

Whoever takes over the company will take on an impressive enterprise. In the last 20 years, Edith has grown the company from a small local trucker to an interstate carrier that services 48 states. And she's not done yet. When describing her mother, Lori said, "Mother has a plan for everything. She has backup plans, too. She may not always be aware of her backup plans, but she has them. Even holiday dinners are thoroughly planned out." I remembered Lori's comments when Edith brought out her building blueprints to show me.

It is a multiphase plan that she started 12 years ago and probably won't finish for another 5 or 6 years.

> For awhile, I ran the office from the house. Then we rented offices. We rented a vacant lot to keep the trailers on, kept the tractors at the old homestead, and rented a gas station where we stored fuel. It was a real patchwork and not a good situation. And I kept adding equipment. Finally, I said, "I just can't go on like this." So I looked for property. When I found this site, everyone told me I was crazy—I was told I was crazy a lot—there were only two other companies here then and nothing else in sight. But it was just a mile from the highway, and I thought it was a good buy. So, in spite of advice to the contrary, I bought seven acres for $9000. Now the property around here is going for $45,000 to $70,000 an acre!

Her property holds office space, a huge garage for the tractors and equipment, and trailer yards. She pointed to another building on the blueprint and said, "This is the next phase. I am going to build a warehouse. That's the next part of the business I want to develop." Remembering the difficulty she had with banks over the years, I asked how she managed to get the funding for such an ambitious undertaking.

> It was very hard, but I just kept pushing. Everyone said you've gotta do this or you've gotta do that, or don't do this, don't do that. I always listen to people, but finally you reach the point when you just have to plug your ears and push ahead. But getting funding was hard. I slowed down on the warehouse plans because I needed to stop for awhile and catch my breath.

It's hard to believe this woman ever stops long enough to
catch her breath. She is a former president of the Michigan Trucking
Association and was also on their board of governors. She has served
on the Motor Carrier Advisory Board and is a frequent speaker
for the trucking industry. Yet, the day we met, she was wearing an
elegant chartreuse suit she had designed and sewn herself. Smack in
the middle of one of the most traditional male industries in America,
Edith Gorter has held on to her own sense of self and has grown a
business that has adapted to her needs and her family's needs.

LEEANN CHIN
Leeann Chin, Inc.

Spinach with plum sauce, lotus root salad, sesame chicken with fun see, Kung pao pork, Mandarin beef, clams with white radishes—all around me, tempting dishes were being served to the crowd at Leeann Chin's Restaurant in Minneapolis. It was noon at midweek. Both regular customers and newcomers were sampling the fare at her third largest restaurant. It is beautiful; set in the entrance to Minneapolis's International Centre, this restaurant looks more like a chic New York eatery than a traditional Chinese restaurant. Soft earth tones and natural textures dominate. Prints and artifacts from Leeann Chin's private collection and trips to China distinguish the walls. Spacious and elegant, the restaurant is arranged in four tiers, which makes it seem more intimate and smaller than it actually is. The restaurant has a capacity of 150, and this day it appeared that all seats were continually filled. And no wonder. Leeann Chin—chef, author, teacher, creator, and businessowner—has spent many years learning what her customers like, how to satisfy them, and how to ensure that they keep coming back. She said, "You have to understand customers' tastes. Even in this city—so small from one part to another—our customers' tastes are a little different. And customers travel more, they are more health conscious, and they have more experiences with Chinese food. We have to keep up with their learning."

She must be keeping up with them. In the last ten years, she has built a business that includes three large restaurants and ten carryouts, all in Minneapolis/St. Paul. Revenues for the restaurants are in excess of $17 million a year. She has also taught over 4000 students the intricacies of Chinese cuisine, published two cookbooks, and now takes groups of interested travelers on "eating tours" in China. But this is a light schedule compared to what she is used to.

Leeann's story is an epic of perseverance, resourcefulness, and rebellion. Within her warm public persona, lies the heart and courage of a rebel. To survive against all odds, she has spent a lifetime resisting the constricting pressures of family, investors, and tradition.

In 1956 Leeann Chin came to the United States with her husband after living for five years in Hong Kong, where they had gone from Canton, China. She was a young wife with a child and a husband from one of China's elite families.

> We left Hong Kong because there were so many people there. It was hard to see a good future for our children. We were like people without a country. We had very little money then.... The way I was brought up, women don't work. You are taught to be a good wife and mother and to obey your husband and mother-in-law. You are a slave and you don't think anything of it. From generation to generation, whether you are rich or poor, you keep doing the same thing your mother and grandmother have taught you—that men have the authority and men are smarter and men have ability and men can do this and men can do that. Women could only stay home with family, all the time. We never dated, we just stayed home. We had to learn to cook and sew and embroider.

Those learned skills were to stand her in good stead later. Leeann and her husband came to America to get a good education for their children. When they finally arrived, the young couple could not speak English. Everything in America was different and hard.

> I started sewing at home, that's how I made money. I did dressmaking. I sewed for a long, long time, day and night, day and night, seven days and seven nights for many, many years. When I had to go to a PTA meeting or take the children to the doctor, I would stay up all night to sew and get my work done so I could take them.

In this way, Leeann helped see her family through the early years in Minneapolis. Her husband, who had been part of the highest social class in China, had a job as a technician at the University of Minnesota, working in the photo lab. Although the work was substantially beneath what he had done in China, it provided income and enabled him to be associated with an academic world—the setting he was most familiar with from his days in China. His English had not improved very much, and this shut him out of most of the opportunities the new country might have offered. Lack of facility with the language and difficulty adjusting to the realities of a different social status prevented him from becoming comfortable with American culture. He also was not happy that his wife was working. Good Chinese women didn't do that. And Leeann worked more and more.

She began teaching classes in Chinese cooking at what was then the General Mills Creative Learning Center—14 classes a week. "That's where I met so many people and learned so much," she said. "After every class you sit down to eat and talk; even when I was teaching I learned so much. And I was making good money, too. It was nice." The relationship in her traditionally arranged marriage began to shift. Leeann was assimilating, exercising her ability, and finding her place in the adopted country.

This young wife and mother, raised to be a good, traditional Chinese woman, was making money, gaining confidence, and feeling increasing competence in her new country. Like a snake crawling out of an old skin, Leeann began to grow out of her traditional persona while developing a new one—one that may have suited her better even when she was a little girl. Listening to Leeann, I had the sense that the role of the quiet, passive, and obedient Chinese daughter and wife would have been hard for her, even if life had unfolded in China rather than the United States. I asked her about the roots of her strength and growing independence.

From the time I was very little, I didn't want people to say bad things about me. I remember when my father told me, "You talk too much. Girls don't do that." And my mother said, "You are such a tomboy. I bet you never can sew." Then when I was eleven, my father's grocery store in Canton got very busy, and he needed me to help him. No matter what I did, he never said, "What a good job." He just said, "You can do better than that." All the time, he would tell me, "You can do better than that." I didn't know I knew how to do anything. So I just kept learning and learning. At the same time, outsiders would compliment me. I was very fast with the abacus, and people came from all around to watch me tally grocery purchases and other things connected to money in my father's store. This made my mother very angry. She would tell me I was the most stubborn person on earth and I didn't know how to dress, I didn't know anything. I was supposed to be a good little girl and sit back and not notice any of the things people said to me. I didn't dare talk back to her, but I determined to learn everything I could and show people what I could do. And those compliments and the attention helped me to know I could do something. Then I wanted to learn everything so I could do anything I wanted.

Leeann uses the words "learn," "learning," and "to learn" often. In her life, learning has been the key to claiming her own abilities and doing whatever she wanted. If knowledge is power, Leeann Chin has a great warehouse of the stuff! Just as she mastered the intricacies of the abacus in her father's grocery store, she mastered the sometimes complex ways of her new culture—and, in the process, she started her business.

By 1980, more than 4000 students had gone through her cooking classes and she had a thriving catering business. The Minneapolis business press began to take note of this young dynamo, and former students and friends encouraged her to open a restaurant. With a growing reputation, a small savings of her own, and five investors (including Sean Connery) who each came up with $25,000, she opened her first restaurant. It seated 80 people. Thus began an odyssey that few people and few businesses could have survived.

Over the next seven years, Leeann bought out those original investors, expanded her original restaurant, opened two more, and then sold her business to General Mills. Three years after selling the company to General Mills, she bought it back from them. Now she is the owner, with a compelling vision: to alter the reality of restaurant life for her employees.

For many, many years the image of working at a Chinese restaurant (and most American restaurants) has been hard work, low pay, long hours, and no benefits. I am changing that. Our managers do not work seven days a week or 15-hour days. We employ enough people that we do not need to do that. Sure it cuts into our profitability now. But it's one of the reasons my business is successful. We are different, we are not running this in the traditional ways. We are training people and promoting them. I travel, in this country and in China, to develop new recipes and learn about new foods and changes in customer taste. I take our people on some of those trips with me. You can't just tell people things and expect them to learn, you have to show them. They have to see; they have to have direct experience. That costs money. But those people are getting better over time. As they improve and as we get more efficient, we will get more profitable. It's a long-term investment in people and the company. You can't provide opportunity, offer good jobs, improve your company, *and* reach maximum profitability quickly. But it will all come.

Such is the sophistication and confidence that Leeann Chin has garnered over the last ten years. Leeann's odyssey with her restaurant began almost ten years ago, shortly after her first investors became involved.

They weren't comfortable with the way I ran the business. They kept telling me, "You only want a little restaurant, we want more." They acted as though they could read my mind and thought that's all I wanted. They didn't bother to ask me or talk to me about what I wanted for my future. Then they hired a manager, but I didn't like the way he did things. They said I didn't like to delegate. I told them I couldn't just let him go ahead and do things I felt were wrong. Finally, we agreed I would buy them out. So I went to the bank, borrowed the money to pay them off, and expanded the restaurant.

Then opportunities opened up. People in the community encouraged me to open a second restaurant. By now I had many people who I had taught in the restaurant. They were doing a good job, and it was time for many of them to be promoted. The way I saw it, I could expand the business and give more people opportunities at the same time. So I said, "Why not?" The second restaurant was even larger than the first. It was also very successful, so I opened another restaurant. This one was smaller, a carryout restaurant, and that did well, too.

Then I got scared. Suddenly I didn't have confidence that I could handle this. I hadn't done such a big business before. I didn't trust myself, and everybody told me, "You can't do it. Don't do it." My husband was constantly after me to give it up.

Everyone experiences crises of confidence from time to time. Those are the times we need someone to say, "Atta girl, you can do it!" Maybe, in line with sociologist Bob Schrank's idea for a tape of applause, we need a national "ATTA GIRL" line—an 800 number anyone can call to get positive reinforcement, which is sometimes harder to find than kangaroos in Kansas. By the time Leeann started to feel scared, she had been hearing "you can't" for most of her life. At the point she was beginning to show "she could," it must have seemed almost too good to be true. Small wonder she began to look for help. It was a perfectly sensible response. But, in this case, normal entrepreneurial anxiety over growth issues was viewed as evidence that she couldn't handle the business. Instead of reinforcing her ability, the people around her reinforced her fears.

So I began to look for a partner—someone with good business experience who also knew the food business. But no one seemed right. Finally, a businessman who's been helpful to me many times over the years suggested we talk to General Mills. The idea was that they would invest and offer some management help and I would continue to be the creator in the company. It seemed like a good idea. At that time, the business was doing just about $5 million a year in revenues. He arranged the talks between General Mills and me, and we negotiated a three-year contract. That was in 1985. At first it was wonderful. They made me president of my own division. I got a lot of support, they did good publicity, they helped me a lot. But, after six months, they moved me from the responsibility of the consumer group, which had actually bought my company, to the restaurant group. I think it was just internal company politics. But once the new group got involved, they hardly paid attention to the restaurants. Every now and then, they would send someone over and we'd get new orders: "Do this. Do that." Then they'd ignore us for a long time. Eventually someone else would show up with with new orders. And all the time they were undermining what I was trying to teach employees. But they were very polite. It wasn't until later that I understood they were telling employees not to listen to me. They actually fired a few employees who continued to insist on following methods of cooking and service which I had taught them. I thought if I had the title of president I was in charge. But it doesn't work that way! Things got progressively worse. Nevertheless, I got the chairman's award for outstanding performance at General Mills. Six months later, they began to talk about selling the company—or at least not putting more time or money into it. Rumors started to fly. A few people came forward with various deals to offer, but nothing looked good. At that point, I thought of my children and my grandchildren, and I realized if I didn't do something the whole thing would die and there would be nothing left. So I negotiated with General Mills to sell the business back to me. Fortunately, I had good standing in the business community by this time and a good reputation with the bank. I was able to get a loan and an investor, and, a short time later, the business was mine again. That was in 1988. Now I own three large Chinese restaurants and ten carryout restaurants.

Leeann's banking transactions sound remarkably easy compared to some of the stories told by other women. I believe that is explained in part by the standing she developed in her community and by the support she received from several professionals familiar with her drive and ability. However, she has endured no small amount of frustration in some of those banking relationships. "They never looked at me when they talked with me," she said. "They would look at the controller or my lawyer. I was paying those people, but they wouldn't look at me." She described talking with one banker who constantly asked questions, challenging her knowledge. "He would ask me a question and then go to work it out on the calculator, but I already had the number figured in my head. He didn't know I spent all those years learning on the abacus." Another banker tried to make her feel uncomfortable about her age. "How old are you?" he asked. "He knew how old I was," she told me. "He was really saying, 'You're 47 and you want to start a business? You're too old.'" Nonetheless, she proved him wrong.

No doubt Leeann learned a great deal in the three years her company was under the aegis of General Mills. It is impossible to say what might have happened had she not given in to her fears and found the resources to help her grow the company some other way. But there is no question that this smart, gutsy lady was able to do whatever she needed to do to keep her company alive—and growing. However, a few strategic "atta girls" from friends, family, or colleagues might have saved her three years of aggravation, caught in a web of corporate politics.

Leeann Chin now employs over 600 people. Clearly, that fact is no longer daunting to her. Now, in fact, she talks about adding more restaurants to the 13 already in Minneapolis/St. Paul and possibly expanding to other cities.

I asked her to talk about the challenges of managing. Instead, she talked about her children. "I have five children. You teach them to be independent and responsible. That was a training ground for managing." Training is a big part of Leeann Chin, Inc.

I really do delegate. I don't delegate until I know it's someone I can delegate to—I am careful. At the same time, you have to let people make mistakes; otherwise, they never learn. You know, even in the very beginning, when those first investors told me I didn't delegate, they were wrong. When the first little restaurant opened, I was doing all the cooking, handling three woks at a time. But, within just six months, I had trained cooks so that I rarely cooked after that. You have to give people time to learn. In more traditional companies, if you don't know what you are doing, you are fired. Here, if we hire someone and they need to learn something, we train them—we give them time to learn, we show them. Our director of quality control and training is a woman who has been with me since I started the catering business. There is still lots of teaching to be done. I want to help my employees learn and develop. As they grow, I know they will understand the business and how to run it most profitably.

Leeann says of her managers:

In this business, there is no room for anybody who doesn't have a good heart. It's a hard business. Employees work hard. It's not the kind of job that is easy. But it can be fulfilling if you enjoy the work. So I want people who are very understanding of people, who know how hard the work is and can have patience. Most of my managers are like that.

Because she had reminded me of her children I asked how they had all turned out. Remember, she had moved to save the company when she realized the legacy she was building for her children and grandchildren might be slipping away. All five children did go to college and graduate school, she told me proudly. The oldest, a daughter, is a lawyer outside of Boston, Massachusetts; her son is a professor at DePaul University in Chicago; her middle daughter, Laura, is vice-president in charge of marketing and advertising for Leeann Chin, Inc.; the next daughter is a doctor—a real doctor—as she put it; and the youngest daughter is involved with film promotion for Disney Studios in Los Angeles.

I don't think the fact that I worked was a problem. I always had the flexibility in my work to take care of them. And I've always helped them when I could. They grew up understanding they had to work hard; they could see that when I worked hard, I got what I wanted. But I could not have started the restaurant ten years earlier. I would not have made it. In this business, the restaurant has to come first. But my kids came first. Something would have suffered. My youngest was 16 when I first started the restaurant in 1980. I'm glad I waited. Up until that time, I was still teaching cooking classes and catering.

Leeann's father died in 1959, not long after the Communist takeover. Her mother recently came to this country and now lives with the daughter she scolded so frequently for her stubbornness. A sister works for her. "Women hold up half the sky," according to a piece of wisdom once popular in China. It seems that Leeann shoulders a little more than that.

Now that Leeann seems comfortable with the responsibilities of a large, growing business, I asked her what else she wanted to accomplish. Expansion is on her mind, as is achieving a larger margin of profitability. She believes these goals will be accomplished as she achieves her vision of a nontraditional company—a company in which people are respected and well trained. Leeann's vision of success is in no small part the dream she has sought all her life: respect, knowledge, and growth. Her achievements, the distance she has come—both geographically and psychologically—are extraordinary. The journey, of course, has exacted costs.

Whenever cultures rub against one another, some things are lost and others are gained. The needs of a traditional marriage and a nontraditional woman conflict. Leeann shed the skin of the obedient wife to help her family survive in a new country. She learned a new language, the culture of business, and the culture of independence; however, while she was gaining, her husband was experiencing loss—loss of status, loss of ease and place in a culture, and loss of profession. It has been a difficult shift for both of them.

I remarked that I thought she had exhibited great bravery over the years. "Brave?" she said. "You think that because I am never afraid to lose things. Material things can always be replaced. If I lose money, I'll make it again tomorrow." Clearly, this philosophy has given her courage to make great leaps across yawning chasms. For the sake of her children's education and her own realization of self, she was—no doubt, still is—willing to take great risks. Leeann Chin seems very calm, very self-assured. It is as though she is absolutely clear that what she has accomplished so far is a prelude to what is coming.

So, there you have it—seven different women, six different businesses, six different stories. But these women have much in common. Each of them has created an enterprise in a way that suits her individual needs and lifestyle. Each has found a way to integrate her values into her business. Each is making money and, to greater or lesser extents, doing good and having fun.

Is it important whether or not any of the businesses described here make it to the *Fortune* 500? Does it matter if any of the women make the *Forbes* "list of billionaires?" And what if they do? What is the value of the self-confidence they each claim, the sense of inner power and competence they each have achieved in the course of growing a business? Where will it all lead?

HERSTORY

Although it may seem like a contemporary phenomenon, the fact is that women have been starting businesses for a very long time. Here is an honor roll of some of those ordinary women who led the way.

Barbara Uttman (1514–1575) was the founder of the lace industry in Saxony. She opened a school in her home; this marked the beginning of a profitable industry throughout Germany. By 1561, lacemaking was an active trade that employed 30,000 people throughout Germany.

Mary Goddard (1736–1816) became the publisher and manager of Baltimore's first newspaper. Her press printed the Declaration of Independence.

Charlotte Guest (1812–1895) inherited and managed the Dowlais Iron Company. She successfully averted a strike by dealing reasonably with the workers' demands.

Madam C. J. Walker (1867–1931) founded the Walker College of Hair Culture and Walker Manufacturing Company. She offered an alternative to domestic service and trained hundreds of women to take control of their destiny. She was the first black woman in America to become a millionaire.

THE VIEW
AHEAD

SEVEN

Tsunami

Tsunami is a great sea wave. Tsunamis are created by submarine earth movements such as earthquakes and volcanoes. You may not be able to see it at first, but it rumbles up from the ocean and arrives on land in the form of a huge tidal wave. Like a tsunami, women are rumbling up from their quiet invisibility and making their mark on the land. Like a tsunami, we are coming.

A QUIZ

The following quiz will test your knowledge of women-owned businesses:

1. Women own how many businesses in the United States?
   a. 2 million
   b. more than 5 million
   c. 6.3 million
   d. over 10 million

2. In 1987 what percentage of businesses were owned by women?
   a. 5 percent
   b. 10 percent
   c. 30 percent
   d. 50 percent

3. What were the total receipts collected by women-owned business in 1987?
   a. $746 million
   b. $278 billion
   c. $477 billion
   d. $965 billion

4. Women-owned businesses contributed how much in federal tax dollars in 1988?
   a. $465 million
   b. $900 million
   c. $3 billion
   d. $37 billion

5. What percentage of government contracts go to women-owned businesses?
   a. 1 percent
   b. 5 percent
   c. 10 percent
   d. 25 percent

According to a study released by the Foundation for the National Association of Women Business Owners in 1992, there are over five million women-owned businesses in the United States. Imagine if those women stood side by side across the country; one woman standing every three feet could span the continent. You could empty the country of Norway, population 4.2 million, and replace the citizenry with all those women who own businesses. That's a lot of women. So what do business reporters, business professors, investors, and others who ought to know better mean when they say they can't find women who own businesses? (The answer to number 1 is b; you receive 5 points if you got it right.)

Maybe these people don't read the news. After all, the *Wall Street Journal,* the *New York Times, Business Week, Nation's Business,* and *Fortune* all reported the staggering jump in the number of businesses owned by women. In 1972 less than 5 percent of all business owners were women. In 1987—less than 20 years later—the figure was over 30 percent. And the news raises some juicy questions for further investigation: Where did those women come from? How many represent exiles from corporate America? What kind of brain drain does that imply for the *Fortune* 500? More importantly, what does this activity foretell regarding the future of our social institutions? (The answer to number 2 is c; you receive 5 points if you got it right.)

Now think about the money those businesses represent. In 1987, according to the *1987 Economic Census—Summary of Findings on Women Owned Businesses,* there were four-plus million businesses that accounted for over $477 billion in gross receipts, which represents the combined amount of all proprietorships, partnerships, subchapter s corporations, and regular corporations. (The answer to number 3 is c; you receive 5 points if you got it right.)

What would happen if those women owners coalesced into a political party? Which politicians would have a record that would warrant the support of that party? And that's not so crazy. In 1988 women-owned businesses accounted for $37 billion in federal tax dollars and another $13 billion in state and local taxes—this is separate from your personal tax dollars, of course. That amount must represent at least as much influence as the National Rifle Association. (The answer to number 4 is d; you receive 5 points if you got it right.)

And what portion of federal contracts did these tax paying businesses get awarded? In any year, it is less than 1 percent. Although women-owned businesses account for 30 percent of the total businesses in this country and pay a whopping $37 billion in federal taxes, for some reason, they are awarded only 1 percent of the government contracts. (The answer to number 5 is a; you receive 5 points if you got it right.)

Did you get all five questions correct? If so, you have earned a full 25 points (and the right to a cup of tea while you continue reading). If you didn't, it's not surprising (so go for the tea anyway). Not many people know the size and scope of women's participation in the world of business ownership. In fact, it is with some trepidation that I devised the quiz at all.

For the most part, the numbers given come from the *1987 Economic Census—Summary of Findings on Women-Owned Businesses,* which was released in 1990. In 1990 the Small Business Administration (SBA) issued its report, *A Status Report to Congress: Statistical Information on Women in Business,* which states that "no federal data series currently covers the entire population of women-owned businesses." In other words, we have better records and data bases on exotic cars in this country than we do on businesses owned by women.

You can see my dilemma. I want to illustrate the size of the tsunami wave I predict, but I am cautious about doing so. Women-owned businesses are not tracked nearly as well as real earthquakes and tidal waves. Within seconds of the eruption of a volcano in Japan or an earthquake in California, we have all kinds of quantifiable data on the force of the action, how long it lasted, what size area was affected, and how much damage was done. However, the federal government has not yet devised a reliable means for providing a full accounting of businesses owned by women; therefore, we can only approximate the true size of the wave. Everything must be qualified by saying, "as far as we know at this time." In part, this is because the power of myth and stereotype has been sufficient to maintain the attitude that there really isn't much to keep track of. According to those who dismiss suggestions to fund a decent survey that would provide a comprehensive accounting, women's businesses are small, service oriented, temporary, and they rarely grow very big.

The purpose of this book has been quite simply to tell the stories of some women who own businesses, not to provide a statistical analysis of businesses owned by women. That is a serious task for another writer. What is currently known about women's businesses is, at best, a picture drawn from fragmented reports that use data that is three to five years old at any given time.

Throughout this book, I have maintained that many women are creating their own businesses and devising their own rules, apart from the organized, traditional world of business. Further, I say every now and then that such a strategy may be good for their businesses and for the long-term future of business and the planet. In a way, women-owned businesses are a kind of "skunkworks" for new models of business. In these "skunkworks" women devise new ways of doing business because they are isolated from the sources of capital and support available to other businesses. Am I trying to have it both ways—to be apart and to be counted? Yes, I guess I do want it both ways. As long as women employ workers, pay taxes, and contribute to the cash circulating in the economy, I think they have some minimum level of expectation that is reasonable. They can expect to be counted properly. The consequences of not being counted properly are continued invisibility, ongoing trivialization, dismissal, and stereotyping, which enjoys an unwarranted lifespan. These consequences don't really affect the tsunami—women's businesses are growing in spite of and, in some cases, because of institutional barriers—but they do affect a woman's quality of life, a business's real opportunities, and the development of policies which affect those businesses.

RECENT HERSTORY

Every five years, the Department of Commerce, Bureau of the Census, issues the *Economic Census*. Almost all the numbers used by business journalists, statisticians, armchair observers, and me to make points regarding the size and impact of women-owned businesses come from this *Economic Census,* as did the numbers in the preceding quiz, which are 1987 figures issued in the 1990 report. In an age when Wall Street can flash financial figures around the world in mere seconds, it is a puzzle to me why it takes three to five years to get reliable figures on business ownership and participation. This lack of timeliness leads to fragmented knowledge.

When it comes to the size of the tsunami wave, reality is hard to grasp. The number of women-owned businesses in 1987 was, according to the *Economic Census,* only 4.1 million. However, if you add the number of regular corporations (which they don't—they use someone else's figures and "fill in") in addition to the number of proprietorships, partnerships, and subchapter s corporations they have officially tallied, the number of women-owned businesses in 1987 is closer to 4.3 million. When I was writing the book, I cautiously used the conservative 4.1 million figure, but my guess, based on the inaccuracies of reporting and growth that must have occurred since 1987, was closer to 5.5 million. Then, like manna from heaven, the NAWBO Foundation released its study and confirmed my estimates.

That study was sufficient to create a major stir in the media. It is one more piece of data that compels a more accurate official counting of women in Washington. The pressure of NAWBO, the Committee of 200, and leaders of women's economic development funds in the country, with the support of women business owners, resulted in Congressional hearings held in 1988 on "New Economic Realities: The Role of Women Entrepreneurs." For six days in April and May of that year, women business owners testified before the Committee on Small Business, chaired by Representative John J. LaFalce from New York. LaFalce opened that hearing with these words:

> In 1980 I initiated hearings to document the difficulties faced by women entrepreneurs ... eight years later many of those problems (access to government contracting opportunities, access to credit, public policies, and programs, the changing nature of the workforce and, the changing nature of the U.S. economy) still persist.

The women testified on a wide range of subjects: credit access, discrimination, contract procurement, myths, and attitudes. They detailed real horror stories and matter-of-fact narratives of grit and sweat expended to realize their business visions. There was no whining, no pleas for special treatment. Indeed, the recurring theme was a plea for equal treatment. Women want to play on a level playing field; they don't want to be forced to swim with one arm tied to their body and then be punished for losing the race.

Polly Bergen, the chairperson of Polly Bergen Company (a manufacturer of shoes, handbags, and accessories) and a spokesperson for NAWBO, told the committee members:

Women business owners have seized every opportunity available to go into business and to be profitable, and the record shows that we have done it with little assistance from the government or from the corporate sector. The record shows that we have done it with the help of family and friends.

Gillian Rudd, then the president of NAWBO, told the committee, "We do not see ourselves as a special issue or social issue. We see ourselves as part of a national economic issue."

Other women gave detailed stories about being denied credit or about getting credit and being charged excessive interest rates and collateral—sometimes up to five times the actual amount of the loan. In contrast, Kathryn Keeley, the president of WOMANVENTURE (an economic development fund in Minnesota) provided examples of what could be done to support women and their businesses.

A major part of our program is financing. We believe an owner should be at risk for their business, but we use creative financing. The most creative business we did was a florist. We did a five-day note on the roses and took the roses as collateral, which we could have sold, because the roses had a life history of ten days. We did it on Valentine's Day. That owner sold $3000 worth of roses, she had $2500 to collateralize her business, and she was in operation. . . . Out of our $1.2 million fund, we have $800,000 loaned out at any one time, and we have only lost $21,000 in three years. We have a loss rate most bankers envy.

As a result of the stories and testimony of the entrepreneurs at the first hearings, a second set of hearings was scheduled. In March 1990, the Subcommittee on Exports, Tax Policy, and Special Problems met to examine the special problems and access to credit issues related to women-owned businesses. The committee chairperson opened with a statement of the findings from the 1988 hearings.

Those hearings identified four barriers to the advancement of women-owned businesses:

1. The need for management and technical training to maximize growth potential
2. Inequity of access to credit
3. Virtual exclusion of women from government procurement activities
4. The inadequacy of information and data on women-owned businesses

The committee once again listened to a distinguished list of witnesses discuss the challenges women entrepreneurs face. One banker stated that:

> women tend to be taken less seriously...the disadvantages are obvious. Referrals for business are not made as often. More lucrative or technically challenging opportunities are sent to other firms, and access to other useful business information is more difficult. And women have lower personal assets and a two-phase problem. Their available resources for equity investment are generally smaller, and their access to financing is restricted to disinterested lenders and angels they cannot meet. And once they do jump the financing hurdle, the bank wants more collateral or security than they would for the same loan to a man.

After these two hearings, Congress finally directed the SBA to do something tangible. The mandate was to conduct a study to determine the most accurate and cost effective means to gather and present data on women-owned businesses. In response, the SBA issued a *Status report to Congress* in December 1990: *Statistical Information on Women in Business.* That report used figures from the *1987 Economic Census* to tell Congress what it presumably already knew—that as of 1987, there were 4.1 million women business owners accounting for $278.1 billion in total receipts. The report mentioned that according to someone else's survey we could estimate that another 184,000 women owned regular (as opposed to irregular, I guess) corporations and that those accounted for another $198.8 billion in receipts, bringing the total to the $477 billion I noted in the quiz.

After detailing all the problems of counting the businesses women own (and forget keeping track of businesses owned by women of color—they get lost no matter how the counting is done), the conclusion sent to Congress in this status report was that "the standard reports of the major federal statistical programs produce relatively little information about women-owned businesses and their changing status over time." A footnote added, "Informed decisions about policy related to businesses owned by women, minorities and veterans are often constrained by a lack of timely and accurate information."

The authors of that status report to Congress noted that existing sources could be developed to provide a better count but that would "require time and money not currently available in the budget of either the Statistics of Income Division or the IRS." (What about that $37 billion in federal tax dollars women are contributing, where's that going?) One suggestion was made to do a survey based on area samples that would provide extensive data on women-owned, minority-owned, veteran-owned, and other small businesses. (What about our large businesses? The sample is flawed and the survey hasn't even been designed yet.) However, the suggestion was dampened by the observation that such a survey would cost at least $1 million, maybe as much as $3 or $4 million—really too expensive, they implied.

The upshot of the 1988 and 1990 hearings was that in spite of the difficulties and barriers women face they are starting and growing businesses in astonishing numbers. For all the talk, the hearings, and the reports, women are still pretty much on their own.

But a tsunami is a powerful wave. With the strength of at least 4.1 million (and another 5.5 million predicted by the end of the 1990s), we have political, financial, and social clout that is washing over the land, regardless of the action or inaction of the agencies that are supposed to serve us and the congressional leaders who are supposed to represent us.

WHAT'S COMING?

Three developments are brewing that will change the business landscape: (1) the expansion of the third generation of women entrepreneurs, (2) the development of social, financial, and political clout by women, and (3) the acceptance of a new style of management that includes the ability to relate. These developments are as inevitable as the wave that follows a submarine movement of the earth, and by now they have acquired a life of their own and are already shaping the future.

The Third Generation

Just because women's business presences grew from 5 percent to 30 percent in less than 20 years, we cannot predict the same linear rate of growth for the next 20 years. However, women's businesses will continue to increase in both real numbers and percent of business ownership—perhaps reaching 40 percent to 50 percent by the year 2010—and our existing businesses will grow. Despite the difficulties, women will find ways to grow businesses on their own terms. Anita Roddick, founder of The Body Shop; Sophia Collier, founder of Soho Cola; Sandra Kurtzig, of ASK Computer; and Frieda Caplan, of Frida's Finest, are just a few of the women leading the way. The third generation of women-owned businesses is a force to be reckoned with.

The first generation, going back to the turn of the century, includes those businesses that were sole proprietorships: the laundries, tea shops, and seamstresses that catered to the personal needs of customers and did not really require start-up capital. There are still many first-generation firms running and starting today. It's one of the ways you start a business if you have no money. Some of the great industrialists of the early part of this century became legends by telling and retelling stories of how they rose from shining shoes to owning huge companies. There is nothing shameful in being a first-generation business.

Second-generation businesses include those being taken over by the daughters of the founding mothers (and fathers) as well as those businesses being started by the MBA generation and women who are leaving high-level jobs in some of America's largest companies to do it different and do it on their own. I call these "second generation" because the entrepreneurs come to their business with a foundation of experience and knowledge that the first-generation entrepreneur usually doesn't have. This second generation may have slightly better access to capital (although not always, as a reading of the congressional hearings mentioned earlier points out) and more knowledge and training about running a business. The second generation is also making significant inroads in manufacturing, technology, transportation, and information age businesses, which they did not have access to earlier for want of capital and contacts. In the course of doing research for this book, I was struck by the number of daughters taking over Mom's (and, in some cases, Dad's) business. Lonear Heard, Edith Gorter, Leeann Chin, and many other entrepreneurial mothers have daughters preparing to take mom's place someday. Some of those daughters are directly involved in their mother's business now; others are off gaining experience to bring back home. Karen Caplan has recently bought her mother's business and is preparing for a period of growth. It appears that woman-controlled capital may not be such a far-out idea after all.

The third-generation entrepreneurs have sold one or more businesses and have sufficient capital (or access to capital) to purchase other businesses (as Sophia Collier sold Soho to Seagram's and purchased Working Assets), invest in other businesses, or otherwise influence the next generation of businesses. The third generation is involved in the leadership of major advocacy and policy-making bodies; they sit on the boards of other corporations. The officers of large urban chapters of the U.S. Chamber of Commerce are often women, and it is no longer uncommon for the president of an industry association to be a woman entrepreneur who is successful in her business and a leader in the industry. Third-generation businesses will more broadly influence mainstream businesses, business practices, and political policy.

The *Savvy* Sixty has included both second- and third-generation businesses in their listings over the last seven years. In the first year that *Savvy* saluted 60 large businesses owned by women, the cutoff for inclusion on the list was annual sales of $5 million. By 1988 the cutoff figure had risen to $24 million, and in 1990 the figure rose again to $39 million. Those 60 businesses accounted for almost 100,000 employees. (What was that about small businesses?)

Generational growth is nonlinear. First-, second-, and third-generation businesses are evolving simultaneously. Sometimes they share common issues and characteristics; sometimes they have wholly different issues and needs. But this multigenerational view of women owned business demands an appreciation for depth and dynamism and rejects a simplistic stereotype of small, service businesses that seldom outlast the tenure of the entrepreneur.

Investors, business schools, researchers, journalists, policy makers—anyone associated with the business of business—will need a more sophisticated understanding of this generational view of women-owned businesses in order to sell to, compete with, or otherwise understand the impact of millions of women-owned businesses. The third generation of women-owned businesses will grow dramatically in the next decade. And the fourth generation? Just imagine the businesses our daughters' daughters will create.

Clout and the Effects of a Dawning Consciousness

I have maintained repeatedly that women have a lesser need for power over and a greater desire for empowerment. But women aren't stupid, and if it takes a strong coalition to obtain a level playing field, I believe women will use their numbers and their financial clout to get it. Up to this point, women have not understood their own force. Hampered by a lack of information, we have politely asked for equity and opportunity. For too many years, women have accepted and incorporated the myths spun about them. Now, women are throwing off the cloak of the weak sister. Empowered, impatient, and finally aware of the contributions they make to federal tax coffers, the general economy, American social institutions, and the future of the country, women business owners will be expecting their fair share of resources, information, capital, and political responsiveness.

At those congressional hearings held in 1988, Gillian Rudd, then the president of NAWBO, told the representatives present that NAWBO wanted four things:

1. A reallocation of resources to benefit women's businesses

2. A greater private role in the public sector (that is, more than 1 percent participation in government contracts)

3. A three-year model program to support women-owned businesses (this in lieu of too many single-shot programs that come and go and are useful primarily in showing how ineffective it is to provide programs for women)

4. A greater emphasis on women-owned businesses in all sectors of the government

Congress finally appropriated $10 million for training programs, SBA staffing, and a Women's Business Council. Although that money is not enough to remedy the situation, the fact that it was appropriated is proof that women have political strength, staying power, and clout. We won't suffer the fate of Rosie the Riveter.

The name Rosie the Riveter was used to describe those women who left their kitchens (or their jobs as waitresses) during World War II to woman the factories and build the planes and other items often credited with helping to win that war. The U.S. government initiated a major campaign to reassure women that it was their civic duty, their patriotic responsibility, to lay aside concerns about their traditional roles as housewives, secretaries, and waitresses and fill in for the men who had gone off to be soldiers. Using ads, posters, magazine articles, and all the other propaganda tools available to the U.S. government, women were encouraged to take up the riveters and the hammers that had previously been the tools of men. The record shows that those women filled the factories and did the job. However, with the end of the war, the propaganda campaign reversed itself. Women were told they had a new patriotic duty. They had to give up those jobs, leave the factories, and go back to their kitchens or their much-lower-paying jobs as waitresses and retail clerks. They had to give the jobs back to the men returning from war. The film *Rosie the*

Riveter details heartbreaking stories of women who were fired or otherwise forced to take off their hard hats, retie their apron strings, and relinquish the first decent money and feelings of competence and worth they had ever experienced.

Conditions are different now. Rosie owns the factory. And the advertising agency. And the freight company. No amount of propaganda will make her disappear. This time, men will have to compete for the jobs, the votes, and the dollars that women increasingly are in charge of. That's the clout women have. As women become more aware of it, they will use that clout in ways that will have a profound and lasting effect on both business and society.

Business guru Tom Peters has seen this coming. In an article in *Nation's Business* in 1989, he said:

> The "mommy track" is not the point. The question is whether there is a job for Daddy in the future. I suggest that women are going to be in the driver's seat of virtually every corporation.... Only 3 percent of us are going to work in factories by 2001.... Mommy in the driver's seat and Daddy at home washing the dishes is the fate we males face in the years ahead.

Peters is overreacting, I think. (Besides, there's a lot more to do at home than just wash the dishes!) But his reaction does signal an intuitive awareness that a shift is happening, that the tsunami is a real phenomenon that is affecting the very basics of life and lifestyle for everyone.

His reaction signals an awareness. The women who have already left corporate America to start their own companies spoke with their feet. They have said they will no longer be "Prisoners of Men's Dreams." They are establishing their own realms and playing by their own rules; they are a virtual siren to other women. Their companies stand as "a city on a hill." The growing presence and visibility of women business owners is having a twofold effect. First, it signals to corporate women that they have a choice—they don't have to suffer the frustration of glass ceilings any longer. That signal is in part driving the growth of women-owned businesses. The second effect will create serious tension in the workplace of the 1990s. Women's growing impatience with explanations of why the glass ceiling never cracks, combined with their awareness that they have the power to do something different, will kindle the fire of their discontent and drive them to throw off the king's rules and demand the creation of new rules—rules that will recognize the needs of women and the reality of their lives.

The simple awareness that they have a choice will give women the courage to speak out. They will begin to demand access past the glass ceiling, flexible work/family policies, and the bounty that accompanies respect. Knowing they can start their own company— whether they do or not—gives women the knowledge that they can survive outside the corporate workplace. Armed with that knowledge, they are transformed from victims—supplicants at the altar of corporate norms and male standards—to equals with leverage and clout. Although one or two million more women will leave companies to start their own businesses (and another million may never enter) in the nineties, others will stay right where they are and demand change.

New Management Styles

There are keys to the future in women-owned businesses. Women have adopted methods and styles that have helped their businesses to survive and flourish under conditions of reduced capital sources, rigorous obstacles, and the multiple responsibilities of work and family. Flexibility and the ability to be responsive to rapidly changing conditions are survival skills that stem from an ability to listen, hear, observe, and connect with the forces of change affecting one's business. Those methods and styles will influence business changes as the broader business community (of both men and women) searches for ways to compete internationally, to improve the quality of life, and to sustain what is left of our planet.

Like water on rock, women-owned businesses are eroding time-hardened beliefs about the way business is and must be done. The different views and perspectives on life that people of different ethnic backgrounds bring to business will also change the old assumptions. The very notion of what constitutes business progress and success is under review. Many of us are questioning old assumptions and getting ready for a future we cannot yet fully describe.

Although we can't really see the future, we can identify some of its aspects. There is a growing understanding that a sustainable planet is not just a hip, new-age sensibility, it is an imperative of survival. One response that business will be able to make to the new imperative is to harken back to the teachings of E. F. Schumacher, author of *Small is Beautiful*. He wrote:

Experience shows that whenever you can achieve smallness, simplicity, capital cheapness and nonviolence, or indeed any one of these objectives, new possibilities are created for people, singly or collectively, to help themselves, and that the patterns that result from such technologies are more humane, are more ecological, less dependent on fossil fuels, and closer to the real human needs than the patterns (or lifestyles) created by technologies that go for giantism, complexity, capital intensity, and violence.

I am not arguing that women are or should be involved only in small works. That would be to feed the old stereotypes about what women CAN do. However, women have learned a great deal about the growth and management of smaller, streamlined, flexible organizations that integrate real life with commerce and are adaptive to the new rules of managing for a sustainable planet. And many of their companies do reflect the values set forth by Schumacher.

Women's businesses provide models for new forms of production, delivery, and employment. Managing complex systems and tasks as well as people and information requires an ever greater ability to relate, communicate, engender trust, and empower. These qualities will be increasingly valuable in the businesses of the coming decades. Authoritarian models of delivering orders and achieving goals will look ever more crude and rudimentary. The capacity to relate and to practice business with integrity will be marks of sophisticated management. Those people who have those qualities and have spent the last 10 or 20 years honing them will have a natural advantage in business relationships and transactions.

Business changes will not arrive with a brass band. Only in looking back will we see how the landscape has changed, how some business practices, once standard operating procedure, will have fallen into disuse. Learning to relate is powerful but rarely dramatic. Learning to relate is not like learning new quality control techniques or even becoming a "one-minute manager." Learning to relate is a subtler and more challenging process of coming to understand self and self in relation to others. There are a lot of people who are real experts in the realm of relationships—people who dare to trust, to be mutual, to empower. People who do not develop these qualities will be stuck with the more primitive tools of authority, coercion, and old punishment and reward systems.

The evolution of the third generation of women-owned businesses, the attendant impact—women's growing consciousness of their clout—and the inevitable changes associated with more sophisticated skills of managing and relating will make the businesses of the twenty-first century very different from those industrial age businesses that feel so familiar (if uncomfortable) now. The companies that will survive and bloom in the coming decades will be those companies that have dared to examine and experiment with new models, regardless of where they originate. Many of the companies that ride healthy into the future will be run by or influenced by the practices employed by women of the tsunami.

A NATIONAL AGENDA FOR WOMEN AND GIRLS

Nevertheless, like the president of NAWBO, I have an agenda, a wish list. What women have asked for to support their entrepreneurial efforts has been reasonable, perhaps overly reasonable. My own desire is for an aggressive national agenda that will enable the nation to tap the riches offered by the talent of entrepreneurial women. Such an effort will need to include more than a few conferences sponsored by the SBA, more than the passage of a few bills intended to protect the rights of women (which should be self-evident anyway), and more than a few congressional hearings that will allow women to express and document their needs yet again. The effort I have in mind is a big one, costing between $10 billion and $20 billion over a five-year period (yes, that's billion, not million). I have been asked where this number comes from. I realize the question arises because it is such a big number—imagine setting aside that much for women and girls! Yet that amount of money over five years pales beside the amounts we still set aside for military expenditures and is comparable to what is allocated to welfare payments over a similar period of time. I am not suggesting a cutback in welfare, but I am suggesting that a serious discussion about investment in women must go beyond welfare support. Women want to be self-supporting, but programs that offer $5 million here and $10 million there, every three to five years, for a few studies and training programs are mere tokenism. The structural change implied by a larger investment in women challenges policy makers to recast their ideas about women's worth. (How much did we pay to put how many men on the moon?)

This five-year investment could be used very productively:

1. *To count.* Women-owned businesses must be counted, tracked, and reported on accurately and properly. Legislation, funding, and policy decisions are made now in a vacuum of information and knowledge. Women business owners will not be valued fully

by others or themselves until there is a clearer picture of who, where, how many, and what they are. More critically, decisions and policies that affect their businesses will be made with wrong or insufficient knowledge. As I travel the country, I have been struck at how shocked women are when I tell them they have counterparts in the millions. It is time women entrepreneurs understood the mass they represent and the power of the federal dollars they contribute in the way of business taxes.

2. *To study*. The models women have devised for holding down costs, managing and motivating employees, and building alliances with partners, suppliers, and customers are just a few of the treasures locked inside their companies. I challenge business schools and researchers to increase funding by at least 40 percent to develop case studies that examine the first, second, and third generations of women-owned businesses. (This 40 percent figure represents somewhat less than the percent of women-owned businesses projected by the end of the 1990s. As it is, cases in business schools on women-owned businesses constitute no more than 2 percent or 3 percent of the examples used to teach modern management techniques. That seems a little outdated in light of current reality. I do not believe that curricula should be devised by quota, but I do believe they should at least be reflective of reality. It doesn't take a rocket scientist to see that current business school curriculum has not kept up with the changing society.)

It is not enough just to rewrite cases with women in the starring roles. These new studies must be approached with an entirely fresh perspective. If examined not as women-owned businesses, but as businesses that happen to be owned by women, the research will yield a wealth of information. Investigating their businesses for new models, structures, and methods, rather than for information about the women themselves (What do they have in common? How are they different from men?), will alter the nature of the research (away from women as specimens) as well as the fruits of that research. Furthermore, studying businesses owned by women on their own terms, not as compared to business as we have known it, will enable researchers to discover the fallibility of some of the assumptions about traditional business that remain unchallenged.

3. *To develop and provide resources*. It is not unreasonable to push for fair and innovative access to resources. If WOMANVENTURE, Inc. can make a loan using roses for collateral, you can be sure there is a lot of room for creative financing that has not yet been explored.

Traditional forms of venture capital, which only fund businesses promising 35 percent to 50 percent return on investment, may be adrenalin-producing, but funds that are structured more like mortgages might encourage a more stable form of business development. The aggressive support of the SBA (rather than the passive, "Gee, we'd like to help, tell us what you need, *again*" game played for the last two decades) is long overdue. Guaranteed loan funds, technical training, and data base support are just a few of the areas that could make a real difference (if initiated with the kind of serious commitment we have seen demonstrated for other missions in this country) and would make good use of that $10 to $20 billion budget.

4.   *To assure access.* If women constitute over 30 percent of all businesses, but receive less than 1 percent of the federal contracts available, something is wrong with the system. For the $40 billion in taxes women's businesses contribute, the system can be changed.

5.   *To create innovative programming.* Two kinds of programming are needed; one is concerned with learning, the other focuses on entrepreneurial support systems. Innovative programming for learning purposes includes conferences, seminars, and curricula that have both specific industry focus (e.g., the Women's Food Service Forum) and more general business focus (e.g., the annual conferences sponsored by the Alliance of Women Entrepreneurs and *Inc.*). Too many of the programs originating in business schools are designed for men, by men, and based on the male experience. For the sake of the general economy we also need programs developed by women and based on women's experience.

Innovative support systems include special insurance and health programs for early-stage entrepreneurs as well as day-care facilities for children. These would go a long way toward encouraging more entrepreneurial ventures for both men and women in this country. For parents with children, the risk of being without proper insurance coverage—health and disability—is a serious impediment to starting a business. Incentives to establish more incubator programs to which women have real access is another support system that could be initiated by state and federal systems as well as private organizations and corporations that wish to encourage entrepreneurs.

6.   *To mine the riches of diversity.* Entrepreneurship is a dynamic force among all people—Hispanics, Asians, African-Americans, and Native Americans as well as Anglo women and men. Furthermore, each of us brings to our businesses knowledge, insights, and practices that are derived from our own cultures and experiences.

Learning more about each other's knowledge, we will no doubt borrow some techniques that may be more effective than some of the habits familiar in our own culture. By sharing business lore, practice, and experience, we may develop hybrid forms of management we might not otherwise have imagined.

American corporations have spent enormous sums of money and time trying to understand Japanese culture and work practices. A more fundamental understanding and respect for cultural differences and riches right here at home would go a long way toward healing some of the racial and ethnic divisions felt in our society. At the same time, it would reveal new and more effective ways of doing business. I call for a biannual "Conference on Entrepreneurial Diversity," which might be jointly sponsored by a group of business magazines, business organizations, and the SBA. A yearly forum for sharing and learning would be a smart way to understand one another's markets as well as differing and similar operating styles and management philosophies.

7. *To develop girls.* We must invest in our girls and young women. Investing in girls is the responsibility we have to the future; it must be an investment of money, programming, and time. It is time for a national agenda to value, invest in, and prepare young girls to be involved in the future of this society. I suggest a two-part program.

First, there should be programs sponsored jointly by the federal and state governments to reach at least three million girls between the ages of 10 and 15. These programs should develop leadership, scholarship, physical development, and the arts. Yes, it would be nice to have such an effort for young boys, too; however, to the extent that we have done anything for our children (and it's not much), boys have generally gotten the lion's share of programs, services, and resources. My focus now is on those girls Carol Gilligan and her colleagues are studying who appear, somewhere between the ages of 11 and 13, to lose the spunk that seems to be present until that time. Over and over women have said to me: "I was told I could be a teacher or a social worker or a nurse." Because medical schools, law schools, and business schools have seen a dramatic increase in female students, it is easy to think that the days of girls being directed into gender-appropriate professions are behind us. Not so. Many young girls still get precious little exposure to options that demonstrate routes to economic independence. Inadequate educational facilities, diminished social services in the inner cities, lack of family resources, and lack of significant mentoring relationships leave young girls vulnerable and poorly prepared for self-reliance.

Second, there should be a national campaign to match at least 30 percent of the four million plus women who own businesses with young women around the country. The program would be a kind of domestic Peace Corps program that would provide young girls between 12 and 17 with relationships with entrepreneurial women. Naomi Farber of the University of Wisconsin has done research that clearly indicates the value of significant adult contact with young women in the inner city. Girls who get the attention, modeling, and encouragement of successful women are likely to perform better educationally, socially, and vocationally. Such a program could be administered by a new "Office for Girls" located in the Department of Education and designed with the aid of an organization such as NAWBO and for the Committee of 200.

I am aware that suggesting we set aside $10 to $20 billion in state and federal dollars to be used for supporting and encouraging the entrepreneurial potential (or any kind of potential) of women and girls may be a bit breathtaking (though still meager from my point of view), particularly in an age of cutbacks and fiscal conservatism. However, support other than welfare payments is long overdue. The investment I recommend will provide a return on investment well within the acceptable rates of the most demanding venture capitalist.

8. *Women investing in women*. The last item on my wish list is separate from this agenda. It is something that can come from no one but women themselves. What I want is a commitment from women to invest in other women. Until now, women have either: (1) not felt secure enough about making their own investment decisions (often delegating them to men), (2) accepted some of the myths about women being a less wise investment, or (3) not thought about or searched out opportunities to invest in other women's businesses. Investing in one another is one of the most important ways we can empower one another.

Kathryn Keeley has called for the growth of women-controlled capital. Increasingly, I hear mothers talking about the importance of providing a nest egg for their daughters—something they can draw on to protect themselves. That is a healthy and exciting beginning, but we need to do more than that. We need funds controlled by women for the purpose of investing in one another's businesses. Those funds need to be innovative and innovating—

funds run for women and by women. Having sufficient capital available to make a real difference will necessitate shifting that capital, now controlled by women, from traditional investments to these new funds. Corporate women, entrepreneurs, women no longer in the work force (but in control of substantial resources), women in the financial sector of the economy (bankers, brokers, investors)—all women—have a responsibility to this bold new movement. Placing money in women's hands, in a form other than welfare checks, is a good investment in the future for everyone. To this end, I will put my money where my pen is and commit a portion of the proceeds from this book to an economic development fund for women.

The tsunami is a mighty force. It has the power to transform the landscape. Powered by their businesses, women entrepreneurs are doing just that. Achieving economic independence, they are finding ways to create a better world for themselves, their families, and their communities. No longer "Prisoners of Men's Dreams," these women are pursuing their own dreams. Four and a half million strong and growing fast, this new constituency has the potential to benefit us all—men and women. How we choose to use our clout and our values will be the story of the coming decades.

IV

RESOURCES: IN LIEU OF A MENTOR

Mentors do a lot of different things. They sometimes lend a shoulder or an ear, often counsel and advise, occasionally argue and direct. If you are lucky, they also open doors and provide connections and introductions. Mentors sometimes save time and provide shortcuts to learning that might otherwise come only after a more circuitous journey. These appendices are intended to provide support in lieu of or in addition to a good mentor. Appendix A, "Before You Write A Business Plan," is a kind of checklist to help you get started on a business. Appendix B, "Books and Organizations," is not intended to be comprehensive, but it may get you started on obtaining the information you need. Appendix C, "More Stories from Entrepreneurial Women," has been included to facilitate a dialogue. Women and their businesses are a dynamic, rapidly growing, and changing phenomenon. I hope you will share your experiences and insights as they evolve.

Before You Write a Business Plan

There are literally hundreds of books devoted to the subject of the business plan. Banks, accounting firms, business schools, and many law firms usually have an outline they recommend to their clients. My business partner, Jane, maintains (rightfully, I think) that doing a business plan is a little like writing a novel. You have to engage the reader in the idea, build an interesting story, make it compelling and convincing, and give them enough good information so you don't lose their attention.

A business plan is written for at least two parties: you and anyone you want to invest in your business. Whether you are financing your idea from personal savings or from investment money from friends, family, or venture partners, you will find that the telling and retelling of the story, sharpens your thinking; new ideas will emerge, and sticky problems will either be resolved or get your attention.

The following questions are intended to start you thinking about your idea. They cover the basics. When you have done your homework, you will be ready to begin on a business plan.

1. *Getting started: the idea.* Consider the idea. Why does it appeal to you? How did it come to you? What makes you think it's an important idea? Could you live with the idea for a long time? How do you know? What difference does this idea make? Can you state the idea in a few words? If your idea was a car, what kind would it be? In other words, what images or associations do you relate to your idea? What other kinds of people might be attracted to the idea, not as customers, but as investors and employees?

2. *First things first: life.* How will you run your life if you accept responsibility for this idea? What do you need to think through in regard to family, friends, and self? What trade-offs are you willing to make? What do you have to plan around? How will you take care of yourself? What are your values? What's important?

3. *Getting info: the market.* Who needs what you want to do? How do you know? How can you get more information? How large is the market? Large pharmaceutical companies can sometimes afford to develop and produce "orphan" drugs—that is, medicines for a very small market. But start-up companies with limited resources need to make sure the market they are targeting is large enough to grow in. What is the benefit of your idea or product to your market? What are the unique features of the product? What other opportunities are related to this idea?

4. *Making money: sales.* How will you reach your market? Who sells products like yours now? How do they do it? How else might it be done? What will you need to sell this product? What will it cost to sell this product? How do you know? How will you figure out a pricing strategy? What's your competition? What's your advantage?

5. *Making it happen: resources.* What do you need and when do you need it? What are the ways you might get what you need? Where will you set up the business? Who will help you? What kind of people will be required to make this happen? What materials do you need? How will you finance your idea? What will others get for investing in your idea?

6. *Avoiding pitfalls: hazards.* What's the worst that could happen? What skills should you improve? What do you need to learn more about? What qualities in yourself do you have to be wary of? What kinds of support systems do you have or do you need to develop? What do you suppose you don't know that you don't know?

7. *What you already know: intuition.* Pay attention to your reactions to the following words:

Selling

Risk

Commitment

Numbers

Conflict

Payroll

Surprise

Teams

Money

Relationships
Decision Making
Debt
Profit
Leadership
Self
Quality
Loss
Fun
Energy
Customers
Responsibility

If you scored over 70 on the right stuff quiz in Chapter 2 and you think you still want to pursue your idea after considering these questions, it's probably time to get started on your business. Good luck. May your wildest dreams come true!

Books and Organizations

The lists below are purely personal and idiosyncratic; the books are ones I have read and feel have some relevance to subjects covered in this book. I have not had personal experience with all of the organizations listed but hope you will find them helpful.

Books and Articles

Bennis, Warren. *On Becoming a Leader.* Reading, MA: Addison-Wesley, 1989.

Bundles, A'Lelia Perry. *Madam C.J. Walker, Entrepreneur.* New York: Chelsea House Publishers, 1991.

DePree, Max. *Leadership is an Art.* New York: Doubleday, 1989.

Hawken, Paul. *Growing a Business.* New York: Simon and Schuster, 1987.

Kantor, Rosabeth Moss. *When Giants Learn to Dance.* New York: Simon and Schuster, 1989.

Klass, Perri. *Other Women's Children.* New York: Random House, 1990.

Kurtzig, Sandy. *CEO.* New York: W.W. Norton, 1991.

Making Connections. Carol Gilligan, Nona P. Lyons, and Trudy J. Hanner, eds. Cambridge, MA: Harvard University Press, 1990.

O'Toole, James. *Vanguard Management.* New York: Doubleday, 1985.

Roddick, Anita. *Body and Soul.* New York: Crown Publishing, 1991.

Rossner, Judy. "Ways Women Lead." *Harvard Business Review,* 68 (November–December 1990), pp. 119–125.

Schaef, Ann Wilson. *Meditations for Women Who Do Too Much.* New York: Harper & Row, 1990.

Schumacher, E. F. *Good Work.* New York: Harper Colophon Books, 1979.

Schumacher, E. F. *Small is Beautiful.* New York: Harper & Row, 1973.

Working Papers

Baker-Miller, Jean. "What Do We Mean by Relationship?" The Stone Center, Wellesley College, Working Paper, no. 22, 1986.

Bergman, Stephen J. "Men's Psychological Development: A Relational Perspective." The Stone Center, Wellesley College, Working Paper, no. 48, 1991.

Surrey, Janet. "The Self in Relation: A Theory of Women's Development." The Stone Center, Wellesley College, Working Paper, no. 13, 1985.

Surrey, Janet. "Relationship and Empowerment." The Stone Center, Wellesley College, Working Paper, no. 30, 1987.

Hearing Proceedings

U.S. Congress, House Committee on Small Business, *New Economic Realities: The Role of Women Entrepreneurs, Hearings before the Committee on Small Business*, 100th Cong., 2d Sess., April 26–27, May 10, 11, 17, and 19, 1988

U.S. Congress, House Committee on Small Business, *Women-Owned Businesses: Special Problems and Access to Credit, Hearings before the Subcommittee on Exports, Tax Policy, and Special Problems*, 101st Cong., 2d Sess., March 12, 1990.

Organizations/Resources

American Women's Economic Development Corporation, 60 E. 42nd Street, New York, New York, 10165. Phone: 212-692-9100.

Association of Black Women Entrepreneurs, 1301 North Kenter Ave., Los Angeles, California 90049. Phone: 310-472-4927

National Association of Women Business Owners, 600 S. Federal Street, Suite 400, Chicago, Illinois, 60605. Phone: 312-922-0465.

National Black MBA Association, 180 N. Michigan Avenue, Suite 1820, Chicago, Illinois, 60601. Phone: 312-236-2622.

National Coalition of 100 Black Women, 50 Rockefeller Plaza #46, New York, New York, 10020. Phone: 212-974-6140.

Office of Women's Business Ownership, U.S. Small Business Administration, 1441 L Street, N.W., Room 414, Washington, D.C., 20416. Phone: 202-653-4000.

Leadership America, 803 Franklin Street, Alexandria, Virginia 22314. Phone: 703-549-1102. Selects 100 talented women to participate in a year-long series of seminars dealing with national and international policy.

SBA Answer Desk: 1-800-368-5855. Experts from the SBA's Office of Advocacy answer phones Monday through Friday from 8:30 A.M. to 6:00 P.M. EST. They are prepared to handle questions connected with your business or the government.

More Stories from Entrepreneurial Women

Do you have a story about your own business that you would like to share? Please fill out the form below and mail (or fax) to me.

Name _____

Company Name _____

    Street _____

    City, State, Zip _____

    Telephone, Fax Numbers _____

Title and relationship to the company _____

Industry and product or services sold _____

Year company founded _____

Source of start-up capital _____

Number of employees _____

Comments on anything you read in *Our Wildest Dreams:*

_____

_____

Tell a story about your business. (What was the inspiration or source of the idea? What are your difficulties, proudest achievements, insights, discoveries about self or business, goals, supports, advice to others? Use additional pages if necessary.)

_____

_____

_____

All information will remain confidential unless express permission is given to share or use in research or business reporting.

Fax to 805-646-4206, or mail to *An Income of Her Own,* 221 Bryant Street, Third Floor, San Francisco, CA 94110

Afterword

Two years of listening to and writing about women and their businesses has taught me humility. I have heard epic stories of courage and strength, funny stories of guile and ingenuity, and surprising stories of discovery and invention. I have met women of all styles, cultures, industries, and ages. I have many new heroines. I am humbled by the very mass of stories I collected. I knew when I started this project that I would have no trouble finding women entrepreneurs—I had no idea that a time would come when I would feel awash in stories. I have an inventory of accounts that will keep me warm—and affirmed—for years. But those stories are rightfully the heritage of the coming generations of young women.

Much of the early history of women has been lost or buried. Fortunately, a few documentaries are beginning to appear. *CEO* is Sandra Kurtzig's account of the growth of her company, ASK Computer. A'Lelia Perry has written a biography of her great-great-grandmother, Madam C.J. Walker, the washerwoman who became a self-made millionaire by marketing and manufacturing a line of hair care and beauty products. It is imperative that we collect, protect, and pass on more "herstories" of the women who, through their entrepreneurial efforts, are even now, shaping the future.

I was thrilled and proud to learn of so many good works that women are initiating through their businesses. Ella Williams is gearing up to establish a second company in the inner city of Los Angeles. With that company, she hopes to employ young people and help revitalize a neighborhood. Gwen Kaplan and Sonia Melara use their businesses to help enfranchise those who have previously been shut out. Nancy Alexander consciously uses her company to "build a better world for her kids." Over and over I heard "I have to give something back." Women define success in terms that reach way beyond net worth statements and photos in *People* magazine. For so many women, when they are able to give something back, they feel successful and fulfilled.

I suspect some readers will finish a chapter or a section and find something missing; she didn't cover this or she didn't spell out that. Women have been starting and running businesses for decades, but little has been written about their activities and there is a great deal to catch up on. We need a whole library of books to pursue some of the topics only referred to here. Perhaps other researchers will study specific personnel policies; another writer might choose to observe and document the process of staff meetings in women-owned businesses. I hope business school professors will start sending their students to intern with women business owners. Maybe a reporter or two will investigate the kinds of good works women initiate as part of the business of business. Obviously, a look at Anita Roddick's book, *Body and Soul,* will be a good place to start that assignment.

In writing this book I had one goal that stretched me considerably. Much of my life has been spent crossing cultures in one way or another. I am conscious of and grateful for the diversity of life in America. So I was determined that in writing about women business owners I would be inclusive of women of many cultures and experiences. The quest for economic independence is one that many women share, and the true story of women business owners in America is a story of diversity. But writing properly about my colleagues, with whom I share common goals, although not always common cultural and racial backgrounds, is so much more complex than mere inclusion — more complex because one woman's story is never *all* women's story, regardless of race or culture; more complex because attention to language, history, values, and experience make the business of checking assumptions a more critical exercise; and more complex because there are assumptions that I share with women of my own background that I do not share with women who grew up in other cultural and racial contexts. I am aware of that.

As women, sometimes we still gloss over our differences with the comfortable veneer of common gender, but our differences do matter. Just as it is important for men and women to learn about and appreciate both our differences and our common ground, as women we must do that among ourselves. The women I met with and talked to in the course of writing this book were all enormously generous and patient with me. I learned a great deal from them, but mostly I learned how much more I have to learn and how much more work there is to do to reveal the exciting world of women and their businesses.

It is with real feeling that I offer my gratitude to those women who took time to describe the various paths they took to the head of their companies. They were all so articulate and open that my task was easy (well easier!). But now I am hooked. I want to go back in another ten years and take a look at the next chapter in their lives and in their businesses — neither of which is predictable now.

Notes

Chapter 1

1. Tom Wolfe, *The Right Stuff* (New York: Farrar, Straus, Giroux, 1979), pp. 186–187.
2. Jean Baker-Miller, "What Do We Mean By Relationship?" The Stone Center, Wellesley College, Working Paper, no. 22, 1986, p. 20.
3. Janet Surrey, "Relationship and Empowerment," The Stone Center, Wellesley College, Working Paper, no. 30, 1987, p.12.
4. Judy Rosener, "Ways Women Lead," *Harvard Business Review,* Vol. 68, Nov.-Dec. 1990, p. 123.
5. Richard Mason and Ian Mitroff, *Challenging Strategic Planning Assumptions* (New York: John Wiley & Sons, 1981), p. 18–19.
6. ©1984 & 1987 by Revelation Music Publishing Corp. and Rilting Music, Inc. A Tommy Valando Publication. International © secured. Made in U.S.A. All rights reserved. Lyrics by Stephen Sondheim.
7. In Laurie Lisle, *A Portrait of an Artist: A Biography of Georgia O'Keeffe* (New York: Seaview Books, 1980), p. 137.
8. Ray Bradbury, "Management from Within," *New Management Magazine, Selections,* 1986.
9. Ibid.
10. James O'Toole, *Vanguard Management: Redesigning the Corporate Future* (New York: Doubleday and Co., 1985) p. 387.
11. Stephen Bergman, M.D., "Men's Psychological Development: A Relational Perspective" (a work in progress), The Stone Center, Wellesley College, Working Paper, no. 48, 1991.

Chapter 2

1. Rosabeth Moss Kanter, *Men and Women of the Corporation* (New York: Basic Books, 1977), p. 210.
2. E. F. Schumacher, *Good Work* (New York: Harper & Row, 1979), pp. 3–4.

3. Douglas LaBier, *Modern Madness* (Reading, MA: Addison-Wesley, 1986), p. 141.

4. Sally Helgeson, "The Pyramid and the Web," *New York Times,* May 27, 1990, p. 13.

5. Ibid.

6. Glenn Rifkin and George Harrar, *The Ultimate Entrepreneur* (New York: Contemporary Books, 1988), p. 35.

7. Ibid.

8. Stanley Rich and David E. Gumpert, "Growing Concerns," *Harvard Business Review,* Vol. 58, July-Aug., 1980, p. 39.

9. Jeanette Scollard, "New Economic Realities: The Role of Women Entrepreneurs," Hearings before the House Committee on Small Business. *Congressional Record.* 100th Cong. 2nd sess., 1988, p. 120.

10. Fran S. Rogers and Charles Rogers, "Business and the Facts of Family Life," *Harvard Business Review,* Nov.–Dec. 1989, p. 121.

11. Jean Baker-Miller, "What Do We Mean By Relationship?" The Stone Center, Wellesley College, Working Paper, no. 22, 1986,

Chapter 3

1. "These Are For Your Consideration" ©1989 by Emily Hiestand. Reprinted from *Green the Witch-Hazel Wood* with the permission of Graywolf Press, St. Paul, Minnesota.

Chapter 4

1. Ray Bradbury, "Management from Within," *New Management Magazine, Selections,* 1986, p. 7.

2. Quoted by K. C. Cole, "Play, by Definition, Suspends the Rules," *New York Times,* November 30, 1988.

Chapter 5

1. Deirdre Carmody, "Beating Warner at Its Own Game," *New York Times,* April 8, 1990, p. F6.

2. Edna St. Vincent Millay, *Collected Poems* (New York: Harper & Row, 1981).

3. *The Avon Report,* New World Decisions, Inc., Avon Products, Inc., 1989, p. 17.

4. Brian Wright O'Connor, "Choosing a Board To Help Grow Your Company," *Black Enterprise,* vol. 21, no. 11, June 1991, pp. 252–256.

Chapter 6

1. Michael Lewis, *Liar's Poker* (New York: W.W. Norton and Co., 1989), pp. 16–17. Reprinted by permission of W.W. Norton (USA, Philippines, and Canada) and Hodder & Stoughton (worldwide).

2. Jean Baker-Miller, "What Do We Mean By Relationship?" The Stone Center, Wellesley College, Working Paper, no. 22, 1986, p. 3.

3. Ibid.

Chapter 7

1. E. F. Schumacher, *Good Work* (New York: HarperCollins Publishers, 1979), p. 57.

INDEX

Peters, Tom, xxiii, 10, 61, 220
Phelps, Regina, 32, 34, 49
Photo Odyssey, xx, 35
Play, 26–30, 83, 94–96. *See also* Fun
  creating a work culture for, 101–3
  determining personal instincts for,
    100–101
Playing around, 92
Polaroid Corporation, xiv, 29, 42, 66
Polly Bergen Company, 213–14
Power, 9, 17, 19, 37, 44, 57, 70, 99
Prins, Garry, 191
Prisoners of Men's Dreams, xvii, 48
Private investors, 136
Process, 17–22
  balance and self-awareness, desire for,
    22–26
  courage, 33–37
  dimensions of, 18–21
  integrated vision of business and ethics,
    30–33
  and passion, 21–22
  sense of artistry, imagination, and
    playfulness, 26–30
Professional organizations, 144
PSL Marketing, 22

Quadracci, Harry, ix

Racism, 129, 140
Rand, Ayn, 47, 52
Real play, 95–96
Rebelsky (Rebel), xv–xvi
Reciprocity, 10, 44
Redken Laboratories, 109
Relating, 6–12, 99, 222
Relational empowerment, 8
Respect, 20, 54, 80
Results, 79
Rich, Matty, 160–61
Rifkin, Glenn, 66
Right stuff
  complexity and process, appreciation
    of, 15–22
  connectedness, 6–12
  head, heart, and hands policy, 12–15
  men and, 41–45
  new definition of, 3–6
  qualities of, 4, 6
  relationships, ease in, 6–12
  self assessment of, 37–40
Risk taking, 34, 36–37, 130
Roddick, Anita, 5, 34, 60, 63, 78, 108,
    216, 238
Rogers, Fran, 69

Role model(s), 34–36, 43, 127
Rosener, Judy, 9, 10, 19, 71, 99
Rosie the Riveter, 219–20
Rudd, Gillian, 214, 219
Rue de France, 59

Sack, Kirby, 80
St. Vincent Millay, Edna, 138
Sarton, Mary, 83
Savvy Sixty, 218
Sawyer, Chips, 120, 121
Schrank, Bob, 20
Schumacher, E. F., 58, 221–22
Scollard, Jeannette Reddish, 68–69
SCS Communications, 68
Second-generation businesses, 217
Self
  becoming, 5, 37–38, 51, 82
  new view of, 70–71
Self-esteem, 8, 12, 37, 80
Self-fulfilling prophecy, 67
Self-in-relation, 9
Sew What, 109
Sexism, 129, 140
Skunkworks, 10, 212
Sky Venture Capital, 131
Sloan, Alfred, 78
Small Business Administration (SBA),
    120, 136, 211, 215, 219, 223, 225
Small business investment companies
    (SBICs), 136
Small Is Beautiful, 58, 221
Smiley, Karen, 125
Smith and Hawken, 53, 78, 125
Smith, Fred, 108, 126
Social activism, 63, 78
Socialization, 10, 99
SoftAd Group, The, 109, 127
Soho Cola, 217
Sondheim, Stephen, 27
Spontaneity, 96, 103
Stand By Me, 42, 44
Stargell, Willie, 159, 160
Starting a business, 27, 29
  adopting a business, 116–22
  balance, 137–40
  coming to a business, 124–27
  following a dream, 112–16
  hardship, 140–44
  money, 127–37
  responding to needs, 122–24
  sources, 111–27
Steiglitz, Alfred, 29
Stereotypes, 48, 50, 67, 109, 161, 211,
    218, 222